THE WAR PREROGATIVE

The War Prerogative

History, Reform, and Constitutional Design

ROSARA JOSEPH

OXFORD
UNIVERSITY PRESS

OXFORD
UNIVERSITY PRESS

Great Clarendon Street, Oxford, OX2 6DP,
United Kingdom

Oxford University Press is a department of the University of Oxford.
It furthers the University's objective of excellence in research, scholarship,
and education by publishing worldwide. Oxford is a registered trade mark of
Oxford University Press in the UK and in certain other countries

© R Joseph 2013

The moral rights of the author have been asserted

First Edition published in 2013

Impression: 1

All rights reserved. No part of this publication may be reproduced, stored in
a retrieval system, or transmitted, in any form or by any means, without the
prior permission in writing of Oxford University Press, or as expressly permitted
by law, by licence or under terms agreed with the appropriate reprographics
rights organization. Enquiries concerning reproduction outside the scope of the
above should be sent to the Rights Department, Oxford University Press, at the
address above

You must not circulate this work in any other form
and you must impose this same condition on any acquirer

Crown copyright material is reproduced under Class Licence
Number C01P0000148 with the permission of OPSI
and the Queen's Printer for Scotland

Published in the United States of America by Oxford University Press
198 Madison Avenue, New York, NY 10016, United States of America

British Library Cataloguing in Publication Data
Data available

Library of Congress Control Number: 2013937828

ISBN 978–0–19–966432–0

Printed and bound in Great Britain by
CPI Group (UK) Ltd, Croydon, CR0 4YY

Links to third party websites are provided by Oxford in good faith and
for information only. Oxford disclaims any responsibility for the materials
contained in any third party website referenced in this work.

Preface

The decision to commit the armed forces to war is perhaps the most momentous any leader can take. It entails the use of force by the state against another state or non-state target; it sanctions the injury and killing of nationals and non-nationals, civilians, and armed forces personnel; and it potentially involves in its consequences the entire community. Yet despite its most solemn and elementary nature, the war prerogative has not been subjected to sustained or in-depth academic examination. The theory and practice of the war prerogative have been taken as axiomatic, and beyond question or doubt. Legal academic work has assumed that the executive holds exclusive power to declare war and deploy the armed forces, without questioning the ideas underlying that assertion or how the power has actually been exercised in practice. This book questions those assumptions. It explores the ideas underlying the constitutional arrangements for the war prerogative and examines the processes and interactions of the governmental institutions involved in its exercise. My research draws on a wide range of material from law, history, political theory, and social science in an attempt to address this lacuna in the literature.

The war prerogative interested me for three reasons: first, I wanted to examine why the powers to make and wage war are identified as the highest and most paradigm of executive powers. What makes the power to declare war such an axiomatically 'executive' power? Why should the executive hold exclusive power over war? I wanted to trace the changes and continuities in theoretical writings about the executive and its powers over war. I was interested to identify the theoretical justifications that have been and are advanced for the constitutional arrangements for the war power.

Secondly, I wanted to learn whether, in practice, the executive really did have exclusive power over the making of war and deployment of force. Did Parliament and the courts have any role to play at all in the exercise and scrutiny of these powers?

Thirdly, I wanted to address future developments. Were there better ways to organize our constitutional arrangements for the exercise of the war prerogative? I thought it wrong that Parliament's involvement in the exercise and scrutiny of the war prerogative depends mostly on whether the government enables such involvement.

I hope that this work will be of relevance and use to constitutional lawyers and those interested in legal and political history. I think that it could also be useful in the context of proposed constitutional and political reform of the war prerogative. As I identify in chapter 6, the exercise of the war prerogative has been the subject of several in-depth reports and inquiries. It continues to be a contentious and topical issue as evidenced by recent reports of parliamentary select committees and debates in the House of Commons and House of Lords.

This book is based on a thesis submitted in partial fulfilment for a DPhil at the University of Oxford. I would like to acknowledge and thank my doctoral supervisor, Professor Paul Craig, for his support, guidance, and enthusiasm; and for being so understanding of my spending too much time racing bikes abroad. I would also like to thank Selby Marshall and my family for their unconditional love and support.

Rosara Joseph
Wellington, New Zealand

Contents

Table of Cases	ix
Table of Statutes, Bills, and International Instruments	xiii

1	**Introduction**	1
2	**Theoretical and Political Discourses: The War and Foreign Policy Powers**	5
	Part I Introduction	5
	Part II Historical Analysis: Objectives and Methodology	5
	Part III The Executive and the War and Foreign Policy Powers	13
	Part IV Conclusion	41
3	**The War Prerogative in Practice**	44
	Part I Introduction	44
	Part II An Extraordinary Historical Period	45
	Part III Interactions	51
	Part IV Conclusion	107
4	**Judicial Treatment of the War Prerogative**	110
	Part I Introduction	110
	Part II The War Prerogative: Existence and Scope	111
	Part III Jurisdiction and Justiciability	124
	Part IV Review on Established Grounds	144
	Part V The War Prerogative and Individual Rights	149
	Part VI Liability in Tort	153
	Part VII Conclusion	154
5	**Institutional Mechanisms**	157
	Part I Introduction	157
	Part II Institutional Design	157
	Part III Application	167
	Part IV Conclusion	179

6 Reform		181
Part I	Introduction	181
Part II	Parliamentary Access to Information	187
Part III	Detail of the Proposed Legislation	201
Part IV	Role of the Courts	211
Part V	Conclusion	215
7 Conclusions		217
Bibliography		221
Index		241

Table of Cases

A v HM Treasury [2010] 2 AC 534 122
A v Secretary of State for the Home Department [2004] UKHL 56, [2005] 1
  AC 68 .... 13, 113, 116, 137, 138 139, 140, 147, 148, 155
A v Secretary of State for the Home Department [2005] UKHL 71, [2006] 1 AC 221 .... 13, 149
Al Jedda v Secretary of State for Defence [2007] UKHL 58, [2008] 1 AC 322 153
Al Rawi v Security Service [2011] UKSC 34 141
Al Saadoon v Secretary of State for Defence [2009] EWCA Civ 7, [2010]
  QB 486 153
Al-Skeini v United Kingdom [2011] 53 EHRR 18 (ECtHR) 151, 153
Amin v Brown [2005] EWHC 1670, [2006] IL Pr 5 .... 118, 121
Associated Provincial Picture Houses Ltd v Wednesbury Corp [1948] 1 KB 223 147
AG v De Keyser's Royal Hotel [1920] AC 508 .... 27, 111, 113, 120, 121, 123, 187
AG v Nissan [1970] AC 179 .... 121, 125
AG v Tomline (1880) 14 Ch D 58 113
Ayliffe v DPP [2005] EWHC 684 (Admin), [2006] QB 227 146

Bate's Case (1606) 2 St Tr 371 112
Bell v Ministry of Defence [2003] EWHC 1134 154
Bici v Ministry of Defence [2004] EWHC 786 154
Blad v Bamfield (1674) 3 Swanst 604 111
Bradlaugh v Gossett (1884) 12 QBD 271 214
BBC v Jones [1965] Ch 32 124
British Railways Board v Pickin [1974] AC 765 214
Broadmayne, The [1916] P 64 120
Burdett v Abbott (1811) 14 East 1 214
Burmah Oil Co Ltd v Lord Advocate [1965] AC 75 .... 111, 118, 120, 123, 147

Calvin's Case (1608) 7 Co Rep 1a, 77 ER 377 .... 16, 112, 121
Canton, The [1917] AC 102 120
Case of Proclamations (1611) 12 Co Rep 74, 77 ER 1352 .... 111, 125
CCSU v Minister for the Civil Service [1985] AC 374 .... 124, 125, 126,
                                    127, 128, 129, 130, 132, 139, 145, 147, 148
Chandler (Terence Norman) v DPP [1964] AC 763 .... 114, 116, 125, 128, 135, 136,
                                                                        138, 140, 148
China Navigation v AG [1932] 2 KB 197 .... 113, 114, 125, 128, 135, 136
Church of Scientology of California v Johnson-Smith [1972] 1 QB 522 213
Crown of Leon v Admiralty Commissioners [1921] 1 KB 59 120
Curtis v Minister of Defence [2002] 2 NZLR 744 (New Zealand) 127

Edinburgh and Dalkeith Rly v Wauchope (1842) 8 Cl & F 710 214
Engel v The Netherlands (1976) 1 EHRR 647 (ECtHR) 152
Ertel Bieber & Co v Rio Tinto Ltd [1918] AC 260 121
Esposito v Bowden (1855) 4 El. & Bl 963, (1857) 7 El & Bl 763 121

Foday Saybana Sankoh (2000) 119 ILR 389 .... 130, 131

Table of Cases

Godden v Hales (1686) 11 St Tr 1165 115

Hole v Barlow (1858) 4 CB (NS) 334. 120
Hoop, The (1799) 1 C Rob 196 121
Horlick v Beal [1916] 1 AC 486 121
Huang v Secretary of State for the Home Department [2005] EWCA Civ 105, [2006] QB 1 .. 138
Hutchinson v Newbury Magistrates (2000) 122 ILR 499 117

JJ [2007] UKHL 45, [2007] WLR 642. 149
Johnson v Pedlar [1921] 2 AC 262 125

King's Prerogative in Saltpetre, The (1606) 12 Rep 1 120
Kuwait Airways Corporation v Iraq Airways Corporation [2002] 2 AC 883 125

Lord Advocate's Reference (No 1 of 2000) 2001 JC 143 (Scotland) 117

MacDonald v Steele (1793) Peake 17 .... 113, 116
Marchoiri v Environment Agency (2002) 127 LR 574 .... 113, 136, 138
Mulcahy v Ministry of Defence [1996] QB 732 154

Operation Dismantle v R (1985) 18 DLR (4th) 494 (Canada) 151

Pepper (Inspector of Taxes) v Hart [1993] AC 593 214
Potts v Bell (1800) 8 TR 548 121
Prebble v TVNZ Ltd [1994] 3 NZLR 1 (New Zealand) 213, 214
Prohibitions del Roy (1607) 12 Co Rep 63; 77 ER 1342 125
Prosecutor v Tadic (1996) 105 ILR 419 (Appeals Chamber of the International
    Criminal Tribunal for the Former Yugoslavia) 202

R (on the application of Abbasi) v Secretary of State for Foreign and
    Commonwealth Affairs [2002] EWCA Civ 1598, [2003] UKHRR 76 ...... 127, 130, 142
R (on the application of Al-Haq) v Secretary of State for Foreign and
    Commonwealth Affairs [2009] EWHC 1910 .... 135, 144
R (on the application of Al Rawi) v Secretary of State for Foreign and
    Commonwealth Affairs [2006] EWCA Civ 1279, [2008] QB 289 .... 126, 135
R (on the application of Al-Skeini) v Secretary of State for Defence [2007] UKHL 26,
    [2008] AC 153 .... 151, 153
R (on the application of Animal Defenders International) v Secretary of State for
    Culture, Media and Sport [2008] UKHL 15, [2008] 2 WLR 781 214
R (on the application of Bancoult) v Secretary of State (No. 2) [2008] UKHL 61,
    [2009] 1 AC 453 .... 124, 129
R (on the application of Campaign for Nuclear Disarmament (CND)) v Prime Minister [2002]
    EWHC 2777 (Admin) 117, 126, 129, 135, 141, 146, 148, 209
R (on the application of Corner House Research) v Director of the Serious
    Fraud Office [2008] UKHL 60, [2009] 1 AC 756 .... 135, 148
R (on the application of Evans) v Secretary of State for Defence [2010] EWHC 1445 144
R (on the application of Gentle v Prime Minister [2008]
    UKHL 20, [2008] 1 AC 1356 .... 117, 136, 146, 150, 151, 152
R (on the application of Jackson) v A-G [2005] UKHL 56, [2006] 1 AC 262 213
R (on the application of Mohamed) v Foreign Secretary (No 2) [2010] EWCA Civ 65,
    [2010] EWCA Civ 158, [2010] 3 WLR 554 .... 135, 136, 149, 155, 196, 197, 201

Table of Cases

R (on the application of Pretty) v DPP [2001] UKHL 20, [2002] 1 AC 800............... 145
R (on the application of ProLife) v British Broadcasting Corporation [2003] UKHL 23,
  [2004] 1 AC 185 135
R (on the application of Purja) v Ministry of Defence [2003] EWCH Civ 1345, [2004]
  1 WLR 289 151
R (on the application of Smith) v Secretary of State for Defence [2010] UKSC 29, [2010]
  3 WLR 223 .... 136, 150, 151, 152, 153
R (on the application of Suresh and Manickavasagam) v Secretary of State
  for the Home Department [2001] EWHC Admin 1028..................... 129, 213
R (on the application of Wheeler) v Prime Minister [2008] EWHC 1409
  (Admin).. 129
R v Bottrill, ex parte Kuechenmeister [1947] 1 KB 41 .... 116, 118, 122
R v Carew Ct of Chancery (1682) 3 Swanst 669, 36 ER 1016 112
R v Commandant of Knockaloe Camp (1917) 117 LT 627 122
R v Criminal Injuries Compensation Board, ex parte P [1995] 1 All ER 845 126
R v DPP, ex parte Kebilene [2000] 2 AC 326 145
R v Earl of Danby (1685) 11 State Tr 600... 239
R v Forsyth [2011] UKSC 9... 122
R v Governor of Wormwood Scrubs Prison [1920] 2 KB 305........................ 116
R v Hampden (1637) 3 St Tr 825...................................26, 28, 112, 113, 119, 120
R v Jones (Margaret) [2004] EWCA Crim 1981, [2005] QB 259..................... 146
R v Jones (Margaret) [2006] UKHL 16, [2007] 1 AC 136 .... 131, 146, 150
R v Ministry of Defence, ex parte Smith [1996] QB 517 .... 132, 136, 150
R v Secretary of State for Foreign and Commonwealth Affairs, ex parte Everett
  [1989] QB 811.. 129
R v Secretary of State for Foreign and Commonwealth Affairs, ex parte Ferhut Butt
  (1999) 116 ILR 607.. 129
R v Secretary of State for Foreign and Commonwealth Affairs, ex parte Pirbhai (1985)
  107 ILR 462... 129
R v Secretary of State for the Home Department, ex parte Bentley [1994] QB 349.......... 145
R v Secretary of State for the Home Department, ex parte Northumbria Police
  Authority [1989] QB 26... 115, 187
R v Spear [2002] UKHL 31, [2003] 1 AC 734....................................... 113
Re a Petition of Right [1915] 3 KB 649 .... 120, 124, 148
R v Vine Street Police Station Superintendent, ex parte Liebmann [1916] 1 KB 268......... 122
Robson v Premier Oil and Pipe Line Co [1915] Ch 13............................. 121
Rustomjee v R (1876) 2 QBD 69.. 113, 125

Secretary of State for the Home Department v E [2007] UKHL 47, [2007] 3 WLR 720 149
Secretary of State for the Home Department v Rehman [2001] UKHL 47, [2003] 1
  AC 153 .... 132, 135, 138
Secretary of State for Foreign and Commonwealth Affairs v Rahmatullah [2012]
  UKSC 48.. 130, 131
Shaw Savill and Albion Co Ltd v The Commonwealth (1940) 66 CLR 344
  (Australia) 154
Smith and Grady v United Kingdom (1999) 29 EHRR 493 (ECtHR)................... 150
Smith v Ministry of Defence [2012] EWCA Civ 1365 .... 152, 153, 154
Stockdale v Hansard (1839) 9 Ad & E 1... 214

Tingle v Mueller [1917] 2 Ch 144 121
Troner v Hassold (1670) 1 Ch Cas 173.. 111

Weymberg v Touch (1669) Ch Cas 123 111
Wilson v First Country Trust Ltd (No 2) [2003] UKHL 40, [2004] 1 AC 816 215

Zamora, The [1916] 2 AC 771. . . . . 20, 147, 148

Table of Statutes, Bills, and International Instruments

STATUTES

13 Car 2 st 1 c 6 .... 106, 114
16 Car I c 32 47
16 Car I c 8 81
16 Car I c 14 81
17 Car I c 14 119
17 Car II c I 86
18 & 19 Car II c 13 86
19 & 20 Car II c I 86
30 Car II c I 86
38 Geo 3 c 27 123
43 Geo 3 c 55 123
Act Abolishing the Office of King 48
Act Appointing a Council of State 48
Act of Settlement 1701 .... 106, 107
Alien Restriction Act 1914 122
Anti-Terrorism, Crime and Security Act 2001 .... 123, 141
Armed Forces Act 2006 107
Bill of Rights 1688 (1 Wm & Mary 2 c 2) 67, 82, 114, 119
   art 4 .... 82, 107
   art 9 .... 67, 214
Civil Contingencies Act 2004 123
Constitutional Reform and Governance Act 2010 186
Counter-Terrorism Act 2008 123
Crown Proceedings Act 1947 153
Crown Proceedings (Armed Forces) Act 1987 153
Defence of the Realm Act 1914 123
Defence of the Realm Consolidation Act 1914 122
Defence (Transfer of Functions) Act 1964 107
Emergency Power (Defence) Act 1939 ... 123
Emergency Power (Defence) Act 1940 ... 123
European Parliamentary Elections Act 2002 213
Export Control Act 2002 122
Freedom of Information Act 2000 ...... 191, 192, 193, 194, 195
   s 23 192
   s 24 192
   s 27 192
   s 53 .... 193, 194
Human Rights Act 133, 149, 150, 151, 153, 160
Intelligence Services Act 1994 .... 111, 215
Justice and Security Act 2013 .... 141, 196
Parliamentary Participation Act 2005 (Germany) 203, 206
Prevention of Terrorism Act 2005 .... 123, 141
Royal Assent Act 1967 186
Statute Law (Repeals) Act 1969 106
Statute Law Revision Act 1863 114
Succession Act 1604 (1 Jac I, c I) 24
Supreme Court Act 1981 144
Terrorism Act 2000 123
Terrorism Act 2006 .... 122, 123
Trading with the Enemy Act 1939 122
United Nations Export Act 1946 122
War Damage Act 1965 121

BILLS

Armed Forces (Parliamentary Approval for Participation in Armed Conflict) HC Bill (2004–05) [31] 182
Armed Forces (Parliamentary Approval for Participation in Armed Conflict) HC Bill (2005–06) [16] 182, 202
Waging War (Parliament's Role and Responsibility) HC Bill (2006–07) [34] 182

INTERNATIONAL INSTRUMENTS

Brussels Treaty 210
Charter of the United Nations 210

Consolidated Treaty on European Union...210
European Convention on Human
    Rights..........................150
Hague Convention.....................76
Geneva Conventions and
    Protocols 131, 202, 203
North Atlantic Treaty.................210
Treaty of Nice........................210

1
Introduction

Introduction

This monograph studies the evolution of the war prerogative in England from 1600–2012. It traces the historical theory and practice of the war prerogative and proposes reform of the constitutional arrangements for its exercise. It addresses three key questions. First, what have writers on political and constitutional theory said about the constitutional arrangements for the war prerogative, and, in particular, what justifications have been advanced for those arrangements? Secondly, in practice, has the executive[1] in fact possessed sole and exclusive powers over war and the deployment of force, or have Parliament and the courts had a role to play in their exercise and scrutiny? Thirdly, are there better ways to organize our constitutional arrangements for the war prerogative, to enable a more substantive role for Parliament (particularly the House of Commons) in its exercise and scrutiny?

On the first question, I show that orthodox theoretical and political discourses have continuously asserted the executive's exclusive power over war, but the justifications advanced for that arrangement have changed over time. Those changes reflect the varying influence of different political theories at different times. On the second question, I find that, contrary to orthodox theoretical and political discourses, Parliament has played an active and substantive role in the exercise and scrutiny of the war prerogative. The courts have refused to intervene in the exercise of the war prerogative, but have been more ready to intervene in cases involving the exercise of powers incidental to the war prerogative. On the third question, I argue that reform

---

[1] I have used various terms to refer to the exerciser of the war prerogative. In the context of examining the period when real political power was exercised by the monarch, I have used the following terms interchangeably: 'monarch', 'king', and 'Crown'. In the context of examining the period when the war prerogative was exercised by ministers responsible to Parliament, I have used the following terms interchangeably: 'Crown', 'executive', and 'government'. The nature of the Crown in the English constitution is complex, and it is unnecessary for the purposes of this monograph to delve into its intricacies.

of the constitutional arrangements for the war prerogative is necessary and desirable. I recommend the use of 'institutional mechanisms': small-scale rules and institutional arrangements within existing institutions which aim to promote certain normative goals. In particular, I propose a statute which would impose conditions on the executive's exercise of its war prerogative. I argue that these proposals show that, through careful institutional design, democratic values, national security, and operational efficiency can each be reconciled and promoted.

The title of this book identifies the key elements of my research. These are as follows.

War Prerogative

I use the terms 'war prerogative' and 'war power' interchangeably to mean the powers, sourced in the prerogative, to declare war and to deploy the armed forces. It does not, unless otherwise indicated, extend to the powers to control or conduct the actual operations of war. The term 'war prerogative' is a useful shorthand, even though states no longer make a declaration of war and the term 'war' is now largely devoid of significance at international law. International law now speaks of situations of 'armed conflict'. 'War', however, was the term used historically, and continues to have colloquial usage.

History

The historical analysis has two distinct focuses. First, chapter 2 is a 'history of ideas' analysis of the political and theoretical discourses about the constitutional arrangements for the war prerogative. I make two findings: first, that political actors and writers on political and constitutional theory from 1600–2012 uniformly identified the executive as possessing exclusive power over the exercise of the war prerogative. Secondly, that the justifications advanced for the executive's exclusive power have changed over time, reflecting the varying influence of different political theories.

My second historical focus is how the war prerogative has been exercised in practice. In chapter 3, I examine how Parliament (in particular the House of Commons) and the executive have interacted in the exercise of the war prerogative. It shows that the House of Commons has played an active and influential role in the exercise and scrutiny of the war prerogative. It also identifies the dichotomy between orthodox theoretical and political discourses as to the war prerogative, and its exercise. The executive has asserted continuously, consistently with those orthodox discourses, that it alone possesses powers over war and peace which it might exercise without the consent or cognizance of Parliament. However, the executive has, through its exercise of these powers, implicitly recognized that it must exercise them in conjunction with Parliament. This dichotomy between the orthodox discourse and the reality of practice is evident throughout the time period under consideration, and is still evident today. Questions as to the proper role of Parliament in the exercise and scrutiny of the war prerogative have been the subject of contestation for over four centuries.

In chapter 4, I identify how the courts have treated the war prerogative. An unbroken line of judicial authority affirms that the Crown possesses, by virtue of the prerogative, exclusive power over the making of war and the deployment of the armed forces. Chapter 4 shows that the courts have consistently refused to intervene in the exercise of the war prerogative. I argue two things: first, the courts possess jurisdiction to review exercises of the war prerogative; but, secondly, in all but the most extreme case, the courts should find issues intimately connected with the exercise of the war prerogative to be non-justiciable. Justiciability is based on an assessment of factors relevant to relative institutional competence and legitimacy over the issue in question.

Reform

In chapters 5 and 6 I argue in favour of reform of the constitutional arrangements for the war prerogative. Chapter 5 sets the theoretical framework for my proposed reform. It explains how institutional mechanisms (small-scale reforms to institutions and practices within the existing large-scale constitutional arrangements) can promote substantive goals. I explain how my proposed institutional mechanisms seek to advance the inherent and instrumental values of democratic decision-making and efficiency in decision-making about war. I argue that the constitutional arrangements for the war prerogative implicitly prioritize operational concerns over all other substantive goals. I argue that we should reconsider this implicit prioritization; we should challenge the assumption that efficiency and democratic values are necessarily in tension with each other. I show that there need not be a trade-off between constitutional arrangements that give effect to democratic values, and constitutional arrangements which address concerns of operational efficiency and effectiveness.

Chapter 6 details my proposed reforms. It advocates a reforming statute which would impose conditions on the government's exercise of the war prerogative. The statute would require the government to obtain in the House of Commons a majority vote in support of deployment of the armed forces, except in identified situations; impose duties on the government to provide Parliament (and the public) with certain information about the proposed deployment; and establish a joint committee of Parliament to scrutinize the relevant information and exercise a general oversight role over the deployment of forces. I also propose a limited role for the courts in enforcing particular aspects of the procedural requirements. These proposals show that, through careful institutional design, democratic values, national security and operational efficiency can be reconciled and promoted.

Constitutional Design

A theme running through the monograph is a focus on the constitutional arrangements for the war prerogative. 'Constitutional arrangements' encompass the institutions, practices, and rules governing how a particular power or function is exercised and controlled. The term 'constitutional design', as used in the monograph title, expresses my interest in the changes and continuities in the design of these constitutional arrangements and their underlying rationales.

This monograph addresses issues fundamental to modern liberal democracies. The state must be able to protect itself, its citizens, and their ways of life. The executive has primary responsibility for protecting national security and the welfare of the community, based on its institutional competencies, expertise, and historical lineage. Although the executive has primary responsibility, Parliament and the courts can and should contribute to the control and scrutiny of those powers. We must enable the executive to deploy the armed forces and wage war when it is deemed necessary. But we must also ensure that Parliament and (to a lesser extent) the courts are able to, and do, insist that the government makes reasoned and justified decisions about war. Relative institutional competency and legitimacy should condition the respective involvement of governmental institutions. The nature of armed conflict and international politics is becoming especially complex and contested. It is vital that decisions about these matters are subjected to reasoned and, where possible, public deliberation.

2
Theoretical and Political Discourses: The War and Foreign Policy Powers

Part I Introduction

The first three chapters of this book present a legal historical analysis of the theory and practice of the powers over war and foreign policy in England from 1600–2012. The analysis has two focuses. The first is an historical analysis of theoretical and political discourses about the constitutional arrangements for the exercise and control of the powers over war and foreign policy.[1] The second is an historical analysis of those powers in practice, concentrating on interactions between the executive and Parliament in the exercise of the powers over war and foreign policy,[2] and judicial consideration of the war prerogative.[3]

Part II of this chapter outlines the general objectives and methodology of my legal historical analysis. Part III then addresses the first of my focuses: an analysis of the theoretical and political discourses about the constitutional arrangements for the exercise and control of the war and foreign policy powers. I will make two findings. The first is that there has been a virtually continuous assertion in theoretical and political discourses of the executive's exclusive control over war and foreign policy, and a denial of a participatory role for Parliament in the exercise of these powers. The second is that, although theoretical and political discourses have continuously asserted executive power over war and foreign policy, the justifications advanced for why this should be so have changed over time and reflect the varying influence of a range of political theories.

Part II Historical Analysis: Objectives and Methodology

Introduction

This part identifies the objectives and methodology of my legal historical analysis. Legal history analyses are 'studies whose primary focus is the development

[1] See ch 2. [2] See ch 3. [3] See ch 4.

or functioning of legal ideas or institutions at some time in the past'.[4] The two focuses of my legal historical analysis are (1) the development of legal ideas (as expressed in theoretical and political discourses[5]) about the constitutional arrangements for the war and foreign policy powers, and (2) the development and functioning of institutions in the exercise of the war and foreign policy powers. This part identifies the objectives of my legal historical analysis and addresses issues of legal historical methodology as relevant to this analysis.

Objectives of Legal Historical Analysis

The historical analysis in this book has two key objectives: the enhancement of understanding of past events, institutions, and practices; and the enhancement of understanding of contemporary institutions and practices.

My historical analysis will enhance understanding of past events, institutions, and practices in two broad ways. First, it will identify the justifications that have been advanced for the asserted exclusive power of the executive over war and foreign policy. Orthodox theoretical and political discourses have, for the past four hundred years, asserted the executive's exclusive powers over these matters. However, there has not been a comprehensive examination of the justifications advanced for this constitutional arrangement. My historical analysis identifies those justifications and explains how they demonstrate the changing influence of various political theories on England's constitution. Secondly, my historical analysis will enhance understanding of past events, institutions, and practices by showing the disparity between orthodox theoretical and political discourses and how these powers were actually exercised in practice. Orthodox discourses rejected any role for Parliament in the exercise of the war and foreign policy powers. In practice, however, Parliament has had an active and substantive role in the exercise of these powers. The interactions of Parliament and the executive in the exercise of the war and foreign policy powers have not been subjected to comprehensive or long-range analysis. My historical analysis will show the error of the commonly held assumptions that the executive has always exercised exclusive power over war and foreign policy and that Parliament has not had a substantive participatory role.

The second objective of my legal historical analysis is to enhance understanding of contemporary institutions and practices. This objective is based on the premise that historical understanding is necessary for present-day understanding: one

---

[4] D Ibbetson, 'Historical Research in Law' in P Cane and M Tushnet (eds), *The Oxford Handbook of Legal Studies* (OUP 2003) 863, 863.
[5] Refer to citations in nn 39–40 for an explanation of what I mean by 'theoretical and political discourses'.

cannot understand the rules of the present without looking at those of the past.[6] Colin Rhys Lovell proffered that 'To understand the history of law is to know much about its present meaning and purpose.'[7] WS Holdsworth agreed. He said that legal history was 'necessary to the understanding and intelligent working of all long established legal systems'.[8] This is particularly true when examining constitutional rules. Vernon Bogdanor has highlighted the 'historic' character of the English constitution, in the sense of being 'original and spontaneous, the product not of deliberate design but of a long process of evolution'.[9] Historical events and practices have shaped the roles, powers, and structures of present-day governmental powers and institutions, rendering historical understanding vital for an understanding of the contemporary English constitution.[10]

Historical analysis might reveal and challenge assumptions that are commonly made about particular constitutional arrangements or the functions of particular institutions. For one author, the value of legal historical analysis is that it can cast doubt on any deterministic or teleological sense of the immutable or inevitable quality of institutions by exposing 'the possible alternatives and reasons for choosing one rather than another'.[11] This can be a useful reminder in the context of proposed constitutional reform. Similarly, historical analysis reveals the shifting influence of political theories and other ideologies. For Smith and McLaren, history's useful role may be in exposing the contingent nature and ideological quality of law-making and constitutional arrangements.[12] For example, our constitution is now founded on and informed by democratic values, yet our constitutional arrangements for the exercise of the war power do not reflect those values; they instead reflect the political theories and practices that exerted influence at previous times in our

---

[6] R Zimmerman, 'Savigny's Legacy: Legal History, Comparative Law, and the Emergence of a European Legal Science' (1996) 112 Law Quarterly Review 576, 602; J Gordley, 'Why Look Backward' (2002) 50 American Journal of Comparative Law 657; J Gordley, 'Comparative Law and Legal History' in M Reimann and R Zimmerman (eds), *The Oxford Handbook of Comparative Law* (OUP 2006) 753, 772.

[7] CR Lovell, *English Constitutional and Legal History: A Survey* (OUP 1962) xi.

[8] WS Holdsworth, *Some Lessons from Our Legal History* (Macmillan 1928) 8–9.

[9] V Bogdanor, 'Conclusion' in, *The British Constitution in the Twentieth Century* (OUP 2003) 689, 719, drawing on unpublished writings of Dicey, where he described the constitution as 'historic' and 'spontaneous' (see GJ Hand, 'AV Dicey's Unpublished Materials on the Comparative Study of the Constitution' in GJ Hand and J McBride (eds), *Droits Sans Frontieres: Essays in Honour of L. Neville Brown* (Holdsworth Club 1991) esp 77–81, 86). Although, see at 689–720, where Bogdanor argues that the constitutional reforms of the past three decades have in fact altered the constitution's 'historic' nature.

[10] See JWF Allison, 'History in the *Law of the Constitution*' (2007) 28 The Journal of Legal History 263 on the importance of historical understanding in the study of English public law.

[11] RG Collingwood, *The Idea of History* (OUP 1946) 283.

[12] KJM Smith and JPS McLaren, 'History's Living Legacy: An Outline of "Modern" Historiography of the Common Law' (2001) 21 Legal Studies 251, 322.

constitutional history. This, too, is an important consideration in the context of proposed reform.

Legal History Methodology

Having established the reasons why I am undertaking a historical analysis, I now turn to the methodology I will employ and identify the key methodological issues relevant to my analysis.

Choices as to type and content of sources are critical, and raise key methodological issues. The historical analysis in this book draws upon primary, secondary, and tertiary historical sources. Primary sources are documents or other sources of information that were created at the time being studied, or afterwards by individuals reflecting on their involvement in the events of the time. I use a variety of primary sources, including contemporary pamphlets and tracts, records of parliamentary debates, statutes, judicial decisions, and royal proclamations and speeches. Secondary sources are documents which relate to or discuss information originally presented elsewhere. Secondary sources involve generalization, analysis, synthesis, interpretation, or evaluation of the primary information, and raise particular issues for historical methodology, which are discussed later on. Tertiary sources incorporate a compilation of primary and secondary sources with commentary and analysis.

The type and content of the sources used reflect the type of legal history being conducted. The legal historical method employed in this book is primarily an example of what has been called a 'lawyer's legal history', or an 'internal' legal history. An internal legal history is[13]

> the history of lawyers' law, of legal rules and principles. Its sources are predominately those that are thrown up by the legal process: principally statutes and decided cases, supplemented where possible with lawyers' literature expounding the rules and occasionally reflecting on them.

An internal legal history typically emphasizes the use of appellate court judgments, statutes, legislative history, and legal text books and treatises. The analysis in this book draws largely on these types of sources, supplemented where appropriate with some non-legal sources, such as contemporary writings on political philosophy. Internal legal histories are to be contrasted with 'external' legal histories. External legal histories typically look at the political, social, and economic impact of people and events on legal institutions and rules, and vice versa. Its sources include personal papers, letters, diaries, and pamphlets.[14]

[13] Ibbetson (n 4) 864.
[14] Ibbetson (n 4) 864. See also J Parrish, 'A Guide to the American Legal History Methodology' (1994) 86 Law Library Journal 105, 106; C McCrudden, 'Legal Research and the Social Sciences' (2006) 122 Law Quarterly Review 632, 633–5.

One of the most prominent criticisms of legal historical methodology focuses on how legal historical writing deals with the nature of the relationship and interaction between 'law' and society: to what extent are legal doctrines and institutions insulated and/or separable from 'external' forces? Internal and external legal histories offer different responses to this issue. A key criticism of internal legal histories is that they try to understand the law of a time or place or nation as an independent object of study.[15] In particular, some internal legal historical work has been criticized for being based upon an assumption of English law's natural and autonomous evolution, independently of extra-legal ideas, events, and influences, or upon an assumption that the law constitutes a sufficiently autonomous field of experience or discourse that can legitimately be described by reference to its own sources.[16] Critics of internal legal histories commend external legal histories for recognizing the broader context in which law operates by shifting the focus from legal rules and discourses to institutional frameworks and the complex situations within which the rules operate.

This book focuses on the institutions, rules, and processes involved in the exercise of the war power, which are, avowedly, the prime focuses of internal legal histories. I recognize the limitations of trying to understand legal practices and institutions in isolation from other events and influences. However, my doctrinal and institutional focus is a conscious and justified choice. For example, my focus on the inter-institutional relationship between Parliament (in particular the House of Commons) and the executive means that I have concentrated on particular historical events and practices which best illustrate the nature of that relationship. That focus necessarily precludes detailed consideration of other potential influences on the formulation of foreign policy.[17] My focus on the orthodox theoretical and political discourses means that I have concentrated on the key authoritative theorists and texts and the statements and writings of leading political actors.[18] Smith and McLaren recognize that legal historical analysis may legitimately confine itself to an internalist investigation, provided that the limitations of the exercise are made clear, that is 'doing no more than to be dealing with the interactive nature

---

[15] Gordley, 'Comparative Law and Legal History' (n 6) 758–9.
[16] See, eg, Smith and McLaren (n 12).
[17] cf J Black, *A System of Ambition? British Foreign Policy 1660–1793* (Longman 1991) 1–2, identifying what he sees as a failing, in many historical accounts of foreign policy decision-making processes and institutions, of over-simplifying the complex processes and institutions involved.
[18] On the danger of overstating the extent to which there was only one climate of opinion or dominant framework, see Ibbetson (n 4) 872–3; J Black, 'Hanover and British Foreign Policy 1714–60' (2005) 120 English Historical Review 303, 303–4; Gordley, 'Comparative Law and Legal History' (n 6) 764. I recognize this danger, but contend that my concentration on the orthodox theoretical and political discourses is justified, for the reasons stated.

of legal assumptions and ideas of the various legal agents and agencies most immediately engaged in the process'.[19] Secondly, there are methodological challenges associated with external legal histories, including needing to understand properly both the legal materials as well as their political, social, and economic contexts, avoiding the risk of selecting sources in order to support a predetermined thesis, and dealing with the interpretative problems that arise. Limitations of space and proficiency, as well as the limited scope of my historical analysis, preclude taking on such challenges.

I now turn from criticisms made of internal legal history specifically, to criticisms made of legal history more generally. One potential issue is employing anachronistic interpretations in historical analysis. Historians are often accused of illegitimately imposing contemporary conceptions onto historical events, institutions, and ideas, or of being 'enticed into carrying concepts and even social frameworks back into periods to which they do not belong'.[20] I am aware of the dangers of, for example, imposing ideas about present-day institutions and their functions onto historical institutions and their functions. It is clear that the institutional structure of present-day governments is very different from that of seventeenth-century governments; as are the environments (political, social, economic, technological, and global) in which they operate. As a specific example, Conrad Russell stresses the importance of avoiding contemporary conceptions of 'Parliament' when evaluating parliaments of the seventeenth century.[21] Today, Parliament is a permanent institution, but in the first half of the seventeenth century, there was no such singular, permanent institution. Instead, there were 'irregularly recurring events called Parliaments'.[22] A related peril is illegitimately carrying contemporary conceptions of ideas or theories into the past. Whig constitutional history has been criticized for being a vehicle for expressing a fervour for something in the present (such as democracy or freedom of thought) and interpreting past events and practices by reference to its value.[23]

I recognize the need to be aware of the dangers of employing ahistorical structures and interpretations when describing and evaluating historical events, institutions, and ideas. However, it is a peril which is difficult to avoid totally,

---

[19] Smith and McLaren (n 12) 312–13. See also JWF Allison, *The English Historical Constitution: Continuity, Change and European Effects* (CUP 2007) xi–xii, 40, 243–4 on 'internal' and 'external' histories.

[20] SFC Milsom, *Historical Foundations of the Common Law*, 2nd edn (Butterworths 1981) vi.

[21] C Russell, 'The Nature of a Parliament in Early Stuart England' in H Tomlinson (ed), *Before the English Civil War: Essays on Early Stuart Politics and Government* (MacMillan Press 1983) 123.

[22] Russell (n 21) 123.

[23] Allison (n 10) 272, citing H Butterfield, *The Whig Interpretation of History* (Norton Library 1931) 96.

and, in some instances, might in fact enhance the usefulness of legal historical analysis. Historical analysis is the product of the research and interpretation of the individual historian: 'history is made by historians and their task is thoroughly interpretative (*i.e.* concerned to generate meaning).'[24] Research and interpretation is unavoidably coloured and shaped by the individual's 'lens' or framework; part of which will be present-day conceptions of institutions, structures, and ideas. Likewise, comparison and evaluation is made by reference to individual preferences, experiences, and environment. Therefore, although one should be aware of the perils of imposing the contemporary onto the historical, one should also acknowledge that it is an inevitable part of historical research and analysis. Further, for some legal historians, explicit focus on the present is not illegitimate but is in fact what makes legal history useful. For Holdsworth, 'effective legal history' (as opposed to 'mere antiquarianism') must be orientated explicitly to the present: 'the legal historian must have his eye on the end of the story, and be able to pick out the beginnings of those principles and rules and institutions which have survived and are operative today.'[25]

Some have also raised concerns about how the contentious and subjective nature of historical analysis poses particular issues for the uses of legal history. One of those issues is the use of secondary sources. Secondary sources represent subjective interpretations of events, motives, and causes, and reflect differing purposes and ideologies; something which should be kept in mind when drawing on such sources in analysis.[26] A prime example is analyses of the causes of the English Civil War: some accounts written soon after the war attributed the war to individual personal failures, while others thought it was the product of long-term social change.[27] Later studies also reveal the impact of political ideology on interpretation and evaluation; for example, Christopher Hill's Marxist account of the Civil War identified social and economic factors as the main causes.[28]

Another potential issue is the use of legal history as a source of authority for present law. Smith and McLaren observe that, when used in this way, legal history searches for certainty and definition, and is premised on an assumption of a recoverable objective and factual past. Smith and McLaren provide as an example the common practice of prefacing expositions of modern law

---

[24] M Loughlin, 'Theory and Values in Public Law: An Interpretation' [2005] Public Law 48, 63.
[25] Holdsworth (n 8) 6. See also Allison (n 19) 20–5.
[26] See, eg, the discussion about the political motivations of Blackstone and Bentham, in Smith and McLaren (n 12) 254.
[27] H Tomlinson, 'The Causes of War: A Historiographical Survey' in Tomlinson (n 21) 7.
[28] C Hill, *The English Revolution 1640* (Lawrence and Wishart 1940).

with summaries of historical precedents and doctrines. These types of legal history are shaped by the fact that the authority given to precedent will turn substantially on demonstrable linear continuity, and may be coloured by the charging of old principles and concepts with new meaning.[29] The postmodern legal historian will be sceptical about the ability to recover a single, authentic, and authoritative meaning, and suggest that there are a potential multiplicity of interpretations of texts and events.[30] The critical legal studies movement also challenges the presumption of objective meaning, and uses history to demonstrate the inherently political nature of law and legal institutions and how the law reflects the dominant ideology and political power at a particular time and in a particular society.[31]

The selection and invocation of particular interpretations of historical events or practices as authority for present law is, at least in part, a normative exercise. It is also the basis of the common law doctrine of precedent, by which 'what is historic is attributed legal authority',[32] and precedents are selected or ignored depending on whether they strengthen or weaken one's case. A historian's history and a lawyer's history might take different approaches to these issues. Some historians warn that broader theorizing on the nature and processes of doctrinal or institutional change carries the danger of predetermining outcomes; Maitland for example warned against using history to promote particular ideological ends: 'If we try to make history the handmaid of dogma she will soon cease to be history.'[33] The lawyer is likely to be far more comfortable with the inherently disputed and selective nature of 'history' and its use as authority for present law. As Allison notes, a Maitland 'document-based best-evidence' history, overwhelming with detail and undirected, is inaccessible and ultimately unhelpful for understanding what is of constitutional legal significance.[34] 'Constitutional myth-making', involving the veneration of

---

[29] Smith and McLaren (n 12) 311.

[30] On the objectivity and interpretation of facts, see Loughlin (n 24) 61–3; GE White, 'Truth and Interpretation in Legal History' in *Intervention and Detachment, Essays in Legal History and Jurisprudence* (OUP 1994) 17.

[31] eg, Morton Horwitz expresses fundamental scepticism over the possibility of objective facts and the ability to separate fact from value. He says: 'As one sees both theories and causes as more contingent, one's belief in one's own objectivity is also drawn into question. Is it just my story, with all the connotations of skepticism and subjectivity that the word "story" implies?' (*The Transformation of American Law 1870–1960: The Crisis of Legal Orthodoxy* (OUP 1992) viii).

[32] Allison (n 19) 25.

[33] FW Maitland, 'Why the History of English Law is Not Written' in H Fisher (ed), *Collected Papers of Frederic William Maitland* (first published 1888, CUP 1911) 488, cited in Smith and McLaren (n 12) 260.

[34] Allison (n 19) 19–20. See also Allison (n 10) 281, where he identifies the complementary and precautionary value of Maitland-style history, in helping to avert the danger of a constitutional historical account contributing to a contortion of history or 'constitutional propaganda'.

a particular conception of a constitutional framework and values, is a prominent feature of English constitutionalism.[35] Constitutional myth-making employs historical narrative to promote particular ideological ends and the validity of particular rules, principles, and values.[36] It is historically-grounded, but based less on a claim of objective historical 'facts', and more on particular (mythical) conceptions of historic values, constitutional arrangements, and practices. Lord Nicholls asserted in the *Torture Evidence* case: 'the precise detail does not matter.'[37]

I have recognized the methodological issues of legal historical analysis and some of the challenges associated with such analysis. While these issues must be given due attention, they should not be overstated to the extent they overwhelm the analysis and its objectives. Legal historical analysis can pursue and attain worthy objectives, and contribute usefully to our knowledge and understanding of the past and the present. I hope that the historical analysis in this work makes a unique and useful contribution to our understanding of the war prerogative.

Part III The Executive and the War and Foreign Policy Powers

Introduction

Orthodox constitutional theory declares that the powers to wage war and to formulate and implement foreign policy lie within the exclusive prerogative of the Crown. This statement described the constitutional position at the start of the seventeenth century, and it has remained the constitutional orthodoxy since. In practice, however, the position is not (and was not) so clear. There has always been disparity between the constitutional orthodoxy and how the war and foreign policy powers were and are exercised in practice. This chapter and the following chapter explore these issues in a historical context, by identifying and evaluating the roles of the executive and Parliament in exercising and controlling the war powers over the past four centuries. I will show that, contrary

---

[35] See, eg, *A v Secretary of State for the Home Department* [2004] UKHL 56, [2005] 2 AC 68 (Belmarsh) [88]–[89], [91], [95] (Lord Hoffmann); *A v Secretary of State for the Home Department (No 2)* [2005] UKHL 71, [2006] 2 AC 221 (*Torture Evidence* case) [11] (Lord Bingham); [65] (Lord Nicholls); [81]–[83] (Lord Hoffmann); [101] (Lord Hope); [152] (Lord Carswell). See also I Ward, *The English Constitution: Myths and Realities* (Hart Publishing 2004).

[36] D Friedman, 'Torture and the Common Law' (2006) 2 European Human Rights Review 180, 199; M Zagor, 'Judicial Rhetoric and Constitutional Identity: Comparative Approaches to Aliens' Rights in the United Kingdom and Australia' (2008) 19 Public Law Review 271, 279.

[37] *Torture Evidence* case (n 35) [65].

to constitutional orthodoxy, Parliament historically had a substantive role in the exercise of the war power and exercised real influence over the Crown's foreign policies through debate, the power of supply, and retrospective scrutiny. Parliament's role in war and foreign policy has changed over time as the nature and functions of Parliament changed and parliamentary government developed. Parliament's role has become largely restricted to scrutinizing and criticizing governmental policies and actions, rather than participating in their formulation and implementation.

The remainder of this chapter sets up the first part of my argument: that, according to constitutional orthodoxy, the executive holds, and always has held, exclusive powers over war and foreign policy. The first section traces the continuous assertion of executive power over war and foreign policy from the seventeenth century to the present. It presents a representative survey of statements from writers on political and constitutional theory and from political actors. I refer to these sources as 'theoretical and political discourses'. The second section switches the focus to the justifications advanced for this constitutional orthodoxy. It will show that, although there has been a continuous assertion of executive power over war and foreign policy, the justifications advanced for why this should be so have changed over time. Chapter 3 will demonstrate the disparity between this constitutional orthodoxy and how the war powers were in practice exercised and controlled.

Some initial notes as to the scope of my historical analysis. First, the time period under consideration is 1600–2012. Secondly, although my focus is the exercise and control of the war prerogative, I extend that focus, where appropriate, to include consideration of the powers over foreign policy more generally. Historically, the powers over war and peace were considered to be an aspect of the king's prerogatives to conduct external relations. The waging of war and brokering of peace were expressions of foreign policy and were interconnected with other aspects of foreign policy, particularly the conduct of foreign relations and the making of treaties. It would therefore be artificial to consider in isolation the specific power over war. Thirdly, my focuses are the domestic legal and political decision-making processes and institutions involved in the foreign policy and war powers. Detailed consideration of the impact of international law and politics on domestic decision-making processes and institutions is outside the scope of this work.[38]

Finally, a note on whose statements and words I draw upon in this chapter. My focus is what writers on political and constitutional theory and political

---

[38] For an examination of the impact of public international law on the UK's deployment of armed force since World War II, see N White, *Democracy Goes to War: British Military Deployments under International Law* (OUP 2009). See also C Ku and H K Jacobson, *Democratic Accountability and the Use of Force in International Law* (CUP 2003).

actors have said about the constitutional arrangements for the war and foreign policy powers. I refer to these sources as 'theoretical and political discourses'. A history of theoretical and political discourses focuses on 'the principal vocabularies or "languages" which were available and exploitable for the conduct, discussion, vindication, and criticism of political action and the principles on which it was seen to be founded'.[39] By 'writers on political and constitutional theory', I refer to those writers who sought to explain and justify these constitutional arrangements in theoretical terms. I accord a broad interpretation to 'writers on political and constitutional theory', to include 'classic' accounts of political authority (such as those of Locke, Montesquieu, and Kant) and also accounts of influential text writers (such as Chitty). It would be artificial and unnecessary to try to divide these theoretical accounts into 'political' theoretical accounts and 'constitutional' or 'legal' theoretical accounts. Political theory tends to have a broader focus than constitutional theory: constitutional theory concentrates on constitutions (their arrangements, practices, rules, institutions, etc), while political theory tends to look to broader questions of political authority, ideas, and practices. However, many of the theoretical accounts examined here contained a mixture of both, and also a mixture of normative and descriptive content. By 'political actors', I refer to individuals involved in the practical exercise of these governmental powers, including members of parliament (MPs), the media, the monarch, and royal officials.[40] I present these theoretical and political discourses as representing the 'constitutional orthodoxy', meaning the position widely accepted. As will be observed, there has been remarkably little dissension from this position.

The Executive's Foreign Policy Powers: Constitutional Orthodoxy

The continuous and virtually unchallenged assertion of the executive's exclusive powers over war and foreign policy is striking. Calls for radical constitutional changes to the way in which the war and foreign policy powers are exercised and controlled have been rare. Even in the mid-seventeenth century, when the king's powers in certain spheres were challenged, the king's unique authority over war and foreign policy was assumed and accepted for a surprisingly long time. Advocates for greater parliamentary involvement in foreign policy have tended to confine their appeals to an extension of parliamentary

---

[39] JGA Pocock, 'Introduction' in JGA Pocock (ed) (with Gordon J Schochet and Lois G Schwoerer), *The Varieties of British Political Thought, 1500–1800* (CUP 1993) 1.
[40] I concentrate in this and the following chapter on what actors in the 'political branches' (the executive and Parliament) thought and said. Judicial treatment of the war prerogative is dealt with in ch 4.

influence within the orthodox constitutional arrangements, rather than a more fundamental challenge to the royal prerogatives over foreign policy.[41]

For most of the seventeenth century, constitutional orthodoxy asserted that matters of war and peace, treaty-making, and foreign policy were paradigm 'kingly powers', and the subject of the inseparable and absolute royal prerogative. This was regarded as axiomatic: these were the king's powers, according to custom and practice and the 'ancient constitution'. Commentators and political actors were united in asserting the king's exclusive competence over war and foreign policy. Sir Thomas Smith, in his *De Republica Anglorum* (circa 1562–5) stated: 'the monarch... has absolutely in his power the authority of war and peace, to defy what prince it shall please him, and to bid him war, and again to reconcile himself and enter into league or truce with him at his pleasure or the advice only of his privy council.'[42] In *Calvin's Case*[43] it was proclaimed that '*bellim indicere* belongth only and wholly to the king.' In 1641, Charles I described his power to deploy and command the militia as 'the just power prerogative which God and the laws of this kingdom have placed in him for the defence of his people'.[44] Sir Walter Raleigh (a writer and historian during the reigns of Elizabeth and James I) identified 'The second mark of majesty is authority to make war, and conclude peace, at his pleasure';[45] and, a writer during the Interregnum recalling learned opinions of earlier times declared that 'The makinge of war, and so likewise of peace, is wholy and absolutely a regall prerogative.'[46]

During the revolutionary period in the mid-seventeenth century these orthodox constitutional principles were challenged; but not until 1641, when the nation was on the brink of civil war. Most of the leaders in the struggle against the king accepted for a surprisingly long time the absolute power of the king within certain realms, one of those being war and foreign policy. It is striking that, during the Interregnum, many still adhered to the orthodox constitutional position and regarded the revolutionary period as a 'temporary exception', justified on the grounds that the king had been misled by 'evil counsellors'. The revolutionary period and the justifications advanced by

---

[41] J Black, *Parliament and Foreign Policy in the Eighteenth Century* (CUP 2004) 3–4; M Judson, *The Crisis of the Constitution: An Essay in Constitutional and Political Thought in England 1603–1645* (Rutgers University Press 1949) 26.
[42] Thomas Smith, *De Republica Anglorum* (Mary Dewar ed, CUP 2009) 85.
[43] (1608) 7 Co Rep 25ba.
[44] Parliamentary History, 28 February 1641, vol 2, col 1107.
[45] Walter Raleigh, 'The Cabinet-Council' in *Works of Sir Walter Raleigh* vol I (T Birch ed, 1751) 42.
[46] Sir Roger Twysden, *Certaine Considerations upon the Government of England* vol xlv (J M Kemble ed, 1849) 21.

parliamentarians for assuming the foreign policy powers, are examined in the following chapter.[47]

With the Restoration and return to monarchical government, the long-standing constitutional orthodoxy was revived, and the king's powers over war, peace, treaties, and foreign policy were again asserted. This position was uncontroversial, and ascribed to by both political actors and commentators.[48] A typical statement on the nature and extent of the Crown's powers over war and foreign policy was made by John Snell in a debate on the Septennial Bill in the Commons in 1716:[49]

by the known and standing law of the land, the right of making peace and war, treaties and alliances, are undeniably the King's prerogative; and most for the good and benefit of his people, without application to Parliament, either to approve or confirm.

Other MPs during the eighteenth century also made statements of similar effect, asserting the Crown's exclusive powers over these matters. Walpole, England's first Prime Minister, said that 'our constitution has trusted intirely to the crown, the power of making peace and war'.[50] In 1743, William Murray said that one of the chief prerogatives of the Crown was that the king had not only the sole power of declaring war but the sole direction of its conduct.[51] In 1755, Lord Chancellor Hardwicke declared that the king was not constitutionally obliged to ask the consent of Parliament to any treaty which he made, or even to communicate it to it, unless a grant or an act of Parliament was required, and even then, not until he applied for the grant or bill which was needed.[52]

Assertions of the Crown's exclusive powers over war and the conduct of foreign relations denied a role for Parliament in their formulation or implementation. As was announced in the House of Commons in 1677: 'The Right of making and Managing War and Peace is in his Majesty: And, if you think He will depart from any Part of That Right, you are mistaken.'[53] Archibald Hutchenson, an MP, in 1716 asserted: 'Surely the executive power is intirely in the prince, there the laws of the land have placed it, and there I hope it will for ever remain: The power of peace, war, and alliances, are the undoubted

---

[47] See citations at n 1 in ch 3.
[48] J Clarke, *British Diplomacy and Foreign Policy 1782–1865: The National Interest* (Unwin Hyman 1989) 44.
[49] Parliamentary History, 24 April 1716, vol 7, col 315.
[50] Parliamentary History, 30 March 1738, vol 10, col 690.
[51] Parliamentary History, 6 December 1743, vol 13, col 246.
[52] Parliamentary History, 10 December 1755, vol 15, col 652.
[53] Cited in ER Turner, 'Parliament and Foreign Affairs, 1603–1760' (1919) 34 The English Historical Review 172, 180.

prerogatives of the crown, and no parliament, I hope, will ever pretend to dispute the same.'[54] Another MP commented that although 'of late years parliaments have thought themselves intitled to interpose their advice' on matters of foreign relations, 'I deny it to be their right'.[55]

The leading writers on political and constitutional theory in the seventeenth and eighteenth century matched these statements of political actors. Locke accorded the executive with total control over foreign policy and war. Locke's analysis of governmental functions was unique in distinguishing executive power (concerned with executing the municipal laws of a system) from what he labelled the 'federative power' (concerned with 'the management of the security and interest of the public without').[56] Locke included within the federative power the powers to make war and peace, to enter alliances, and to enter other transactions with all persons and communities outside the state.[57] Locke explained that the exercise of the federative power and the executive power each requires the force of the commonwealth, and therefore it would be impracticable and undesirable to place the two powers in separate hands, for they might act separately and divide the force of the commonwealth.

Writing later in the eighteenth century, Montesquieu and Blackstone each proclaimed the king's exclusive powers over war and foreign policy both as a matter of description and as a matter of normative principle. According to Montesquieu, making peace or war, sending or receiving embassies, and protecting against invasions were executive powers held by the king.[58] This distribution of the executive power was desirable: 'The executive power ought to be in the hands of a monarch; because this branch of government, which has always need of expedition, is better administered by one than by many'.[59] The executive should also possess exclusive control over the army, thought Montesquieu: 'once an army is established, it ought not to depend immediately on the legislative, but on the executive power; and this from the very nature of the thing; its business consisting more in action than in deliberation.'[60]

Blackstone took a similar approach. He identified the powers over 'intercourse with foreign states' as direct prerogatives of the king. Direct prerogatives

---

[54] Parliamentary History, 24 April 1716, vol 7, col 864.
[55] Parliamentary History, 24 April 1716, vol 7, col 315.
[56] John Locke, 'Two Treatises of Government', ch XII [146]–[147] in S M Cahn (ed), *Classics of Modern Political Theory: Machiavelli to Mill* (first published 1689, OUP 1997). See also MJC Vile, *Constitutionalism and the Separation of Powers*, 2nd edn (Liberty Fund 1998) 65. For a contemporary analysis and application of Locke, see D Jenkins, 'The Lockean Constitution: Separation of Powers and the Limits of Prerogative' (2011) 56 McGill Law Journal 543.
[57] Locke (n 56) [146].
[58] Montesquieu, 'L'Espirit des Lois' (1748) in Cahn (n 56), 347.
[59] Montesquieu (n 58) 347.   [60] Montesquieu (n 58) 352.

are those which are 'such positive substantial parts of the royal character and authority, as are rooted in and spring from the king's political person'.[61] These powers of intercourse with foreign states included sending and receiving ambassadors, making treaties and alliances, making war and peace, and admitting foreigners. In the exercise of these powers, Blackstone declared, the king is the delegate and sovereign representative of his people.[62] In the exercise of his war prerogative, the king is the 'generalissimo, or the first in military command, within the kingdom'.[63] His position as 'general of the kingdom' accords the king 'the sole power of raising and regulating fleets and armies'.[64] Blackstone emphasized this point, perhaps in response to the lingering memories of the Civil war when Parliament sought to wrest military control from the king: he declared military command 'ever was and is the undoubted right of his majesty, and his royal predecessors... and that both or either house of parliament cannot, nor ought to, pretend to the same'.[65]

By the nineteenth century, Whig thought and theories of representative government started to replace the portrayal of the English constitution as one of mixed and balanced monarchical government. However, the executive's exclusive powers over war and foreign policy continued to be asserted. Chitty's monograph on prerogative power, written in 1820, was the seminal influence on nineteenth and early-twentieth centuries' analyses of prerogative power. He declared that '[a]s representative of his people, and executive magistrate, the King possesses... the exclusive right to make war or peace, either within or out of his dominions'.[66]

Whig thought's major contribution to discourse about the war and foreign policy powers was the recognition that although the formal legal distribution of powers accorded to the monarch powers of government (including powers over war, peace, and foreign policy), in practice, the monarch exercised those powers on the advice of his or her ministers.[67] Writing on the nature of parliamentary government in 1858, Earl Grey observed:[68]

---

[61] Sir William Blackstone, *Commentaries on the laws of England, in Four Books* vol 1, 13th edn (E Christian ed, Strahan 1800) 239–40.
[62] Blackstone (n 61) 252, 256–7.
[63] Blackstone (n 61) 261.
[64] Blackstone (n 61) 261.
[65] Blackstone (n 61) 261–2.
[66] J Chitty, *A Treatise on the Law of the Prerogatives of the Crown: And the Relative Duties and Rights of the Subject* (Butterworth 1820) 43.
[67] cf later accounts, which argue that Whig writers overstated the extent to which the monarch was politically powerless, particularly in the realm of foreign policy. See HJ Hanham (ed), *The Nineteenth-Century Constitution 1815–1914: Documents and Commentary* (CUP 1969) 24 and the citations at n 70 in ch 3.
[68] Henry Grey, 'Parliamentary Government' (1858) in Hanham (n 67) 13–14.

> It is the distinguishing characteristic of Parliamentary Government, that it requires the powers belonging to the Crown to be exercised through Ministers, who are held responsible for the manner in which they are used, who are expected to be members of the two Houses of Parliament, the proceedings of which they must be able to generally guide, and who are considered entitled to hold their offices only while they possess the confidence of Parliament, and more especially of the Houses of Commons.

Bagehot and Dicey stressed the unreality and fiction of those accounts of English constitutional arrangements which identified the king as exercising real political power. For example, in reference to Blackstone's praise of the English constitution's placement of the executive powers in the hands of one individual (the king), Dicey said: 'It has but one fault; the statements it contains are the direct opposite of the truth. The executive of England is in fact placed in the hands of a committee called the cabinet. If there be any one person in whose single hand the power of the State is placed, that one person is not the king but the chairman of the committee, known as the Prime Minister.'[69]

Political actors and commentators continued to assert that the decision to go to war was, formally at least, outside the sphere of parliamentary action or influence. Constitutional historian FW Maitland said: 'Without the consent of parliament he [the King] can direct the invasion of a foreign country...and practically a ministry has a great deal of power as regards foreign affairs, and might even force a reluctant nation into a war from which it would be impossible to withdraw.'[70] One contemporary wrote in 1882: 'The Cabinet as adviser to the Sovereign retains the conduct of Foreign affairs in its own hands.... It can and does undertake delicate and important negotiations with other States on the issue of which may hang peace or war not only on its own responsibility but without the knowledge of the House of Commons'.[71] In 1864, Disraeli said in debate in the House of Commons that 'If there be a prerogative of the Crown, which no one has ever challenged, it is the prerogative of the Crown to declare peace or war without the interference of Parliament, by her Majesty alone, under the advice of her responsible Ministers.'[72]

Today, the orthodox constitutional position regarding the war and foreign policy powers remains largely unchanged as from the statements made in the nineteenth century. The Crown wages war and makes peace, deploys the armed

---

[69] AV Dicey, *Introduction to the Study of the Law of the Constitution* (first published 1895, 10th edn, Macmillan 1959) 8.
[70] FW Maitland, *The Constitutional History of England: A Course of Lectures Delivered by F.W. Maitland* (CUP 1913) 423–4.
[71] Anon, 'Our Foreign Policy' (1882) 5 Scottish Review 332, 342.
[72] HC Deb 4 February 1864, vol 173, cols 97–8.

forces, directs the conduct of war, and conducts foreign relations. Parliament has no formal role in their exercise, although possibly a constitutional convention in favour of parliamentary consultation before deployment has developed.[73] In 1909, a commentator stated: 'The King and his Foreign Minister can make war and peace, they can annex and alienate territory, they can assume obligations which may oblige not only us, but our children, to go to war in support of an ally in a quarrel not our own.'[74] O Hood Phillips, writing in 1939, said that these prerogatives are '*legally* vested in the King, though this is a matter of form. By custom and convention prerogative powers must be exercised through and on the advice of other persons'.[75] Contemporary textbooks tend to adopt a shorthand, by talking of the powers over war and foreign policy as simply being exercised by 'the government'.[76] However, in a formal conceptual sense, these powers are powers of the royal prerogative, and the government is exercising the royal prerogatives in the name of the Crown.[77]

This brief survey of theoretical and political discourses concerning the war and foreign policy powers has identified a constant and forceful assertion of the executive's exclusive authority over their exercise. This arrangement has often been considered axiomatic: to be assumed and unquestioned. However, brief consideration of some other analyses of constitutional design shows it was not inevitable in any teleological or axiomatic sense. Immanuel Kant thought that the decision to wage war should be made by the people (by their representatives), not by the head of state.[78] He observed that in systems where the power to wage war was under the control of the head of state, there had been a multiplication of wars and constant increases in the number of standing soldiers, weapons, and costs. He said '[T]he people are hardly likely to plunge themselves into penury—which never touches the head of state—out of sheer lust of expansion or because of supposed purely verbal insults.'[79]

---

[73] See ch 3, 105–6. See, as a survey of constitutional texts, O Hood Phillips, *The Principles of English Law and the Constitution* (Sweet & Maxwell 1939) 237; Sir WR Anson, *The Law and Custom of the Constitution* vol II, 4th edn (Clarendon Press 1935) 136–7; *Halsbury's Laws of England* 'International Relations Law', vol 61, 5th edn (2011) [26]; 'Constitutional Law and Human Rights', vol 8(2), 4th edn (1996 reissue), [809]; 'War and Armed Conflict', vol 49(1), 4th edn (2005 reissue) [406]; A Le Sueur, 'The Nature, Powers, and Accountability of Central Government' in David Feldman (ed), *English Public Law*, 2nd edn (OUP 2009) [3.77], [3.80]–[3.84].
[74] HN Brailsford, 'The Control of Foreign Affairs: A Proposal' (1909) 4/13 *English Review* 122, 124. See also Lord Courtney, *The Working Constitution of the United Kingdom and Its Outgrowth* (London 1910) 348.
[75] Hood Phillips (n 73) 234–5 (emphasis the author's own).
[76] Le Sueur (n 73) 3.77.
[77] See Ministry of Justice, *The Governance of Britain* (Green Paper) (Cm 7170, 2007) 15.
[78] Immanuel Kant, 'On the Old Saw: That May be Right in Theory but It Won't Work in Practice' in Cahn (n 56) (translated by EB Ashton) 568; 'Perpetual Peace' in Cahn (n 56) (translated by M Campbell Smith) 574.
[79] Kant, 'On the Old Saw' (n 78) 568.

Under a republican constitution the consent of the people is required in the determination to go to war: 'nothing is more natural than that they should weigh the matter well, before undertaking such a bad business. For in decreeing war, they would of necessity be resolving to bring down the miseries of war upon their country.'[80]

The United States also diverged from the English orthodoxy. During the Founding debates, the allocation of the powers to conduct external relations was a key issue of contention. In a letter to Thomas Jefferson, James Madison explained why the Constitution allocated to Congress the power to declare war.[81] He wrote that the Constitution 'supposes, what the History of all Governments demonstrates, that the Executive is the branch of power most interested in war, & most prone to it. It has accordingly with studied care, vested the question of war in the Legislature'.[82]

The Justifications for the Executive's Powers over War and Foreign Policy

1 Introduction

This section identifies the key justificatory arguments advanced for the asserted exclusive powers of the executive over war and foreign policy. It moves the focus from how political and theoretical discourses have described the constitutional arrangements for the war and foreign policy powers, to their arguments as to why these arrangements should be so. This analysis will show that the justificatory arguments have changed over time, even though the assertion of the exclusive executive powers has remained constant. The changes in these justifications reveal the shifting influence of political theories on English constitutional and political thought. In the seventeenth century, justifications for executive power over war and foreign policy emphasized divine right, mixed government, the art of governing, and inseparable prerogative. These justifications were replaced in the eighteenth and nineteenth centuries by arguments based on the constitutional ideas of mixed and balanced government. By the nineteenth and twentieth centuries, justifications for the executive's war and foreign policy powers were founded on arguments of institutional expertise and representative government.

I have structured the discussion by looking at each justification separately and in roughly chronological order. My presentation of the justifications in this way should not be taken to suggest that each justification was neatly

---

[80] Kant, 'Perpetual Peace' (n 78) 574.   [81] US Constitution, art I, s 8.
[82] Letter from James Madison to Thomas Jefferson (2 April 1798) cited in JH Ely, 'Suppose Congress Wanted a War Powers Act That Worked' (1988) 88 Columbia Law Review 1379.

confined to a particular time period, or that only one argument was influential at a particular time. Justificatory arguments for the executive's war and foreign policy powers overlapped and were variously picked up and discarded, as different political theories became more or less influential. The history of English political thought is not one of straight-line development: it is not the history of successive modes of expressing political relationships, each succeeding its predecessor.[83] Varying and competing concepts coexisted. However, as the following discussion shows, it is possible to identify trends in the political theories and justificatory arguments that were influential at particular times.

2 Divine Right

In the first part of the seventeenth century, the theory of divine right was used to justify the king's exclusive authority over certain realms and to explain his particular competence over the conduct of government. The ideas that the king's authority came from God, that he was divinely charged with the responsibility for the general welfare of all, and that he should not be resisted were constitutional principles accepted by most Englishmen in the early-seventeenth century; including by moderates, members of the parliamentary opposition, and leading Puritan clergy.[84] It was generally agreed in the early decades of the seventeenth century and the decade following the Restoration that kings held their thrones by the will of God alone, and not by the wills of the people or of Parliament. Francis Bacon, an MP during the Restoration period, declared: 'the King holdeth not his prerogatives of this kind mediately from the law, but immediately from God, as he holdeth his Crown.'[85]

Monarchs were said to be divinely endowed by God with the 'art of governing'. These were qualities of love and wisdom that only kings possessed, and which made the king peculiarly competent in and solely responsible for the exercise of the powers of government. In certain realms—foreign affairs, questions of war and peace, the army, the navy, and coinage—the king was practising the 'art of governing', and his authority was accepted as absolute, and not shared with Parliament.[86] Roger Maynwaring, an English bishop known for his support of absolutism, praised 'the high discourse and deep

---

[83] N Phillipson, 'Politeness and Politics in the Reigns of Anne and the Early Hanoverians' in Pocock (n 39) 214, 221.

[84] Judson (n 41) 111–12; J S Hart Jr, *The Rule of Law 1603–1660* (Pearson Education 2003) 11, 79–82.

[85] J Spedding, *The Letters and Life of Francis Bacon* vol III (London 1861–74) 371, quoted in Judson (n 41) 138.

[86] Judson (n 41) 25, 82; J Goldsworthy, *The Sovereignty of Parliament: History and Philosophy* (Clarendon Press 1999) 79.

counsels of Kings, seeing their hearts are so deep, by reason of their distance from common men, even as the heavens are in respect of the earth'.[87]

Divine right was a generally accepted theory, but its use by the Stuart Kings to address specific legal questions involving prerogatives and liberties was more contested. Of particular controversy were the assertions that divine right accorded the king with absolute power over certain subjects and that the king should not be resisted when exercising those powers.[88] The Stuart Kings claimed divine right ordained them with absolute power over particular realms, including war and foreign policy. James I, a strong proponent of divine right,[89] argued that it was not lawful to dispute the 'absolute prerogative' of the Crown: because the king held his power by divine right, to disobey the king was to disobey God.[90] In a speech to Parliament in 1610, James said that 'Kings are not only God's Lieutenants upon earth, and sit upon God's throne, but even by God himself they are called Gods'. He concluded that 'to dispute what God may do is blasphemy' and thus it is 'sedition in Subjects, to dispute what a King may do in the height of his power'.[91]

In the lead-up to the Civil war and during the Interregnum period, parliamentarians used divine right arguments against the king to justify their radical actions in assuming the paradigm 'kingly' powers, including those over war and foreign policy. For example, Harbottle Grimston, in an address in April 1640, referred to the biblical instructions given to Ezra by King Artaxerxes, whose 'state was as much out of frame and order as ours is at this presente': 'whosoever hath not done the Lawes of God and the King, lett Judgement bee speedily executed upon him.'[92] Oliver Cromwell propagated the idea of parliamentarians as being 'servants of God', and repeatedly reinforced their sense of religious

---

[87] 'A Sermon Preached Before the King' (4 July 1627) in JP Kenyon, *The Stuart Constitution, 1603–1688: Documents and Commentary*, 2nd edn (CUP 1986) 13.

[88] Scholars have been divided on the practical implications of the assertions of absolute divine authority. JR Tanner says that the theory of divine right gave an intellectual justification to the claims of the Stuart Kings to exclusive competence in the powers of government: 'The Succession Question and Divine Right—Commentary' in Tanner (ed), *Constitutional Documents of the Reign of James I 1603–1625* (CUP 1960) 9. cf Kenyon, who interpreted James' absolutism as confined to the realm of theory, and argues that James was always very careful to respect and act within the laws and customs of England: Kenyon (n 87) 8. See also G Burgess, *Absolute Monarch and the Stuart Constitution* (Yale University Press 1996) 104, who takes the same approach as Kenyon.

[89] In 1598 James anonymously published *True Law of Free Monarchies*, which set out the theory of divine right and, amongst other things, claimed an independent legislative power for the Crown.

[90] See, eg, King James I, 'The Works of the Most High and Mightie Prince James' (1616), in Tanner (n 88) 531; Succession Act 1604 (1 Jac I c I), in Tanner (n 88) 12. For comment, see Tanner (n 88) 14.

[91] Quoted in Tanner (n 88) 17. [92] Quoted in Hart (n 84) 166.

mission. Charles' defeat in the Civil war was seen as evidence that God had abandoned him.[93]

Divine right received a mortal blow by the execution of Charles in 1649. Although there was a fervent revival of divine right theory with the Restoration,[94] it was short-lived and diluted in form. Divine right theorists of this era tended to ascribe to a weaker form of the doctrine, known as 'none resistance' or 'passive obedience', which, unlike earlier versions of the theory, did not claim absolute and uncontrolled powers for the king, but instead said that all Christians owed the king obedience.[95] It was not used specifically to justify the king's powers over foreign policy or war.

Divine right was laid to rest in orthodox constitutional theory by the Revolution of 1688–89, which heralded a major change in the theoretical underpinnings of the office and powers of king.[96] The Revolution replaced divine right monarchy with parliamentary monarchy on the basis that the new King and Queen had not succeeded to the throne in the natural order of events but because the Convention Parliament had made the offer of the Crown to William and Mary. The people replaced God as the source of the monarch's legitimate authority and powers.[97]

3 A Paradigm 'Kingly' Power

The second justificatory basis for the executive's powers over war and foreign policy was that these were paradigm 'kingly' powers, constitutive of kingship. They were essential to monarchical government: 'so inherently part of kingship that a ruler, even if he would, could not disassociate them from himself.'[98] William Camden, a historian writing in 1614–15, considered '[t]he making league or war with any foreign Prince or State' to be a general privilege of all kings.[99] James I, in a reply to a petition of the Commons in 1621, described

---

[93] Hart (n 84) 225.

[94] Most Englishmen of the time regarded hereditary kingship as having been restored by the 'manifest purpose of Providence', proven by its eventual triumph over the temporarily successful rebellion: see DL Keir, *The Constitutional History of Modern Britain 1485–1937* (Adam and Charles Black 1938) 238.

[95] An example of an explication of such theory is Robert Filmer, *Patriarcha* (1680). See Lovell (n 7) 361.

[96] GC Gibbs, 'The Revolution in Foreign Policy' in G Holmes (ed), *Britain after the Glorious Revolution 1689–1714* (Macmillan 1969) 60.

[97] H Nenner, 'The Later Stuart Age' in Pocock (n 39) 197; J Carter, 'The Revolution and the Constitution' in Holmes (n 96) 47; GM Straka, 'The Final Phase of Divine Right Theory in England, 1688–1702' (1962) 77 English Historical Review 638.

[98] Judson (n 41) 33. See also JP Somerville, *Politics and Ideology in England 1603–40* (Longman 1986) 83, 85; Goldsworthy (n 86) 92.

[99] FS Fussner, 'William Camden's "Discourse Concerning the Prerogative of the Crown"' (1957) 101 Proceedings of the American Philosophy Society 204, 210.

the powers over war and foreign policy as historically and by custom the 'most undoubted and regal prerogative'.[100] Even fervent opponents of the king recognized his competence over foreign relations. In the 1628 parliament, Sherland, one of the most zealous supporters of Parliament's cause said: 'The Kinge may make warr, may make peace, call parliaments, and dissolve them, these are of the highest nature, for there the Kinge is the lex loquens.'[101]

In the first half of the seventeenth century, the concept of absolute prerogative overlaid the identification of certain powers as paradigm kingly powers. The concept of absolute prerogative held that uniquely governmental powers exercised by the king were not governed by legal requirements or subject to legal challenge. Foreign affairs was one of the special spheres of government in which the king's powers were absolute and his prerogatives inseparable.[102] In a speech to Parliament in 1610, James I declared that it was 'sedition in subjects to dispute what a King may do in the height of his power'.[103] In argument in *Hampden's Case*, Attorney General Banks contended that the king had absolute authority and discretion in times of war and emergency. This authority was 'innate in the person of an absolute King, and in the persons of the Kings of England'.[104]

The demise of the early Stuart Kings also saw the demise of the concept of absolute prerogatives as kingly powers beyond the control or challenge of the courts and Parliament. It was not advanced again as a serious theory of government in England.[105] However, a modified concept of inseparable discretionary prerogative lived on, with certain powers said to be paradigm kingly powers, inherently part of the office of king. Monarchs no longer asserted absolute power over war and foreign policy, but they did continue to claim special competence and to assert exclusive discretion over their control.

Monarchs used the blunt assertion of their unique kingly powers to justify their exclusive competence over war and foreign policy and to deny parliamentary involvement. For example, in May 1677, when the Commons presented a memorial threatening to withhold supply unless the king made an alliance with Holland against France, Charles II's Secretaries of State protested that this was an invasion of one of the most paradigm and cherished prerogatives of the Crown. One of the Secretaries said in the Commons' debate that the king had only a few prerogatives, including coining money and making peace and war. These were 'landmarks', he said, and 'a curse is upon him that

---

[100] 'King's Answer of 11 December 1621', in Tanner (n 88) 283.
[101] Quoted in Judson (n 41) 26. See further the citations at nn 42–46.
[102] Judson (n 41) 33.
[103] 'Speech to Parliament, 21 March 1610', in Kenyon (n 87) 13.
[104] *R v Hampden* (1637) 3 St Tr 825, 1017.
[105] Judson (n 41) 387.

removes them'.[106] Charles II objected to the Commons' address, declaring that the matters were unfit for the Commons to meddle in, and that the prerogative of making peace and war had been dangerously invaded. He identified the powers to make war and peace and to enter alliances as an 'essential part of the monarchy'.[107] He asserted that while the Commons could advise him in general terms, they could not force him to make specific alliances or direct what sort of leagues he may enter. If such limitations were permitted on his powers of making war and peace, he declared, no other prince or state would believe that the sovereignty of England lay in the king.

The idea of the powers over war and foreign policy being an essential part of monarchy weakened during the eighteenth and nineteenth centuries with the gradual shifting of real political power from the monarch to a responsible cabinet. William III continued to assert unique competence over war and the formulation and implementation of foreign policy.[108] By the Georgian era this claim had weakened, although the monarch continued to exert influence over foreign policy for longer than in respect of domestic policy, in part because of the historical and theoretical claims of these powers being paradigm and unique kingly powers.[109] It has since been held that the Crown has no powers that are 'inseparable'—that is, none which cannot be taken away by Act of Parliament.[110] The contention that the powers over war and foreign policy are uniquely 'executive' powers, however, continues to live on, based in part on an appeal to these historical precedents, and in part on the institutional features of the executive.[111]

4 General Welfare

The king's responsibility for the general welfare founded the third basis for the king's prerogatives as head of state, and, more particularly, for his powers over matters of war, peace, and foreign affairs.[112] The king's obligation to protect the welfare of his subjects meant that the king and his government were expected to ensure the preservation of the subject's person, the protection of his goods and property, and the promotion of his well-being. From

---

[106] 'Commons' Debate on the Address, 25 May', in Kenyon (n 87) 399.
[107] 'The King's Reply, 28 May', in Kenyon (n 87) 400.
[108] Carter (n 97) 52; SB Baxter, 'Recent Writings on William III' (1966) 38 Journal of Modern History 256.
[109] HJ Hanham, 'Cabinet Government: The Monarchy' in Hanham (n 67) 29; T Blanning, '"That Horrid Electorate" or "Ma Patrie Germanique"? George III, Hanover, and the *Fuerstenbund* of 1785' (1977) 20 Historical Journal 20; the works cited in J Black, *British Foreign Policy in the Age of Walpole* (John Donald Publishers 1985) 36.
[110] *Attorney General v De Keyser's Royal Hotel* [1920] AC 508.
[111] See text to n 149.   [112] Judson (n 41) 27.

these responsibilities flowed the king's powers to maintain internal law and order, protect against threats from abroad by securing military preparedness and managing foreign policy, and protect England's investments in overseas trade.[113]

The king's responsibility for the general welfare justified his discretionary power in certain subject areas, including in defence and foreign affairs. The king could do whatever necessary for the common good: *salus populi suprema lex* ('the safety of the people is the paramount law'). For example, in *Hampden's Case*, Solicitor General Edward Littleton argued that the king's responsibility to defend the kingdom gave the king absolute discretion to respond to imminent danger and anticipate potential future threats.[114]

The general welfare rationale continued to have resonance even after the age of absolute prerogative. Blackstone relied on it to explain the powers of government and the king's power over the deployment and command of the armed forces. He considered the principal objective of government was to direct the united strength of the society to protect that society. Monarchial government, he said, was the 'best and most effectual' at achieving this end. It followed that the king possessed the prerogative of command of the military and the sole power of raising and regulating fleets and armies.[115]

As the role of monarchy changed, so did the concept of the general welfare as justifying the allocation of the war and foreign policy powers. Royal power became to be replaced by cabinet government, and the monarch could no longer claim to exercise powers over war and foreign policy on the grounds of general welfare. However, some have suggested that the Crown retains a guardianship role, although it is contested whether this is merely symbolic or involves substantive reserve powers.[116] A type of general welfare argument continues to be used to justify the executive's powers over war and national security, as evidenced, for example, in the assertion that the 'first duty' of the state is to protect its citizens.[117] A recent government report reviewing executive royal prerogatives declared '[t]here is no higher duty on a Government than that to guarantee the safety and security of its citizens'.[118]

---

[113] Hart (n 84) 3.
[114] *R v Hampden* (1637) 3 St Tr 825, 894. See also Judson (n 41) 270.
[115] Blackstone (n 61) 261.
[116] See the discussion in PA Joseph, *Constitutional and Administrative Law in New Zealand*, 3rd edn (Thomson Brookers 2007) 715, 717–19. See also SA de Smith and R Brazier, *Constitutional and Administrative Law*, 8th edn (Penguin Books 1998) 122.
[117] See the discussion of the courts' identification of the guardianship role in the citations at nn 9, 12–16 in ch 4.
[118] Ministry of Justice, 'The Governance of Britain. Review of the Executive Royal Prerogative Powers: Final Report' (October 2009) [76].

5 'Ancient Constitution'

The concept of the 'ancient constitution' was another theoretical justification advanced for the king's powers over foreign policy in the seventeenth century. The ancient constitution was an imprecise and mythical creation which proclaimed unchanging constitutional arrangements and customs from time immemorial. 'Balance' was its essential characteristic.[119] According to the ancient constitution, the monarch had certain prerogatives, the subjects certain rights, and neither could be infringed without causing dangerous imbalance.[120] A classic exposition of these ideas is that of Bacon, who declared that the king's prerogative, the subject's liberty, and the laws existed side by side, each one complementing and strengthening the others and working together to produce a balanced harmony: 'The King's Sovereignty and the Liberty of Parliament...do not cross or destroy the one the other, but they strengthen and maintain the one the other.'[121] In this balanced ancient constitution, the powers over war, peace, treaties, and foreign policy were the subjects of the king's prerogative, and inalienable attributes of his sovereignty.

In the lead-up to the Civil war, both supporters and opponents of the king invoked the ancient constitution to justify their actions. Even in the midst of the bitter conflict, many of the parliamentary leaders expressed the beliefs that prerogative and liberty were compatible and necessary and that a balanced polity was best.[122] Some parliamentarians who sought greater parliamentary power over foreign policy claimed they were endeavouring not to change the nature of the state, but to restore the 'ancient constitution' of a century prior and ensure the protection of their ancient liberties.[123] Invocation of the rhetoric of ancient constitutionalism played to the popular antipathy to change and innovation. However, political actors and commentators were far from united on what constituted innovation, since they had radically different ideas on the past and present constitution of the realm, and the concept of the 'ancient constitution' itself. Despite the imprecise and mythical nature of the concept, however, the idea of the ancient constitution had rhetorical force and served a variety of political ends.[124] By using the rhetoric that the ancient constitution (whatever that was) was in mortal danger, one could characterize

---

[119] The concept of 'balance' was formulated in different ways: balance as between prerogative and law, balance between prerogative and liberty, and balance as between allegiance and protection. See Burgess (n 88).
[120] Kenyon (n 87) 9; see also JG Pocock, *The Ancient Constitution and the Feudal Law* (CUP 1957).
[121] Quoted in Judson (n 41) 62–3.
[122] Judson (n 41) 62–4.
[123] King Charles, 'A Proclamation for the Establishing of the Peace and Quiet of the Church of England' 16 June 1626, in Kenyon (n 87) 154; Pym's speech at Maynwaring's impeachment, 4 June 1628, in Kenyon (n 87) 16.
[124] M Schwartzberg, *Democracy and Legal Change* (CUP 2007) 80–3.

opponents as seeking to subvert the ancient order, claim to be seeking to protect and defend that order, and assert political authority and dominance.[125]

The concept of the ancient constitution also had resonance in the Restoration period. The revolutionary period of the 1640s–50s left the majority of the population in favour of returning to the classical or 'ancient' constitutional arrangements.[126] The roles of governmental institutions, according to these conceptions, were that Parliament alone made the law, the courts alone interpreted it, and the king conducted his government through a council. Powers over foreign policy and war were inseparable from the office and person of king. This theory of the constitution held that Parliament might offer criticisms, but it trespassed beyond its proper sphere if it sought to dictate to the king what policy he must follow and what executive acts he must perform. Clarendon, adviser to both Charles I and Charles II, ascribed to such a view of the constitution. However, as Keir observes, such a conception was wholly unrealistic. Not even the Elizabethan constitution, which Clarendon imagined had embodied constitutional ideas like these, had ever worked in such a way.[127]

6 Mixed Government

A constitutional idea related to the balanced ancient constitution was the theory of mixed government. It was particularly influential in the latter part of the seventeenth century and into the eighteenth century. The theory of mixed government identified different types of government, and assigned different functions to those types according to their relative strengths and weaknesses. Although there were early articulations of the theory in the late-sixteenth century,[128] one of the first prominent articulations was in King Charles I's reply to the Nineteen Propositions of 1642. The Nineteen Propositions represented the high-water mark in the Commons' claims: the Commons demanded royal surrender to Parliament of control over, inter alia, all governmental appointments, the militia, the 'great affairs of the kingdom', and the marriage of the king's children. Charles' reply rejected the Nineteen Propositions, and said that to cede more power to Parliament would upset the historical balance of power between the king, Lords, and Commons.[129]

---

[125] Pocock, *The Ancient Constitution* (n 120); Somerville (n 98) 107; Schwartzberg (n 124) 80–3.
[126] J Miller, 'The Later Stuart Monarchy' in JR Jones (ed), *The Restored Monarchy 1660–1688* (MacMillan Press 1979) 30–1.
[127] Keir (n 94) 231, 244. On Clarendon's conception of the constitution, see EI Carlyle, 'Clarendon and the Privy Council, 1660–67' (1912) 27 English Historical Review 251.
[128] See, eg, John Aylmer, *An Harboure for Faithfull and Trewe Subjects* (1559), cited in C Weston, 'English Constitutional Doctrines from the Fifteenth Century to the Seventeenth: II. The Theory of Mixed Monarchy under Charles I and after' (1960) 75 The English Historical Review 426, 427.
[129] 'The King's Reply to the Nineteen Propositions, 18 June 1642', in Kenyon (n 87) 21.

Charles' response to the Nineteen Propositions is important for its invocation of the constitutional theory of mixed and balanced government as justification for the powers possessed by the Crown. The theory of mixed government identified three types of government—monarchy, aristocracy, and democracy—and claimed that mixed government combined the convenience of all three, without the inconveniences of any. Charles' reply identified the strengths and weaknesses of each type of government: the monarchy gave a focal point for national unity but could lead to tyranny; the aristocracy provided counsel from the ablest persons of a state but could lead to faction and division; and democracy encouraged liberty, courage, and industry, but could lead to tumults, violence, and licentiousness. According to the theory (as stated in Charles' reply), the English constitution combined elements of these major types of government so as to have the benefits of all without the dangers of any. The working of the system depended upon balance between the three estates and each running jointly in their 'proper channel'.[130]

Charles also set out the powers and responsibilities of each of the three estates according to the theory of mixed government. Charles claimed that the 'powers of government' had been entrusted to the king. These included the powers to make treaties of war and peace; to make war abroad; to create peers; to choose and appoint officers and councillors for state, judges, and military officers; to prevent or provide against invasions or insurrections at home; and to pardon. Charles recognized he must exercise these powers in the public interest. Charles cautioned that the Nineteen Propositions aimed to transfer to Parliament powers which historically it had never possessed; the Commons had the sole power to initiate money bills and to impeach officials, but it was never intended, he said, to share in government or choose those who govern. If the Commons did extend its powers and roles into government it would encroach on the powers of the others and upset the balance by reducing the strength of the monarchy and therefore the rallying point for national feeling, while possibly stimulating factionalism (the inherent evil of aristocratic government). Parliament's possession of executive powers could also produce conflicts between its two Houses, with the potential that the Commons would have increasing advantage over the Lords, until the elective body would obliterate the aristocratic element of the constitution leaving it with total legislative and executive power. Further, the size of the Commons, according to Charles' reply, rendered it incapable of transacting affairs of state 'with the necessary service and expedition'.[131]

---

[130] For identification of the difficulties with the theory of mixed government, see JGA Pocock 'Introduction' in Pocock (ed), *The Political Works of James Harrington* (CUP 1977) xiii.

[131] 'The King's Reply to the Nineteen Propositions, 18 June 1642', reproduced in Kenyon (n 87) 23.

The idea of the balance achieved by a system of mixed government, in which the constitution depended on the interaction and balance of opposing elements, continued to have resonance in the eighteenth century. In 1791, a mechanical metaphor was used to describe this system and its virtues:[132]

> that firmness, beauty, and magnificence of our excellent Constitution, founded on the mutual consent of Prince and People; both moving, as it were, in one orb, reciprocally influencing, attracting, and directing each other; whose united power may be compared to a machine for the determining the equality of weights; the Sovereign, and the representative Body, counterpoising each other, and the Peers preserving the equilibrium.

The theory of mixed government dominated constitutional writing of the eighteenth and early-nineteenth centuries, in the works of Blackstone and Harrington, among others.[133] Blackstone, writing in the mid-eighteenth century, championed the theory of mixed government and its practice in England. He described mixed government as a system based upon the combination of the three ways for allocating sovereign authority (monarchical, oligarchical, democratic), with balance being achieved by combining the qualities of each type of government and by the three elements sharing legislative power.[134] Within this system, Blackstone identified the monarchical part of government as best suited to controlling matters of war and peace, foreign policy, and diplomacy, because its institutional features meant it could best deal with their particular demands.[135]

By the nineteenth century, the king's powers over war and foreign policy were no longer justified by reference to the particular distribution of powers according to the theory of mixed government. Whig writers (including James Mill, Bagehot, and Dicey) argued that a mixed and balanced constitution was not possible to achieve in practice, because in the long run one of the elements would be bound to predominate and negate or eliminate the other two.[136]

7 Social Contract

Some writers relied on a social contract-type argument to explain the king's power over war. Blackstone said that in the law of nature each individual

---

[132] *Senator* (1791) I (iii), cited in Black (n 41) 200.

[133] Harrington, 'The Commonwealth of Oceana' in *Pocock* (n 130); J de Lolme, *The Constitution of England, or an Account of the English Government* (Robinson 1796). For comment see C Weston, *English Constitutional Theory and the House of Lords 1556–1832* (Routledge and Kegan Paul 1965) 3–4, 125–75.

[134] Blackstone (n 61) 48–52. See also G Marshall, *Constitutional Theory* (OUP 1971) 101.

[135] See citations at nn 150–174.

[136] HM Magid, 'Jeremy Bentham and James Mill' in L Strauss and J Cropsey (eds), *History of Political Philosophy*, 2nd edn (Rand McNally 1972) 682; W Bagehot, *The English Constitution* (OUP 1867) 2. See also Hanham (n 67) 2–3.

inherently possesses the right of making war. That right was surrendered up by individuals and by the entire body of people upon entering a society, and is vested in a sovereign power. Blackstone explained that it would be improper for individual citizens to have the power of binding the supreme magistrate and putting him in a state of war against his will. The king, therefore, as holder of the sovereign power, exercised the power to wage war as the 'delegate or representative of his people'.[137] According to Blackstone '[w]hat is done by royal authority, with regard to foreign powers, is the act of the whole nation: what is done without the king's concurrence is the act only of private men'.[138]

Chitty also described how the king acted on behalf of the nation in foreign affairs. He identified this as the key reason why formal declarations of war should be made before the commencement of hostilities: a declaration made it clear that the war is undertaken not by private persons, but by the will of the whole community, which is transferred to and vested in the king.[139] In employing this social contract-type analysis, it is likely that Blackstone and Chitty were influenced by Grotius' work *Law of War and Peace*. Grotius said that the purpose of a declaration of war was to make it clear that the war is not undertaken by private citizens but by the will of the whole community, whose rights have been transferred to the supreme magistrate.[140]

8 Whig Parliamentary Government

The Whig school dominated constitutional thinking in the nineteenth century. It identified as the key feature of the constitution the limitation of the powers of the monarch, who as a constitutional ruler was bound to accept the recommendations of such ministers who could command a majority in the House of Commons. Whig thinking held that the prerogatives over war and foreign policy were formally allocated to the monarch, but were, and should be, exercised by ministers responsible to Parliament.

Whig theory advanced two main justifications for these constitutional arrangements. The first justification focused on their pragmatic political advantages, based on the relative institutional strengths and weaknesses of the executive and the legislature.[141] According to Whig theory, parliamentary government ensured the effective and efficient exercise of executive powers, subject to parliamentary oversight. The third Earl of Grey, writing in 1858, asserted that parliamentary government enabled the executive to act with necessary vigour and effectiveness.[142] In relation to matters of war and foreign

---

[137] Blackstone (n 61) 252.   [138] Blackstone (n 61) 257.   [139] Chitty (n 66) 44–5.
[140] H Grotius, *Law of War and Peace* (1625), in particular book I, ch 3.
[141] On these institutional arguments, see citations at nn 150–174.
[142] Grey (n 68) 14.

policy, the executive had exclusive control; the government was able to act without any impediment by or prior sanction of Parliament.[143] Parliament's involvement in matters of war and foreign policy was confined to being informed about the key issues and concerns with which the government has to deal, and to scrutinizing the policies and actions of ministers.

Whig thinkers' emphasis on the efficiency and vigour of parliamentary government demonstrated the primacy given to concerns of pragmatism and political expediency. This extract from the *Edinburgh Review* in 1858 summarizes these sentiments well:[144]

The triumph of the Reform Act of 1832 consists not so much in the recognition of certain abstract principles, or in the readjustment of the franchise as in the fact that for a quarter of a century Parliamentary Government has been established in this country with greater purity and efficiency than it ever possessed before, that during this period innumerable measures of unequalled public importance have been adopted in rapid succession by the legislature.

The second justification advanced by Whig theory for vesting in ministers responsibility for war and foreign policy was that it enabled the governors to be scrutinized and held accountable by the governed. Whig constitutional thinking proclaimed the English constitution's features of regular and free elections and the supremacy of Parliament as promoting representative government—even though the Commons in the nineteenth century was far from representative of the population of England, and there were major deficiencies in the electoral system. Representative government was said by its proponents to solve the constant quandary of societies: given that the people cannot themselves govern, how do they ensure that the governors advance the interests of the people rather than their own? James Mill found the solution in having the people elect representatives to check the governors. He proclaimed the system of representation as the 'grand discovery of modern times' and the 'solution of all the difficulties, both speculative and practical'.[145]

John Stuart Mill expanded on the work of James Mill in *Considerations on Representative Government* (1861).[146] JS Mill's account of representative

---

[143] Grey (n 68) 15.

[144] Anon, 'Earl Grey on Parliamentary Government' Edinburgh Review (July 1858) 272, quoted in A Hawkins '"Parliamentary Government" and Victorian Political Parties, c. 1830–c. 1880' (1989) 104 The English Historical Review 638, 640.

[145] J Mill, *An Essay on Government* (1820) (CUP 1937) vi. See D Judge, *Representation: Theory and Practice in Britain* (Routledge 1999) 15–20 for an overview of the development of the theory and practice of representation in Britain.

[146] JS Mill, 'Considerations on Representative Government' in *Three Essays: On Liberty, Representative Government, the Subjection of Women* (first published 1861, introduction by R Wolheim, OUP 1975) 179–98, 211–14, 226, 233–5.

government sought to address what he considered the error of most other accounts of representative government, which was to hold that the representatives of the people should actually govern. Mill drew a distinction between governing and controlling. According to Mill, experts should govern, subject to the control of the representatives of the people. The functions of government, he thought, are highly skilled activities which require experienced and well-trained individuals which the general community is not qualified to select. Those governing experts were subject, in a democracy, to the people as the 'ultimate controlling power'. Not being able to exercise the controlling power themselves, the people periodically elect deputies who exercise the power on their behalf. In England, Parliament, composed of elected representatives, served in the interests of the people as the controller of the government. Representative government thereby ensured that the powers over war and foreign policy were vested in expert individuals with the necessary competence and aptitude to exercise those powers, while also enabling their scrutiny by representatives of the governed.

9 Democratic Justifications?

Although Whig theory proclaimed the virtue of the English constitution as being a system of representative government, it was not 'democratic' in our sense of the term—in fact, Whigs proclaimed that one of its key virtues was its narrowly limited notion of popular sovereignty. Earl Grey recognized the key distinction between giving the people the power of nominating their rulers by direct election, and an indirect control, through their elected representatives to Parliament, over the selection of ministers.[147] During the nineteenth century, Whig liberalism began to decline, and constitutional theory became more focused on democratic principles, the reform of governmental institutions, and social reform.[148] The increasing influence of democratic thought did not, however, materially impact constitutional thinking about the allocation of responsibility for the war and foreign policy powers. Orthodox constitutional thinking and political practice continued to identify these powers as paradigm executive powers, but the justifications for this arrangement were not explicitly based on democratic principles.

Today, justifications based on democratic mandate or responsibility are still not prominent. The key justificatory arguments advanced for the executive's powers are 'institutional' reasons (the argument that the institutional features of the executive mean that it is best suited to exercising powers over war and foreign policy: see section headed 'Institutional Arguments') and historical reasons

[147] Hawkins (n 144) 659. See also JS Mill (n 146) 179–98 and 211–14.
[148] AF Pollard, *The Evolution of Parliament* (Longmans Green 1920) 340.

(the executive holds the exclusive powers over war and foreign policy because these powers have historically been exercised and controlled by the executive[149]). Sometimes, an 'indirect' democratic argument is used to justify the executive's powers, similar to older theories of representative government: that in the exercise of the powers over war and foreign policy, the executive is subject to the scrutiny of Parliament, which is representative of the people. However, more direct democratic arguments are rarely used to justify governmental control over war and foreign policy. It is not argued, for example, that the executive holds the war and foreign policy powers because it has a democratic mandate by holding the confidence of the democratically elected Commons.

10 Institutional Arguments

The final and perhaps most dominant justification for the executive's possession of exclusive power over war and foreign policy is that its institutional features make it best-suited to that responsibility. Institutional arguments have been incorporated into broader political theories justifying governmental authority, such as the theories of the king's inseparable prerogative, mixed government, and Whig constitutional monarchy. Their common theme is that the executive's decision-making processes, composition, and structure mean that it is most efficiently and effectively able to formulate and implement foreign policy and conduct war. Institutional arguments from the eighteenth century to the present have made the same assumptions about the unique nature and subject-matter of the war and foreign policy powers, the special decision-making processes they demand, and the particular institutional competence of the executive.

Institutional arguments from across the three centuries have contended that the war and foreign policy powers need to be exercised in secret, flexibly, quickly, and by a small number of people. In 1635, William Lambarde explained why discretion and flexibility were necessary in this particular subject area:[150]

As in the government of all *Common-weales*, sundry things doe fall out both in *Peace* and *Warre*, that doe require an extraodinarie helpe, and cannot awaite the usuall cure of common *Rule* and settled *Justice*, the which is not performed, but altogether after one sort, and that not without delay of helpe, and dispense of time . . . yet have there

---

[149] See, eg, Ministry of Justice, *The Governance of Britain* (n 77) [20]: 'A distinguishing feature of the British constitution is the extent to which government continues to exercise a number of powers which were not granted to it by a written constitution, nor by Parliament, but are, rather, ancient prerogatives of the Crown. These powers derive from arrangements which preceded the 1689 Declaration of Rights and have been accumulated by the government without Parliament or the people having a say.'
[150] William Lambarde, *Archeion, or a Discourse upon the High Courts of Justice in England*, 78–9, quoted in Judson (n 41) 29.

alwayes arisen, and there will continually, from time to time, grow some rare matters met (for just reason) to be reserved to a higher hand, and to be left to the aide of absolute *Power*, and irregular Authoritie.

A statement by the leading London ministerial paper, the *Daily Courant*, in 1734, identified the key reasons why the king controlled foreign policy and military issues: (1) the situations and issues that arise in the context of these subjects tend to be individual and specific, and therefore general or prescribed rules are not normally applicable and flexibility is required; (2) these matters need to be dealt with promptly and decisively; and (3) secrecy is necessary. The statement read:[151]

> In the military Part of the domestick indeed, and in both the military Branches of our foreign policy or Government, which regulates our Leagues and Treaties, our Wars or Peace with other States, the King has a greater Latitude; for, as they are almost all of them individual points or cases, which admit of very few, or no invariable general Rules, and do also require the utmost Dispatch, and the greatest secrecy, he is therein invested with the intire power of determining both what shall be done, and who shall execute those Determinations.

And another statement, from a periodical in 1882, pointing to institutional reasons as justifying the cabinet's total control over matters of foreign relations and war, and the exclusion of Parliament:[152]

> The apology for this system is that diplomacy can only be successfully carried on by a small and select body of experts, inasmuch as secrecy is an important element in the conduct of delicate negotiations, which must therefore be committed to a Cabinet armed with discretionary powers and permitted to withhold information from the Houses until it is considered expedient to impart it.

The leading political theorists of the eighteenth and nineteenth centuries, including Locke, Montesquieu, and Blackstone, identified institutional reasons as justification for the king's powers over war and foreign policy. Locke in particular gave detailed consideration to the particular features of what he called the 'federative power', and the special decision-making process which it demanded. Locke thought that the federative power, unlike the executive power, was less capable of being subjected to prospective positive laws, and so therefore 'must necessarily be left to the prudence and wisdom of those hands it is in, to be managed for the public good'.[153] The federative power was less suited to prospective control because decisions and actions made in relation to foreign states and individuals depended largely upon the actions

---

[151] Quoted in Black (n 109) 37. [152] Anon (n 71) 332, 346.
[153] Locke (n 56) [146]–[147]. See also Vile (n 56) 65.

and interests of those foreign states and individuals. It was difficult to foresee the appropriate action and response, and therefore it was necessary to have a flexible and responsive federative power left largely to the prudence and discretion of those in whom the power is entrusted. Writing two hundred years later, the political scientist Samuel H Beer echoed Locke's words as to the special demands of decision-making concerning the military and war: 'they...require a kind of specific and *ad hoc* action which can hardly be derived from the application of general rules and which therefore comes more readily from the executive than the legislature.'[154]

Another common argument was that powers over war and foreign policy need to be exercised by an individual or small group, which necessarily ruled out Parliament being in charge of their conduct. It was asserted that certain activities such as diplomacy and leadership in war could be performed better by one person than by many.[155] Entrusting one person with these powers avoided the dangers and inconveniences that flow from the openness and delays inherent in popular councils.[156] Earl Grey, writing on parliamentary government in 1858, said that the legislature does not interfere directly in the business of executive government, and it is right that it does not, since 'experience has demonstrated the unfitness of large deliberative assemblies for this function'.[157] Blackstone had employed a similar analysis, explaining that, in transactions and interactions with foreign nations, it is impossible that the individuals of a country, in their collective capacity, could transact the affairs of that state with another community also made up of individuals. The British constitution wisely placed the executive power in a single hand, for the sake of 'unanimity, strength and dispatch'.[158] Montesquieu also stressed the need for executive powers to be exercised quickly and with flexibility, which pointed to the powers being exercised by a single person: 'The executive power ought to be in the hands of a monarch; because this branch of government, which has always need of expedition, is better administered by one than by many.'[159] Chitty too said that strength and dispatch are especially necessary in the execution of foreign policy powers, and experience had shown that the rapidity and secrecy required will 'never be found in large assemblies of the people'.[160]

The assertion that the powers over war and foreign policy are better exercised by a single person or by a small group was based on several related

---

[154] SH Beer, 'The British Legislature and the Problem of Mobilising Consent' in E Frank (ed), *Lawmakers in a Changing World* (Englewood Cliffs 1966) 30, reprinted in P Norton (ed), *Legislatures* (OUP 1990) 62, 65.
[155] Miller (n 126) 32.
[156] James Erskine, *The Fatal Consequences of Ministerial Influence* (London 1736) 17.
[157] Grey (n 68) 14.   [158] Blackstone (n 61) 252.
[159] Montesquieu (n 58) 347.   [160] Chitty (n 66) 39.

arguments. The first was that, if foreign policy powers were vested in a large group of people, it is inevitable that there will be deliberation and differences of opinion. This was assumed to be undesirable. Blackstone, Montesquieu, and Chitty, for example, thought it undesirable for parliamentary assemblies to be involved in the exercise of war and foreign policy powers because it would lead to delay in the formulation and execution of decisions. Blackstone thought that if such powers were placed in many hands they would be subject to many wills, which, if not united, could lead to weakness in government. The effort in uniting those different wills could take more time and delay and undermine the exigencies of state.[161] Rousseau, also, noted that public matters are expedited more slowly the more people that are charged with them, which can result in missed or lost opportunities.[162] Chitty expanded on this point, saying that '[w]avering with doubts, and distracted by the jealousies and the animosities of party, such assemblies would be discussing the propriety of the step after the opportunity and occasion for its adoption had transpired'.[163]

A connected argument was that vesting power in a single person increases the strength and dispatch of the exercise of the power. Chitty said strength of execution was of particular importance in relation to the foreign policy powers, for it inspired the people with confidence and struck the enemies with awe.[164] Rousseau considered strength and dispatch of execution to be linked to the number exercising the governmental function or power. He thought it possible, as a general rule, to say that when the functions of government are divided among several institutions, eventually those institutions with the fewest members will acquire the most authority because they can better expedite public business: 'Thus the more numerous are the Magistrates, the weaker the Government.'[165]

Another reason given for the institutional advantage of the executive was the executive's claim to specialist expertise in matters of war and foreign policy. When foreign policy was controlled by the king and his advisers, the 'expertise argument' contended that, because the king and his council corresponded all over the world, they were well informed about matters material to foreign policy, such as the personalities of foreign leaders, relations between foreign leaders, and the key members of foreign courts and governments.[166] James I, in a reply to a petition of the Commons in 1621, claimed that the king had superior experience and knowledge over issues of foreign policy. He wrote 'who can have wisdom to judge of these things of that nature but such as are

---

[161] Blackstone (n 61) 252.
[162] Jean-Jacques Rousseau, *Of the Social Contract* book three, section II in Cahn (n 56) (translated by GDH Cole) 447.
[163] Chitty (n 66) 39.   [164] Chitty (n 66) 39–40.
[165] Rousseau (n 162) 447.   [166] Turner (n 53) 178.

daily acquainted with the particulars of treaties and of the variable and fixed connexion of affairs of State, together with the knowledge of the secret ways, ends, and intentions of princes in their several negotiations?'[167] This expertise argument was bolstered by the practicalities of European relations. Many European monarchs conducted their own foreign policies and wished to deal directly with other heads of states, not with ministers who came in and out of office. Further, the royal families of Europe were often interrelated, which influenced the formulation and execution of foreign policy.[168]

When the real powers over war and foreign policy began to lie with the cabinet rather than the monarch, the expertise argument continued to be strongly used as justification for executive primacy over war and foreign policy. Arguments as to personal relationships with foreign ruling families were not so relevant, but the cabinet, and in particular the Prime Minister and Foreign Minister, developed extensive experience and knowledge in foreign policy issues. The executive had access to all relevant information, and developed knowledge and experience that others, such as MPs outside of cabinet, could not. In a debate on an address to the Queen on the provision of information concerning the Denmark–Germany crisis in 1864, Mr Disraeli had this to say about the qualities necessary to the successful conduct of foreign affairs: 'that sagacity, that prudence, that dexterity, that quickness of perception, and those conciliatory moods which we are always taught to believe necessary in the transaction of our foreign affairs.' In addition, he emphasized the need for specialist knowledge: 'that knowledge of human nature, and especially that peculiar kind of science most necessary in these affairs—an acquaintance with the character of foreign countries and of the chief actors in the scene.'[169] These expertise arguments were used to restrict attempts by MPs to influence foreign policy or to obtain information about foreign policy issues. In a debate in 1717 on a grant of supply to enable the Crown to maintain a standing army, Mr Hanmer said it would be an 'endless thing for the House of Commons to enter into the secrets of state, and to debate upon the different views, and interests, and intrigues of foreign courts; what jealousies are among them, and what treaties are on foot to reconcile them', and therefore the House must 'put an absolute trust in government, because they only know the truth of such matters, and from them we must be content to receive whatsoever account they think fit to give us of them'.[170]

Finally, it was argued that foreign policy powers had to be exercised in secret; which pointed to the powers being managed by a single person or a

---

[167] 'King's Answer of 11 December 1621', in Tanner (n 88) 286.
[168] Clarke (n 48) 42.   [169] HC Deb 4 July 1864, vol 176, col 744.
[170] Parliamentary History, 3 May 1717, vol 7, col 519.

small and constant group of people exactly informed. Governments rejected MPs' requests for information about treaties, negotiations, or other accounts of foreign relations, on the grounds that its release would endanger national security and interests.[171]

These arguments of relative institutional competence continue to be relied upon today to justify executive control over war and foreign policy. Opponents of proposals to increase parliamentary involvement in the exercise of the war power have relied on arguments of institutional competence, making the same contentions as have writers from the past three centuries: that war and foreign policy powers need to be exercised with flexibility, secrecy, and speed, and by people with special expertise and experience.[172] Tony Blair, in a written answer in the House of Commons on 15 June 2005, said that a formal requirement to consult Parliament before deploying the armed forces 'could prejudice the Government's ability to take swift action to defend our national security where the circumstances so require'.[173] And, in response to the Lords Constitution Committee inquiry, the then government declared that 'the ability of the executive to take decisions flexibly and quickly using prerogative powers remains an important cornerstone of our democracy'.[174]

Part IV Conclusion

This chapter has shown that, while orthodox theoretical and political discourses have for the past four centuries consistently asserted the executive's exclusive control over war and foreign policy powers, the reasons advanced for those constitutional arrangements have changed. These changes reveal trends as to the influence of different political theories at different times. Three further observations can be drawn from this analysis. First, from the eighteenth century onwards, primacy has been accorded to 'institutional arguments' as justifying the vesting of responsibility for war and foreign policy in the executive. Institutional arguments have been incorporated into broader political theories justifying governmental authority. For example, they were part of the conception of the king's inseparable prerogative, the theory of mixed and balanced government, and Whig theories of parliamentary government.

---

[171] For more on secrecy of information about war and foreign policy, see citations at nn 120–148, ch 3.
[172] See the discussion of these concerns of efficiency and operational effectiveness, in the citations at nn 33–45, ch 5.
[173] HC Deb 15 June 2005, vol 435, col 348W.
[174] Secretary of State for Constitutional Affairs and the Lord Chancellor, *Government Response to the House of Lords Constitution Committee's Report, Fifteenth Report of the Session 2005–06* (Cm 6923, 2006) [5].

The use and prominence of institutional arguments demonstrates adherence to an assumption that the powers over war and foreign policy are unique amongst governmental functions, posing particular demands and requiring special decision-making procedures. Although they have been incorporated within broader governmental theories, institutional arguments are directed to pragmatic concerns (such as how to ensure that powers can be exercised secretly, or quickly) and concerns of efficiency and effectiveness, rather than with more normative arguments justifying governmental authority or the proper distribution of governmental functions.

Secondly, the type of the justifications advanced for the executive's primacy over war and foreign policy reflect a broader tendency within English constitutionalism of drawing normative conclusions from a descriptive analysis and/or historical practice: legitimacy is derived from the fact of practice, or, more accurately, a particular conception of the fact of practice.[175] This was a particular feature of the political theories of ancient constitutionalism and mixed government. The idea of the ancient constitution sourced its legitimacy in a system and arrangement that had existed since 'time immemorial', while the theory of mixed government sought to justify the allocation of powers in government by reference to some pre-existing constitutional balance. One of the key justifications advanced today for executive control over war and foreign policy is the fact of historical precedent for this practice. These theories mix the descriptive and the normative, by contending that the legitimacy of particular constitutional arrangements derives from the fact of their long existence. Burke referred to this as the 'prescriptive' feature of the English mixed and balanced constitution: 'it is a constitution whose sole authority is, that it has existed time out of mind.'[176] Pocock called it the 'philosophy of custom': a view of institutions as based purely upon immemorial usage and experience, with no conscious beginnings and nothing more to justify an institution than the presumption that, being immemorial, it must on innumerable occasions have proved satisfactory.[177] These theories which draw on historical practice involve some type of constitutional 'myth-making': the veneration of selected (mythical) conceptions of historic values, constitutional arrangements, and practices.

The final observation is about the role that political theories have played in shaping the values, arrangements, and practices of the English constitution.

---

[175] The Whig writers, led by Dicey, claimed to move away from the historical focus of previous accounts of the English constitution, to study the law 'as it now stands.' However, Allison has shown how Dicey was unsuccessful in this endeavour: see Allison (n 10).

[176] Edmund Burke, *The Works of the Right Honourable Edmund Burke* vol 10 (Rivington Edition 1826) 96.

[177] JGA Pocock, 'Machiavelli, Harrington and English Political Ideologies in the Eighteenth Century' (1965) 22 The William and Mary Quarterly 549, 571–2.

Some writers have argued that political theories and normative values have played little or no role in the English constitution. For example, Sir Stephen Sedley has asserted that the English constitution is empty of normative content:[178]

> our constitutional law, historically at least, is merely descriptive: it offers an account of how the country has come to be governed; and, importantly, in doing so it confers legitimacy on the arrangements it describes. But if we ask what the governing principles are from which these arrangements and this legitimacy derive, we find ourselves listening to the sound of silence.

A related argument is that English constitutional arrangements and practices have been shaped by purely pragmatic political concerns, and by a reliance on hard-headed de facto empiricism, which means one need only pay attention to what is required in the necessities of the situation.[179]

The analysis in this chapter disproves these arguments. Theoretical writers and political actors have advanced justifications for why the executive should have certain powers and have drawn on political theories in doing so. Even arguments based on pragmatic concerns (such as arguments as to relative institutional competence) have been incorporated into broader political theories. In some cases, the use of justifications informed by political theories may have taken the form of *ex post facto* legitimization and justification for existing arrangements and practices. However, whether or not the normative justifications had causative effect, it is clear that normative justifications, drawing on various political theories, were and are part of theoretical and political discourses about the English constitution. To say that English constitutional values, arrangements, and practices have been shaped purely by a political free-for-all is inaccurate, as this chapter has demonstrated.

---

[178] Sir Stephen Sedley, 'The Sound of Silence: Constitutional Law without a Constitution' (1994) 110 Law Quarterly Review 270.

[179] See, most prominently, JAG Griffith, 'The Political Constitution' (1979) 42 Modern Law Review 1. For comment on the work of proponents of the political constitution, see G Gee and GCN Webber, 'What is a Political Constitution?' (2010) 30 Oxford Journal of Legal Studies 273. For commentary on the historical context of such thinking, see Pocock, 'Machiavelli, Harrington and English Political Ideologies in the Eighteenth Century' (n 177) 571–2.

3

The War Prerogative in Practice

Part I Introduction

This chapter examines the war prerogative in practice from 1620–2012. It focuses on the ways that the House of Commons and the executive have interacted in the exercise and scrutiny of the war prerogative. It will show that the House of Commons has played an active and influential role in the exercise of the war prerogative, despite the common assumption of an exclusive executive power. The examination identifies the dichotomy between orthodox theoretical and political discourses on the war power and the exercise of that power in practice. The executive has continuously asserted, consistently with the orthodox discourses, that it alone possesses powers over war and peace and that it can exercise those powers without the consent or cognizance of Parliament. However, the executive has, by its practice, implicitly recognized that it must exercise those powers in conjunction with Parliament. This dichotomy between the orthodox discourses and the reality of practice is evident throughout the time period under consideration, and is still evident today.

Part II describes an extraordinary period in English constitutional history, during which the House of Commons assumed responsibility for the war and foreign policy powers and experimented with several different constitutional arrangements for their exercise. Part III, which is the main focus of this chapter, identifies the ways that the Commons and the executive have interacted in the exercise and scrutiny of the war prerogative. I group those interactions into five types:

- freedom of speech and debate,
- the power of supply,
- retrospective scrutiny,
- parliamentary consultation before going to war, and
- legislation.

This chapter traces the continuities and changes in the institutions, rules, and processes in the interactions between the Commons and the executive. With this focus on the inter-institutional relationship, I have concentrated on particular historical events and practices that best illustrate the nature of the relationship. That focus necessarily precludes consideration of other potential influences; for example, the internal workings of the executive in the exercise of these powers, or how other phenomena (such as public opinion, other countries, or regional or international organizations) have influenced how the war prerogative was exercised.

Part II An Extraordinary Historical Period

Introduction

The Civil Wars were waged over an nine-year period between 1642 and 1651. Although the fighting disrupted normal constitutional and political arrangements, systems of government and administration continued to operate. The 'Long Parliament' was in existence through the Civil Wars and the Commonwealth, and it assumed many of the standard governmental and administrative functions, including the powers over war and foreign policy. This section outlines how and why Parliament assumed authority over war and foreign policy and describes the constitutional arrangements experimented with for their exercise. The revolutionary period was clearly an extraordinary time in English constitutional history, but it left at least two important legacies relevant to future arrangements for the powers over war and foreign policy.

Government by Parliament 1642–49

For the first part of the Civil Wars period, the powers of government, including powers over war and foreign policy, were assumed and exercised by Parliament or by smaller committees appointed by and responsible to Parliament. Those powers included (1) the raising and control of the armed forces, (2) the raising of funds for the armed forces, (3) the conduct of war, and (4) the conduct of foreign affairs and relations.

Parliamentarians and their supporters relied on several justifications for the assumption and exercise of the powers of government.[1] Most of these justifications were structured to conform with orthodox constitutional theory, and defended Parliament's radical claims by emphasizing the exceptional nature of

---

[1] For more detailed considerations of these issues, see MA Judson, *The Crisis of the Constitution: An Essay in Constitutional and Political Thought in England, 1603–1645* (Rutgers University Press 1949); M Mendle, 'The Great Council of Parliament and the First Ordinances: The Constitutional Theory of the Civil War' (1992) 31 The Journal of British Studies 133; JS Hart Jnr, *The Rule of Law 1603–1660* (Pearson Education 2003).

the situation and the need to restore the previously existing constitutional balance. The 'king's two bodies' theory was a prominent justification for parliamentary assumption of the paradigm kingly powers of war and foreign policy.[2] The two bodies theory drew a distinction between the natural person of king and the public authority and powers of his office. Separating the king's authority from the person of Charles enabled MPs to defy the king's commands while claiming to defend the integrity of the royal office. Parliamentarians and their supporters argued that the person of king had been misled by evil counsel, who had committed treason by telling the king his prerogative was above the law.[3] Another prominent justification was the appeal to necessity. Parliamentarians claimed that Parliament, as the representative institution, was responsible for the general welfare of all and could employ drastic action in case of necessity for the preservation of the greater good.[4]

Parliament claimed and exercised a power normally reserved to the king when it raised a special force of 10,000 men in the London area. An ordinance of 24 February 1643 declared that the Lords and Commons were 'fully satisfied and resolved in their consciences that they have lawfully taken up arms' for their necessary defence and for the protection of the kingdom from foreign invasion.[5] In 1645, Parliament created by ordinance the 'New Model Army', an army of mercenaries that replaced the volunteer armies of the counties.

As well as establishing an armed force, for a short period Parliament itself conducted war. However, there was widespread acknowledgment that Parliament was ill-equipped to conduct war efficiently: the key problems were indecisive leadership and slow and public decision-making. Parliament transferred the conduct of war to a small group of selected men. There were various manifestations of such a group over the years 1642–49: the Committee of Safety, the Committee of Both Kingdoms, the Derby House Committee, and the Council of State. They shared common functions and powers, being

---

[2] JP Kenyon, *The Stuart Constitution: Documents and Commentary* (CUP 1966) 270; Hart (n 1) 166, 208–10.

[3] A good example of the 'king's two bodies' theory was the oath imposed by Parliament in 1643, which declared that the orders and ordinances of Parliament must be obeyed as orders and ordinances of former parliaments would have been, 'because the king's authority and power is there, though his person be not': see 'Declaration to be Tendered to Officers and Members of the Committee and Those Rated to Lend to Parliament, April 27 1643', in Kenyon (n 2) 285.

[4] Judson (n 1) 364–5, 376. Some parliamentarians and military leaders were particularly influenced by the Levellers, whose political programme was founded on the assertion that all just authority derives from the people. The House of Commons was the supreme authority of England, as it was chosen by and representative of the people. See the key documents and proposals of the Levellers in Kenyon (n 2) 302–8.

[5] Kenyon (n 2) 274–7.

tasked with virtually unlimited authority 'to order and direct whatsover doth or may concern the managing of the war'.[6]

Parliament also took on the raising of money to fund the war and the armed forces. Although the Commons had long asserted its power over supply, the processes of fund-raising during this period were different because Parliament not only voted for supply, but also initiated and executed the fund-raising. The escalating costs of war caused Parliament to employ a series of fund-raising activities, including taxes, voluntary contributions, weekly assessments, and excises on items such as tobacco, imported fabrics, soap, and industrial chemicals.[7] For example, in March 1642 it passed an Act, modelled on ship money, to raise £400,000 to pay troops.[8] There were serious deficiencies in the machinery of the Parliament's wartime administration, and unpopularity, abuse, and corruption flourished in the absence of uniform procedures and standards and a lack of effective oversight.[9]

In addition to Parliament's assumption of powers over war and the raising of funds for the armed forces, Parliament also undertook the general conduct of foreign affairs. Parliament dispatched representatives abroad, sent and received complaints and communications, and gave audience to ambassadors—such as the Swedish minister, who addressed a memorial to the 'Most Illustrious peers, Honourable Knights, and the Renowned Estates of this Most Noble Court', and the ambassador of the States of Holland, who delivered a paper 'To the Honourable Parliament of England, at Westminster'.[10] Foreign states were sometimes unsure with whom to deal, and so communicated with the king, Parliament, or both.[11]

In the following revolutionary years, despite Parliament's efforts to keep control of foreign relations, increasing control was yielded to small committees, and eventually, to Cromwell (as Protector) and his council.

The Constitutional Experiments of the Commonwealth and Protectorate

In January and February of 1649, in quick succession, the Rump Parliament tried, convicted, and executed Charles I; abolished the House of Lords and monarchy; and established the Commonwealth.

---

[6] J Adamson, 'The Triumph of Oligarchy: The Management of War and the Committee of Both Kingdoms, 1644–45' in CR Kyle and J Peacey (eds), *Parliament at Work: Parliamentary Committees, Political Power and Public Access in Early Modern Britain* (Boydell Press 2002) 101.

[7] Kenyon (n 2) 270–87.   [8] 16 Car I c 32, in Kenyon (n 2) 270–1.

[9] Hart (n 1) 217.

[10] Cited in ER Turner, 'Parliament and Foreign Affairs, 1603–1760 (1919) 34 The English Historical Review 172, 175.

[11] Turner (n 10) 175.

These radical constitutional changes meant radical changes to the arrangements for the exercise and control of the powers over war, peace, and foreign policy. Initially, the executive functions were vested for a year in a forty-strong statutory Council of State, composed mostly of MPs.[12] Separate committees were established to deal with particular subject-matters, including foreign affairs, the army, and the navy. One of the Council's members said that its establishment 'was the only way to adde strength thereto, and to make their motion more quick and vigorous'.[13] The Council was responsible for most of the day-to-day direction and management of policy in defence, trade, and diplomacy. It oversaw military campaigns in Ireland and Scotland, managed the invasion crisis of 1651, organized a massive expansion of the English navy, and conducted a war with the Dutch. The Council was also responsible for the conduct of foreign relations, including the sending and receiving of ambassadors.[14]

The Act abolishing the office of king explained the reasons for vesting these powers in a Council of State.[15] The Act declared that it had been found by experience that allocating to one person the powers that the king possessed was unnecessary, burdensome, and dangerous to the liberty, safety, and public interest of the people. It was usual and natural, the Act stated, that where one person has so much power, he is inclined to encroach on the freedom and liberty of the people and to advance his own will and power above the laws. It followed that the office of king should not reside in or be exercised by a single person.

The Commons continued to play a key role in the conduct of foreign policy. It received ambassadors and conducted diplomacy according to rules and procedures set out in resolutions of the House. The resolutions provided that ambassadors should be admitted to public audience in the House when the House thought fit, while other foreign ministers should have audience with a committee, who would report back to the House. For example, in June 1650, the House heard from the Commissioner from the States of Holland. The House responded to the Commissioner's address by way of the Speaker reading an Address of the House while the Commissioner sat in the House.[16]

The Commonwealth ended in April 1653, when the Rump Parliament proposed the dismissal of Cromwell from the post of commander-in-chief.

---

[12] The Council of State was established and empowered by the Act Appointing a Council of State, February 13, 1648/9<http://www.constitution.org/eng/conpur086.htm>.

[13] Earl of Pembroke, quoted in S Kelsey, 'The Foundation of the Council of State' in Kyle and Peacey (n 6) 145.

[14] Act Appointing a Council of State, February 13, 1648/9.

[15] Act Abolishing the Office of King, March 17, 1649 <http://www.constitution.org/eng/conpur088.htm>.

[16] Parliamentary History, 11 June 1650, vol 3, cols 1348, 1359, 1360–1.

Cromwell responded by bringing his troops down to Westminster and dispersing Parliament. A series of constitutional experiments then followed, initiated by Cromwell and his officers. The first was the Nominated Assembly (known as the Barebone's Parliament). It was short-lived.

The second was the Instrument of Government. The Instrument created a Lord Protector who exercised executive powers, advised and assisted by triennial parliaments. The Instrument granted huge powers to the Protector, including powers over the armed forces, war, and foreign policy. When Parliament was sitting, the Protector exercised the power to deploy the armed forces with the consent of Parliament; when Parliament was not sitting, the Protector could deploy the armed forces with the advice and consent of the 'major part of the council'.[17] The Protector directed and controlled the nation's foreign policy and, with the consent of the major part of the Council, exercised the powers of war and peace.[18]

The creation of the Protectorate in December 1653 meant that Cromwell, as the Lord Protector, controlled both the armed force of England and the policy-making bodies that determined how that power would be used. Cromwell's power was extensive, but not absolute, as it was subject to some degree of control or influence by the Council and Parliament.[19] The first Protectorate Parliament in particular sought to exert influence over issues reserved to the Protector under the Instrument of Government. For example, it attempted to establish a militia under parliamentary and local civil control and reduce the army by almost half.[20] It also used its power of supply to good effect. In 1655, Cromwell unsuccessfully sought financial support from a hostile Parliament for his ambitious 'Western Design' foreign policy (an attack on the West Indies). Cromwell attempted to limit Parliament to a more passive role in foreign policy.[21] He accepted that Parliament should be informed of the major foreign policy decisions taken by the Council, but he asserted that Parliament was not to have a substantive role in formulating or implementing that policy.[22]

The 'Rule of the Major-Generals' was established in 1655. The fifteen-month period of direct military government bolstered the growing opposition to the political presence of the army.[23] It was abandoned in 1657 and replaced by a new constitution: the Humble Petition and Advice. The

---

[17] Instrument of Government, art IV <http://www.constitution.org/eng/conpur097.htm>.
[18] Instrument of Government, art V.
[19] CP Korr, *Cromwell and the New Model Foreign Policy* (University of California Press 1975) 101.
[20] JR Western, *The English Militia in the Eighteenth Century: The Story of a Political Issue 1660–1802* (Routledge and Kegan Paul 1965) 6.
[21] Korr (n 19) 121.   [22] Korr (n 19) 123.
[23] CH Firth, *The Last Years of the Protectorate 1656–1658* vol 1 (Longmans, Green and Co 1909) 124.

Humble Petition initially offered Cromwell the Crown, but after he declined the offer, he was appointed Lord Protector. Pursuant to the Humble Petition, the standing forces of the Commonwealth were to be disposed of by the Protector with the consent of both Houses of Parliament if Parliament was sitting, or with the consent of a council of state if Parliament was not sitting.[24]

The constitutional experiments of the revolutionary period were brought to an end in 1660, when the Long Parliament was recalled and Charles II restored as King.

Legacies of the Revolutionary Period

Although the revolutionary period was an extraordinary time in English constitutional history, it left two key legacies relevant to future arrangements for the exercise of the war and foreign policy powers. First, following the Restoration it was generally accepted that Parliament could properly debate any topics relating to war and foreign policy. It was difficult for future monarchs to contend that any topic existed where Parliament had no authority to act, or had to wait for royal initiative before doing so.[25] The raising and spending of revenue, the control of the armed forces, and the conduct of war and foreign policy had been brought within the purview of the revolutionary Parliament. As DL Keir observes, '[t]o preserve these topics as pertaining solely to the "mystery of Kingship" was no longer possible now that the veil which protected them had been rent in twain.'[26]

The second legacy was the lessons learnt from the experimental arrangements for the exercise and control of the war and foreign policy powers. First, in the Commonwealth, the executive powers over war and foreign policy were vested in a council of forty men, with the express objective of avoiding the tyranny associated with vesting such powers in a single person. However, merely vesting the executive powers in a council, rather than a single person, is no guarantee against tyranny as John Lilburne, one of the leaders of the Levellers, observed. He cautioned that the Council's command of the kingdom's land and sea forces meant that 'they will have great opportunities to make themselves absolute and unaccountable'.[27] Secondly, the trend over the

---

[24] Humble Petition and Advice, May 25, 1657 <www.constitution.org/eng/conpur102.htm>.

[25] DL Keir, *The Constitutional History of Modern Britain 1485–1937* (Adam and Charles Black 1938) 231, 233. See the citations at nn 28–54 on the nature and extent of the House of Commons' freedom of speech prior to the Civil war.

[26] Keir (n 25). See also FW Maitland, *The Constitutional History of England: A Course of Lectures Delivered by F. W. Maitland* (CUP 1955) 308; Turner (n 10) 176.

[27] John Lilburne, 'England's New Chains Discovered: Or the Serious Apprehensions of a Part of the People in Behalf of the Commonwealth; Presented to the Supreme Authority of England, 26 February 1649' <http://www.constitution.org/lev/eng_lev_10.htm>.

period was for these powers to be vested in institutions composed of increasingly fewer numbers of people. The revolutionary experience showed that some functions are likely to be more efficiently and effectively exercised by a single person or a small group: the conduct of diplomacy and the command of the armed forces are two particularly apt examples. Thirdly, the revolutionary experience suggests there is a tendency for the individual or small group with primary responsibility for war and foreign policy to desire increasingly greater discretionary powers and to resent interference from other bodies in their exercise.

Part III Interactions

Introduction

The remainder of the chapter turns its focus to the interactions of the executive and the House of Commons in the exercise of the war prerogative in the time period 1600–2012. I focus on five types of interaction, debate, the power of supply, retrospective scrutiny, parliamentary consultation before going to war, and legislation. The analysis will show how, by these interactions, the Commons has played an active and influential role in decision-making about, and the conduct of, war.

Freedom of Speech and Debate

1 Introduction

Parliament's right to freedom of speech was hotly contested through the seventeenth century. The proper scope and initiation of parliamentary debate was a source of tension between the monarchs and their parliaments, and freedom of speech as to matters of war and foreign policy was often at the centre of these battles. The first section examines how Parliament's right to freedom of speech evolved through the seventeenth century and how the Commons during this time used its rights to free speech and debate to try to participate in the making of decisions about war and foreign policy. The second section examines the functions of parliamentary debate in the age of parliamentary government. The roles and functions of parliamentary debate changed, as parliamentary government replaced monarchical government and democratic theories of government altered perceptions of the relationship between the governors and the governed. The third section examines the various limitations on parliamentary debate in the context of war and foreign policy. Legally, Parliament's right to free speech is unrestricted, but in practice there are various limitations or restraints (some self-imposed, others imposed

2 Freedom of Speech in the Seventeenth Century

Parliament's freedom of speech was secured over time by a process of constitutional evolution.[28] During the seventeenth century, there were two key issues of contention regarding Parliament's freedom of speech on topics of war and foreign policy. The first was whether or not Parliament was free to debate issues of any subject-matter, including those related to royal prerogatives. The second was based on a distinction between debate and advice: was Parliament limited merely to debating an issue, or could it properly give advice to the monarch?

Parliament could, when invited to do so by the monarch, debate on any topic, even those relating to the prerogatives of war and foreign policy. The belief that a good ruler took counsel from a wide range of sources was central to medieval political thought.[29] A monarch would be expected to invite debate in Parliament on an issue as important as war. The writs of summons of Parliament supported this policy, stating that Parliament was called to treat and consent about difficult and urgent business concerning the state and defence of the kingdom and the Church of England.[30] For Parliament's part, the broad function of parliamentary debates was to communicate parliamentary opinions to the monarch in the hope of influencing his or her decision. The political strategy of parliaments was to try to persuade the monarch to adopt different counsels, as parliaments were not a rival power centre to the monarch, but just one among the several pressures that the monarch reacted to when choosing his or her course of action.[31]

At the start of the seventeenth century, therefore, it was accepted that Parliament could, on the invitation of the monarch, debate any topic. Much more contested, however, was whether Parliament could discuss such matters on its own initiative. Parliaments from as far back as the reign of Henry III had on occasion opposed the king's will and tried to persuade kings to do things which were contrary to the king's preferences. In 1559, the Crown

---

[28] PA Joseph, *Constitutional and Administrative Law in New Zealand*, 3rd edn (Brookers 2007) 410–38.

[29] C Russell, 'The Nature of a Parliament in Early Stuart England' in H Tomlinson (ed), *Before the English Civil War: Essays on Early Stuart Politics and Government* (MacMillan Press 1983) 123.

[30] In the original Latin: '*ad tractandum et consentiendum pro quibusdam arduis et urgentibus negotiis statum et defensionem regni et ecclesiae Anglicanae tangentibus*', Public Record Office C218/1, cited in Russell (n 29) 128–9.

[31] Russell (n 29) 130.

granted the Parliament's formal request of the privilege of freedom of speech. However, that privilege was granted subject to the condition that members be 'neither unmindful nor uncareful of their duties, reverence, and obedience to their sovereign'.[32] The privilege was also limited by subject-matter. Topics touching on the prerogative were excluded from its protection and Parliament required leave from the Crown to introduce such topics. On a number of occasions Elizabeth stopped a debate which she considered touched on her prerogative. Elizabeth maintained that the Commons could speak as they wished to the business before them, but (apart from a reserve right to raise 'commonwealth matters' in which the public safety was involved) only the Crown could decide what that business should be.[33]

The scope of Parliament's freedom of speech on foreign policy topics became more complex under James I and Charles I. Parliament increasingly debated matters of foreign policy and sought to exert influence and control over the king's choices and actions. Issues of foreign policy, in particular war, relations with Spain, and the marriage of Charles I, were topics at the heart of the debate about the extent of Parliament's freedom of speech. The monarchs' approach to the proper scope of Parliament's freedom of speech was inconsistent and reactive to the particular circumstances and political exigencies. In some situations James permitted and encouraged Parliament's discussion of foreign policy issues, while in others he refused Parliament's competence to do so. For example, in June 1607, the Earls of Salisbury and Northampton delivered a formal lecture to a joint committee of Lords and Commons on the incompetence of the Commons to discuss major affairs of state. But three years later, in June 1610, Salisbury reversed his position and tried to persuade the Commons to grant a subsidy for the support of James' military intervention in the Cleves-Juelich crisis by appealing to them as[34]

men of extraordinary quality...we deal not with you economically, we talk not of corn or grain, but as with statesmen and wish you to bend your cogitations to view how foreign states stand and how their affairs have relation to the state of this kingdom.

Parliament could properly debate matters of war and foreign policy when invited to by the king. However, in the absence of such an invitation, the Commons' debate of war and foreign policy would probably have been regarded as improper constitutional encroachment of the prerogative.[35] Another improper

---

[32] 'Answer to Petition for Privilege' (22 February 1593) in JR Tanner, *Tudor Constitutional Documents A.D. 1485–1603 with an Historical Commentary* (CUP 1922) 552.

[33] Kenyon (n 2) 25.

[34] Quoted in ER Foster (ed), *The Proceedings in Parliament: 1610* vol II (New Haven 1966) 136–7.

[35] C Russell, 'The Foreign Policy Debate in the House of Commons in 1621' (1977) 20 The Historical Journal 289, 296.

encroachment was the giving of unsolicited advice about issues of foreign policy and war. The Commons was generally regarded as overstepping constitutional boundaries when, in 1621, after being invited to discuss a local war for the recovery of the Palatinate, it tried to turn it into a general war against Spain.[36]

The difficult distinction between debate and advice was illustrated later in 1621 in a series of petitions and replies between the Commons and James I. It started with the Commons sending a petition to James setting out the Commons' advice on foreign policy.[37] The advice was detailed, and the recommendations for future actions and policies were stated in firm terms. For example, the first recommendation was the king must go to war: 'seeing this inevitable necessity is fallen upon your Majesty which no wisdom or providence of a peaceable and pious King can avoid, your Majesty would not omit this just occasion speedily and effectually to take your sword into your hand.'[38] The petition also communicated the Commons' wish that James would publicly support the Protestant princes and urged that 'to frustrate their [Spain's] hopes for a future age, our most noble prince may be timely married to one of our own religion'.[39] While forcefully expressing its opinions and calling for action by the king, the Commons made sure to pay lip-service to the accepted constitutional rules, with the concluding paragraph of the petition stating: 'This is the sum and effect of our humble declaration, which we (no ways intending to press upon your Majesty's undoubted and regal prerogative) do with the fullness of our duty and obedience humbly submit to your most princely consideration.'[40]

By this petition, the Commons took the step from mere debate to advising the king on matters of war and foreign policy. James and Charles responded angrily. In a letter to the Commons, James rebuked it for 'argu[ing] and debat[ing] publicly of the matters far above their reach and capacity, tending to our high dishonour and breach of prerogative royal' and commanded it not to 'meddle with anything concerning our government or deep matters of state', matters which were the business of the Privy Council.[41]

In response to James' angry letter, the Commons sent a second petition to the king, which drew a distinction between 'discourse' (protected by

---

[36] R Zaller, *The Parliament of 1621: A Study in Constitutional Conflict* (University of California Press 1971) 145–51; but see Russell (n 35) 303, where he points to evidence that the Commons debated this issue on the basis of official encouragement to do so, and with the belief that they had been invited to do so.

[37] 'Commons' Petition, 3 December 1621', in JR Tanner (ed), *Constitutional Documents of the Reign of James I 1603–1625* (CUP 1960) 276.

[38] 'Commons' Petition, 3 December 1621' in Tanner (n 37) 276, 277.

[39] Commons' Petition, 3 December 1621' in Tanner (n 37) 276–9.

[40] 'Commons' Petition, 3 December 1621' in Tanner (n 37) 277.

[41] 'King's Letter to the Speaker, 3 December 1621' in Tanner (n 37) 279. See also Mendle (n 1) 137.

Parliament's 'ancient liberty' of freedom of speech) and 'determination' (which would improperly intrude on the 'sacred bounds' of royal authority).[42] The Commons acknowledged that the king had the sole powers to make peace and war and to organize the marriage of the prince. They claimed again, however, the Commons' power to discuss and inform the king on these matters. The petition articulated two foundations for its power: first, the Commons' position as representatives of the 'whole commons of the kingdom'; and secondly, its ancient and undoubted right to free speech inherited from the Commons' ancestors.[43] In another reply, James dismissed the Commons' purported advice about the marriage of Prince Charles and war with Spain, and rejected the Commons' competence to give advice about such issues. He declared that the powers over war and foreign policy were historically and by custom the 'most undoubted and regal prerogative',[44] and, further, Parliament lacked the expertise and knowledge necessary to advise on foreign policy.[45]

Despite this angry exchange, after 1621 the Commons was often consulted by James on matters of policy and government. Buckingham (James' chief adviser) undertook not to harm members who discussed matters of state,[46] and sought (but reserved the right not to follow) the 'advice' of the Commons in matters of foreign policy and war.[47] For example, at the opening of Parliament in 1624, James asked the Commons' advice on relations with Spain and the proposed match of the prince.[48] James said that although war and peace were the prerogatives of the king, he would not make decisions on these matters without first informing the Commons and hearing their advice.[49] Parliament was not being asked to rubber-stamp an arrangement agreed upon by the king and his advisers, but to arbitrate in a matter on which the Privy Council and the royal family itself were deeply divided. Parliament advised him to break off all negotiations with Spain. James abandoned the pro-Spanish policy to which he had devoted a large part of his energies for many years, and one which he most likely sincerely believed in.[50]

While pushing the accepted boundaries of its privileges, the Commons was careful to acknowledge, at least in form, the Crown's exclusive prerogatives. The Commons continued to employ the political strategy of paying proper

---

[42] Tanner (n 37) 282–3.
[43] This second justification was reiterated in the Commons Protestation of 18 December 1621, in Tanner (n 37) 288.
[44] 'King's Answer of 11 December 1621' in Tanner (n 37) 283.
[45] 'King's Answer of 11 December 1621' in Tanner (n 37) 286.
[46] Mendle (n 1) 138.   [47] Tanner (n 37) 296–302.
[48] GL Mosse, *The Struggle for Sovereignty in England* (Michigan State College Press 1950) 116.
[49] 'The King's Answer, 8 March 1624' in Tanner (n 37) 296, 299.   [50] Kenyon (n 2) 30.

lip-service to the king's prerogatives, while at the same time attempting to influence how the king exercised those prerogatives. In November 1621, when James gave to the Commons an account of foreign business and sought their advice and supply, MPs praised his 'wise and gracious condescension' in doing so. Sir Dudley Digges said: 'Though his majesty be not tied to give account of his actions to any but to God, yet it hath pleased him to descend from his royal prerogative therein so low, as to acquaint his houses of parliament with his proceedings in this business.'[51] In a session in 1626, in the midst of the war against Spain, the Commons was eager to assure the king that although the Commons had debated 'some business that were partly foreign, and had some relation to affairs of state', it was not their intention 'either to traduce your counsellors, or disadvantage your negotiations'.[52]

Charles was not as receptive to parliamentary debate or advice as James. He asserted that the 'greatest council of state' was the Privy Council, not Parliament, and that the Privy Council was above the general interference of the Commons.[53] By the last Parliament under Charles the Commons was still unable to defend their privilege of free speech; but the general privilege of discussing any matter they chose, in any order, had been virtually conceded in practice, with Charles' only response being prorogation or dissolution.[54]

Post-restoration, the rules and practices regarding Parliament's freedom of speech had changed.[55] In practice, the scope of Parliament's freedom of speech was relatively settled: Parliament could debate any topics of its choice. The key issue of contestation now was whether Parliament could and should go beyond mere debate and advice to the monarch, and seek to exert control over foreign policy. As an aspect of its freedom of speech, MPs would criticize the king's decisions and actions and make clear their opinions on the course of action they thought he should pursue. The Commons insisted on a share in foreign policy if they were to supply the means of carrying it out. On some occasions the Commons offered advice about war and alliances, and even sought to prescribe the terms of alliances which the king was to make. In 1664 the Commons requested that the king take action against the United Provinces and promised their support. The following year, Charles II told them 'I entered upon this War by your Advice and Encouragement', and asked them for their 'chearful Supply for the carrying it on'.[56] However,

---

[51] Parliamentary History, 21 November 1621, vol 1, col 1303.
[52] Parliamentary History, 5 April 1626, vol 2, col 69.
[53] SR Gardiner (ed), *The Constitutional Documents of the Puritan Revolution, 1625–1660*, 3rd edn (OUP 1906) 4–5.
[54] Kenyon (n 2) 32.
[55] The impact of the revolutionary period on the scope and nature of Parliament's freedom of speech has been discussed in citations at nn 25–26.
[56] Quoted in Turner (n 10) 176–7.

despite such instances of clear advice and attempts to control, MPs were divided on whether Parliament should actually exert control over the king's foreign policy decisions. Some did not support attempts to force the king to act on their advice. In a debate on foreign policy in 1677, one MP said: 'The prerogative is not at all encroached on, nor do we pretend to treat or make alliances. We only offer our advice about them and leave it with the King to do as he pleases, either make them or not make them.'[57] Another said: 'Though we are his [the king's] great council, we are not his directors.'[58]

Despite the reluctance or uneasiness of some MPs with giving advice to the king the practice continued under William III. The Commons continued to use its freedom of speech to communicate its wishes to the king and its opinions on his foreign policy. For example, in 1689, the Commons sent an address to William requesting that he declare war on France. It insisted that the Crown communicate relevant information, such as the terms of treaties, the conduct of affairs, and the management of military expeditions, and then gave counsel about them.[59] Some MPs continued to express their concern that Parliament was improperly encroaching upon the king's prerogatives. According to them, the king should personally formulate and execute foreign policy, and although he was supposed to ask for advice on important matters he was not bound either to ask advice of any particular person or body or to accept any such advice.[60]

By the reign of Anne, most MPs considered it properly within their scope to give advice on matters of foreign policy. A minority of parliamentarians adhered to the old view that, because war and peace were prerogatives of the Crown, Parliament should not offer advice unless it was asked for. For example, during the reign of Anne, a dissent was recorded during a debate over the Treaty of Utrecht, on the grounds that 'we look upon it as an Encroachment on the Royal Prerogative, in so hasty a Manner to declare our Opinions, and on no better Grounds, in a Thing so essentially belonging to the Crown, as making Peace and War'.[61] However, the more dominant approach held that it was proper for Parliament to offer advice and that no prerogative could be above advice.[62] Diplomacy and military and naval operations were all subjected to parliamentary scrutiny and oversight. The Commons asked for papers and information relating to the terms of alliances, military

---

[57] Quoted in J Miller, 'The Later Stuart Monarchy' in JR Jones (ed), *The Restored Monarchy 1660–1688* (MacMillan Press 1979) 30, 41.
[58] Parliamentary History, 23 May 1677, vol 4, col 874.
[59] Turner (n 10) 181–2.
[60] GC Gibbs, 'The Revolution in Foreign Policy' in G Holmes (ed), *Britain after the Glorious Revolution 1689–1714* (Macmillan 1969) 59, 66.
[61] Quoted in Turner (n 10) 182–3.   [62] Turner (n 10) 182–3.

strategy, troop numbers, and the conduct of war, and there were lengthy and heated debates on these matters.[63]

The Crown's duty to seek advice and Parliament's right to give such advice was said to stem from Parliament's historic function as the supreme council of the kingdom.[64] Speaking to the Commons in 1743, Solicitor General Murray identified the emergence of the 'right' of the Commons to give advice: 'it is very certain, that this House was not designed, by its original institution, to advise, but to consent, as appears from the very words of the writ, the ancient form of which is still preserved. However, the practice has been so frequent for a century past, that we seem to be in possession, and therefore I shall not dispute our right.'[65] In the same debate, another MP dismissed the contention that it was an encroachment of the prerogative for the Commons to give advice to the sovereign on matters concerning war and foreign policy; the exertion of the prerogative and the advising how to exert the prerogative, he said, are two very different things.[66]

3 Debate in the Age of Parliamentary Government

Introduction

The emergence of parliamentary government and the increasing influence of democratic thought changed the relationship between the government and the House of Commons and the nature and functions of parliamentary debate. In this section, I examine the broader themes of parliamentary debate in the age of parliamentary government, focusing on the changing functions of parliamentary debate. Later in the chapter I will examine how the Commons used debate and other mechanisms of parliamentary procedure to scrutinize government policies and actions,[67] and how governments have used debates to consult with Parliament about war.[68]

First, a short summary of the development of parliamentary government. A cabinet composed of selected MPs emerged in the 1690s as a response to particular practical problems existing under the rule of William and Mary, which included William's frequent absences from the country, the need for Mary to have systematic advice while she was nominally ruling, and the necessity for coordinated wartime planning. Initially the cabinet's role focused on the administration and execution of the monarch's powers, with the big decisions about

---

[63] Turner (n 10) 185–6.
[64] GC Gibbs, 'Laying Treaties before Parliament in the Eighteenth Century' in R Hatton and MS Anderson (eds), *Studies in Diplomatic History: Essays in Memory of David Bayne Horn* (Longman 1970) 116, 120.
[65] Parliamentary History, 6 December 1743, vol 13, col 252.
[66] Parliamentary History, 6 December 1743, vol 13, col 264.
[67] See citations at nn 231–276.   [68] See citations at nn 277–334.

peace, war, and foreign policy being made by the monarch and his or her Privy Council.[69] Under Anne, the practice of a cabinet council continued and grew in strength, and its functions evolved from administrative duties to being a material participant in decision-making. In conjunction with the monarch, the cabinet council decided all questions of policy, relegating the Privy Council to the tasks of routine business and administrative duties. Although the reign of Anne was not an example of cabinet government in the modern sense, ministers were developing a dual function of conducting executive business and winning parliamentary support for what they did. By the time of the first two Hanoverian kings, the cabinet and parliamentary government were firmly established in respect of domestic affairs and administration. The monarchs continued to play a material, if hidden, part in the direction of foreign affairs,[70] but real political power lay increasingly with the government composed of ministers responsible to, and holding the confidence of, the Commons.

The gradual transfer of political power from the monarch (and his or her officials) to ministers sitting in Parliament changed the nature and functions of parliamentary debate. During the seventeenth century, the Commons had used debate and freedom of speech to try to exert influence on the monarch's decisions about war and the formulation and implementation of foreign policy. It was proactive in seeking to participate in the exercise of those powers through debate and other mechanisms (in particular the power of supply). The development of parliamentary government altered the relationship between the Commons and the government. MPs still tried to influence the direction and conduct of foreign policy through debate in the House. However, as parliamentary governments became stronger and more coherent, the capacity of the Commons as an institution to initiate policy or influence decisions made about foreign policy became increasingly limited. The cabinet was where the real power lay. This changed the nature and functions of parliamentary debate. Governments used parliamentary debate to defend their policies and actions and to persuade the Commons (and, increasingly,

---

[69] J Carter, 'The Revolution and the Constitution' in Holmes (n 60) 39, 52; SB Baxter, 'Recent Writings on William III' (1966) 38 Journal of Modern History 256.

[70] Although Whig theory characterized the monarchy as a mere figurehead, the monarch played a real political role in government during the nineteenth and early-twentieth centuries, particularly in relation to foreign policy. For further, see Turner (n 10) 189–90; HJ Hanham, 'Cabinet Government: The Monarchy' in Hanham (ed), *The Nineteenth-Century Constitution 1815–1914: Documents and Commentary* (CUP 1969) 24, 29; F Hardie, *The Political Influence of the British Monarchy: 1868–1952* (BT Batsford 1970) 42–5; T Blanning, ' "That Horrid Electorate" or "Ma Patrie Germanique"? George III, Hanover, and the *Fuerstenbund* of 1785' (1977) 20 Historical Journal 20; works cited in J Black, *British Foreign Policy in the Age of Walpole* (John Donald Publishers 1985) 36.

the public) of their merits, and the Commons used parliamentary debate to scrutinize the government's conduct of war and foreign policy.

With these developments, the Commons took on what is commonly considered the paradigm characteristic of legislative institutions as being responsive, rather than initiating.[71] According to this conception, the function of legislatures is to respond to the initiatives and actions of the government and to scrutinize the exercise of governmental power. Bernard Crisk summarized the role of Parliament thus: 'influence, not direct power; advice, not command; criticism, not obstruction; scrutiny, not initiation; and publicity, not secrecy'.[72] This conception of parliamentary function is quite different from that of seventeenth-century parliaments. As the examination of the Commons' use of freedom of speech and debate in the seventeenth century demonstrated, the Commons had a parliamentary stance on a range of foreign policy issues and sought to participate in and influence governmental action in the realm of foreign policy.

The increasing influence of democratic principles led to the second major change in the function of parliamentary debate. In the early part of parliamentary government, the Commons was still seen to reflect the medieval conception of Parliament as a gathering of wise men. Its function was to shape, rather than reflect, public opinion. Through the nineteenth century, conceptions of Parliament's role and the role of the people in government changed, with the effect being that the Commons came to be seen as the organ of government which reflected the popular will.

The following discussion focuses on these two developments: the scrutiny function of parliamentary debate; and parliamentary debate as shaping, and later reflecting, public opinion.

The Scrutiny Function

There are two key aspects to the scrutiny function of parliamentary debate. The first aspect is that governments used debate in the Commons to explain and defend its decisions and actions in war and foreign policy. Particularly in the early years of parliamentary government, governments took very seriously the need to explain and defend government policy and to respond to criticism

---

[71] For more on the functions and roles of Parliament, see P Norton, 'Parliament and Policy in Britain: The House of Commons as a Policy Influencer' (1984) 13 Teaching Politics 198, reprinted in P Norton (ed), *Legislatures* (OUP 1990) 177; R Blackburn and A Kennon, *Parliament: Functions, Practice and Procedures*, 2nd edn (Sweet and Maxwell 2003) [1-009]. For a more expansive examination on the functions of legislatures, see, eg, RA Packenham, 'Legislatures and Political Development' in A Kornberg and LD Musolf (eds), *Legislatures in Developmental Perspective* (Duke University Press 1970) 521, reprinted in Norton, *Legislatures* (n 71) 81.

[72] B Crick, *The Reform of Parliament*, 2nd edn (Weidenfeld and Nicholson 1968) 80.

in the Commons.[73] Ministers were aware that parliamentary support bolstered their position both domestically and abroad.[74] As part of explaining and defending their policies and actions, governments would also, on either the request of an MP or on their own initiative, provide information to the Commons about war and foreign policy. Such information was communicated to the Commons through a variety of procedural mechanisms, including the speech from the throne (which was written by ministers), statements to the House, question time, the laying of papers before the House, and 'Blue books' (compilations of official information).[75]

The second aspect of the scrutiny function of parliamentary debate was that, through debate and other parliamentary procedures, the Commons reviewed, questioned, and challenged the government's exercise of powers over war and foreign policy. In 1739, a pamphlet writer stated what had come to be generally admitted:[76]

> the Right of making Peace and War is universally allowed to be the Prerogative of the Crown, as the Power of examining whether this Prerogative be properly or improperly exercised, remains in the King's hereditary great Council, and in the Representatives of the People.

In 1802, in a debate about the government's conduct of a war against France, one MP strongly defended the constitutional role of the House of Commons as scrutinizer of the government: 'the House of Commons, which according to the constitution, should be the jealous observer and controller of the acts of the executive, the protector and guardian of the people and the laws.'[77] Another MP, in a debate in 1803 on the king's message announcing the raising of a large armed force, praised the 'wise purpose' of the constitutional arrangement whereby the king exercises the prerogative to declare war on the advice of his ministers who are responsible to Parliament. This arrangement, he said, enables the Commons and the nation to know 'how to direct their inquiries, and where to fix their censure, if bad advice should appear to have been followed.'[78] Government ministers, too, recognized the constitutional scrutinizing role of the Commons. In a debate on the Crimean war of 1853–54, Lord Palmerston said that the debate was 'one of the most

---

[73] GC Gibbs, 'Parliament and Foreign Policy in the Age of Stanhope and Walpole' (1962) 77 The English Historical Review 18; Gibbs, 'The Revolution in Foreign Policy' (n 60) 59, 72; Turner (n 10) 182.
[74] Black (n 70) 77.
[75] ZS Steiner, *The Foreign Office and Foreign Policy 1898–1914* (CUP 1969).
[76] Anon, *Miscellaneous Reflections upon the Peace, and Its Consequences* (London 1749) 3, quoted in Turner (n 10) 195.
[77] Parliamentary History, 12 April 1802, vol 36, col 492.
[78] Parliamentary History, 18 June 1803, vol 36, col 1682.

solemn and important occasions which can fall to the lot of Parliament to deliberate on a momentous occasion'. The government lays before the House relevant information and diplomatic correspondence 'for the express purpose of affording Parliament an opportunity of fully considering and reviewing the conduct of the Government and if it thought fit, of expressing an opinion thereupon'.[79]

In the eighteenth and nineteenth centuries particularly, debates in the House of Commons on issues of foreign policy and war were frequent and in-depth. The debates were motivated by a mix of reasons—sometimes by a serious disagreement about policy, and sometimes by an attempt to harass political opponents.[80] The king's speech always prompted a lengthy discussion on foreign affairs, and foreign policy was also prominent in debates on the army and navy and the mutiny bill. Particular events also prompted debate on issues of foreign policy or war. For example, in the debate in November 1761 on the king's speech, the government's strategy in waging a controversial war against Germany came under serious attack and numerous MPs rose to criticize Britain's involvement. The leading opposition spokesman urged the immediate recall of British forces serving abroad and the resumption of peace negotiations with France. Government ministers responded to the criticism, with the elder Pitt delivering a long speech comprehensively reviewing and justifying his ministry's programme and defending the war as vital for the king's honour and national interests.[81] In June 1850 the government's conduct of the Greek crisis was the subject of a four-day debate. The debate also encompassed more general thematic issues, such as whether British foreign policy should be interventionist and whether Britain should adhere to international law and morality.[82]

The Commons has taken seriously its role in pressing governments on their conduct of wars. Despite the unwritten but generally acknowledged limitations on the scope of parliamentary speech in the context of war,[83] there are many instances where the Commons has scrutinized, criticized, and questioned choices made by governments in the conduct of war, including matters of military strategy,[84] the suitability of the equipment of the

---

[79] HC Deb 20 February 1854, vol 130, cols 1029–30.   [80] Turner (n 10) 192.

[81] K Schweizer, 'An Unpublished Parliamentary Speech by the Elder Pitt, 9 December 1761' (1991) 64 Historical Research 98.

[82] HC Deb 25 June 1850, vol 112, col 444. See also G Hicks, 'Don Pacifico, Democracy, and Danger: The Protectionist Party Critique of British Foreign Policy 1850–1852' (2004) 26 The International History Review 515.

[83] See citations at nn 115–180.

[84] During WWII, the Commons, in the wake of defeats in Libya, Greece, and the Balkans, questioned whether the government had pursued the proper strategy: see H Finer 'The British Cabinet, The House of Commons and the War' (1941) 56 Political Science Quarterly 321, 348. In debates

armed forces,[85] the efficiency of arrangements within government for the direction of war,[86] and the necessity of measures taken at home during wartime.[87] Speaking in the midst of World War Two, Winston Churchill praised the role of the Commons in scrutinizing the conduct and operations of the war effort:[88]

I think I have said before that to try to carry on a war, a tremendous war, without the aid and guidance of the House of Commons would be a super human task. I have never taken the view that the Debates and criticisms of this House are a drag and a burden. Far from it. I may not agree at all with the criticism—I may be stunned by it, and I may resent it; I may even retort—but at any rate Debates on these large issues are of the very greatest value to the life-thrust of the nation, and they are of the very greatest assistance to His Majesty's Government.

Parliamentary Debate and Public Opinion
Since the eighteenth century, conceptions of the function of parliamentary debate vis-a-vis public opinion have shifted. Although the Commons in the eighteenth century claimed to be representative, the claim was not framed in democratic terms. Parliamentary debate was regarded as serving the function of shaping public opinion. The increasing influence of democratic thought altered conceptions of the purpose of parliamentary debate, with the consequence that the Commons was seen as the organ for the expression of public opinion and Commons' debate was said to reflect public opinion. This section outlines

---

during the Falklands war, many MPs criticized the government's conduct, questioning why it was not better prepared for an Argentine attack and alleging failures of intelligence and strategy: see HC Deb 3 April 1982, vol 21, cols 633–68. During the Kosovo crisis, the opposition questioned the government's strategy of employing airstrikes and not sending in ground troops: HC Deb 26 May 1999, vol 332, cols 355–72.

[85] In a debate during WWII about the disastrous campaign in Norway, MPs questioned why soldiers had not been provided with white cold weather clothes, skis, or snowshoes: see HC Deb 6 May 1940, vol 360, col 1083.

[86] During the first years of WWII, the Commons focused on the government's organization and structure for the coordination of the war effort. MPs were particularly concerned with the absence of a War Cabinet, and then later, once a War Cabinet had been established, with its composition and size. See the discussion in Finer (n 84).

[87] In 1802, during the war with France, MPs expressed concerns about the excessive violation of constitutional freedoms during the war effort: Parliamentary History, 12 April 1802, vol 36, col 492. During WWII, the House of Commons rejected the Defence Regulations introduced in 1939, which contained provisions for 'detention on suspicion', prohibition on propaganda 'prejudicial to the defence of the realm', and unrestricted press censorship. See Finer (n 84) 356. Recent measures taken by governments in the 'war against terror' (such as control orders and detention without trial) have been subject to heavy criticism in Parliament. For example, on 9 November 2005 the government's proposals to extend detention without trial to ninety days were defeated in the Commons.

[88] HC Deb 22 January 1941, vol 368, col 258.

these changes in the perceived functions of parliamentary debate vis-a-vis public opinion.

The Commons in the eighteenth century regarded itself as representative of the nation. The Commons was drawing on a long history in claiming to be representative. Since at least the seventeenth century the Commons had proclaimed itself the voice of the nation,[89] and constitutional concepts such as the 'ancient constitution' and mixed and balanced government treated the Commons as contributing the 'democratic' mode of government to the English constitution.[90] Writing in 1643, one commentator declared 'the Parliament be the Representative Body of the Kingdom'.[91] As the representative body, it was said to be concerned with the welfare of the kingdom. Accordingly, Parliament was the place where the king and his subjects, lords and commons, came together in a common council to discuss and act upon matters common to all. Bacon described Parliament as 'the great Council of the King, the great Council of the Kingdom, to advise his Majesty of those things of weight and difficulty which concern both the King and kingdom'.[92] Eighteenth-century conceptions of Parliament were very similar. Parliament regarded itself as the 'great council' or the 'national council', a place where great matters of state were deliberated. As one commentator asserted in 1760: 'The wisest Measures have often been pointed out in the Course of parliamentary Debate.'[93]

The seventeenth- and eighteenth-centuries' conceptions of Parliament's representative and deliberative nature were not, however, framed in democratic terms. Apart from a brief time during the revolutionary period there was never any suggestion by the leaders in Parliament that the nation at large possessed active political power. Various radical groups during the mid-seventeenth century (most prominently the Levellers and the Diggers) had campaigned for the realization of democratic representation but, post-Restoration, their ideas were not accepted in mainstream thought.[94] Instead, Parliament seemed to assume without question that its voice was truly the voice of the nation.

---

[89] Judson (n 1) 274–310; J Goldsworthy, *The Sovereignty of Parliament: History and Philosophy* (Clarendon Press 1999) 96–7; D Judge, *Representation: Theory and Practice in Britain* (Routledge 1999) 15–17.

[90] See the citations at nn 119–127 in ch 2 on the ancient constitution and the citations at nn 128–136 in ch 2 on the mixed and balanced government.

[91] *An Exact Collection of the Remonstrance, Declarations . . . between the Kings Most Excellent Majesty and His High Court of Parliament . . . Dec. 1641 . . . Mar. 21, 1643* (London 1643) 697, cited in Judson (n 1) 373.

[92] J Spedding, *The Letters and Life of Francis Bacon* vol VI (London 1861–74) 38, quoted in Judson (n 1) 70.

[93] J Douglas, *A Letter Addressed to Two Great Men* (London 1760) 1–2, cited in Turner (n 10) 195.

[94] See M Loughlin, 'Constituent Power Subverted: From English Constitutional Argument to Constitutional Practice' in M Loughlin and N Walker (eds), *The Paradox of Constitutionalism: Constituent*

Whig theory continued this tradition. It claimed parliamentary government to be a representative system, but the theory was not framed in democratic terms.[95] Government was not considered the concern of the people. Ministers were changed, policies adopted, war declared, and peace made, without reference to the voters.[96]

With these conceptions of Parliament as a deliberative and representative (but not democratic) 'council', the perceived function of parliamentary debate was to shape, rather than reflect, public opinion. The public was said to look to Parliament: in 1800, Pitt asserted that 'with regard to the large and complicated question of peace and war, as on every other point of national interest, the eyes of the people are trained upon parliament'.[97] Jeremy Black identifies Parliament in the eighteenth century as a setting in which ideas and policies were debated and took on coherence and legitimacy.[98] The function of this debate was not to act as an organ for popular expression, but to shape and define extra-parliamentary debate and opinions.[99] Burke's famous speech to his constituents in Bristol in 1774 illustrated these ideas well: 'parliament is a deliberative assembly of one nation, with one interest, that of the whole; where, not local purposes, not local prejudices ought to guide, but the general good, resulting from the general reason of the whole.'[100]

During the second part of the nineteenth century conceptions of Parliament's role and the public's role in government evolved. Driven by the increasing influence of democratic principles, an increasing number of groups, societies, petitions, and other organizations acted as modes of expressing common opinion and exerting active influence on national policy.[101] This evidenced an increasing interest in national questions and an increasing desire to have a voice in decision-making. Public opinion became a very real pressure on government.

Perceptions of Parliament's role evolved, from the medieval idea of Parliament as a gathering of wise men to the idea that the function of Parliament (and in particular, the Commons) was to put into legal form the decisions which the

---

Power and Constitutional Reform (OUP 2006) for an examination of the Levellers' assertion of the House of Commons as the supreme authority of England, on the basis that it was chosen by and representative of the people.

[95] For more on the Whig theory of government, see citations at nn 141–146 in ch 2.
[96] AF Pollard, *The Evolution of Parliament* (Longmans, Green and Co 1920) 339.
[97] William Pitt, *Orations on the French War* (JM Dent 1906) 369, quoted in P Towle, *Going to War: British Debates from Wilberforce to Blair* (Palgrave Macmillan 2009) 126.
[98] J Black, *Parliament and Foreign Policy in the Eighteenth Century* (CUP 2004) 8.
[99] Black (n 98) 6.
[100] F Canavan, 'Edmund Burke' in L Strauss and J Cropsey (eds), *History of Political Philosophy*, 2nd edn (Rand McNally and Co 1972) 659, 672. See also Judge (n 89) 47–69.
[101] GB Adams, *Constitutional History of England* (Jonathan Cape 1921) 416–17.

nation had reached elsewhere.[102] In 1861, Prime Minister Palmerston referred to this as the 'mouthpiece' function of the Commons. The Commons, he said, was 'highly conducive to the public interests—namely, that of being the mouthpiece of the nation; the organ by which all opinions, all complaints, all notions of grievances, all hopes and expectations, all wishes and suggestions which may arise among the people at large, may be brought to an expression here, may be discussed, examined, answered, rejected, or redressed'.[103] Bagehot, writing in 1867, called it the House of Commons' 'expressive function': 'it is its office to express the mind of English people on all matters which come before it.'[104]

The increased emphasis on the Commons as a mouthpiece for the nation influenced the content of debate. Rather than debate serving to shape public opinion, debate in the Commons started to reflect public opinion and to refer to public sentiment and opinions on particular issues. For example, in a debate in 1854 as to war with Russia, MPs referred to the 'popular feeling' on the subject, and 'policy worthy of the nation'.[105] One MP asserted that, as 'the representatives of the people of England', the Commons was bound to consider what the interests of the people require.[106] Late in the nineteenth century, a government minister, in outlining government policy with regard to China, recognized that 'the public mind had been in a condition of considerable anxiety' about developments in East Asia.[107]

This development continued into the twentieth century. In debates about war, MPs often referred to the opinions of their constituents and general public sentiment. One MP, on the eve of Britain's entry into World War One, asked the government 'whether they are not compelled, by their highest duty, to consider their obligations to the people of this country'.[108] Another MP, commenting on the popular feeling about going to war said: 'Certainly last week, if you asked any man in this country, whatever his politics might be whether he would calmly contemplate the entrance of this country into this quarrel, he would have said, "No".'[109] In a debate on action in Korea, one

---

[102] Although, see Judge (n 89) 19–20, where he identifies the paradoxes replete in discussions of 'representation' in Britain. He writes: 'Representation both serves to include "the people" in decision-making—infrequently and indirectly through the process of elections—yet, simultaneously, to exclude them from direct and continuous participation in the decision-making process.' Also, see 58–69 on the modern application of the 'trustee' (Burkean) conception of representation.

[103] HC Deb 3 May 1861, vol 162, col 1492.

[104] W Bagehot, 'The House of Commons' (1867) in Norton, *Legislatures* (n 71) 36, 38.

[105] HC Deb 27 March 1854, vol 132, col 242.

[106] HC Deb 27 March 1854, vol 132, col 261.

[107] HC Deb 5 April 1898, vol 56, cols 225–39. See further TG Ottee, 'Avenge England's Dishonour: By-Elections, Parliament and the Politics of Foreign Policy in 1898' (2006) 121 English Historical Review 385.

[108] HC Deb 3 August 1914, vol 65, col 1851.   [109] HC Deb 3 August 1914, vol 65, col 1859.

MP said he thought it was true that most people in the country supported the government's action: 'I certainly found that in my constituency last weekend, particularly when talking to what one might call ordinary, non-political people.'[110] In a debate on the Suez crisis in 1956, one MP in debate referred to the 'large number of people in this country' who had felt that the government was dragging the country into war without enabling the 'representatives in this House...to comment in any way in reflecting public opinion upon these decisions'.[111] During debate about British military intervention in Libya in 2011, one MP observed that: 'Talking to constituents over the weekend, I discovered that they had great concerns about our involvement, and about the length and level of that involvement. A great deal is needed from the Government to reassure the public about that involvement, not just now but over the coming weeks and months.'[112]

The media has developed as a crucial conduit between Parliament and the public. Much public debate takes place in media forums, such as talk shows, blogs, and other online forums. Politicians will monitor the media for a measure of the public mood.[113] One MP warned during the debate on Kosovo in March 1999: 'on Radio Five this morning the airwaves were blocked with people of Serbian background and people of Albanian background phoning in. The hatred that they felt for each other was so poisonous...that it would have given even the most gung-ho supporter of the Government's policy [in favour of intervention] second thoughts.'[114]

4 Limitations on Parliamentary Debate

Introduction

Article 9 of the Bill of Rights 1688 codified and affirmed Parliament's privilege of free speech. Parliament had a constitutional right to debate on any subject of its choosing, and—legally—was not restricted from talking about any matters, including those of war and foreign policy. However, despite Parliament's legal rights, MPs did not (and sometimes could not) talk completely freely about matters of war and foreign policy. In practice, there were limitations on the freedom of speech and debate in the Commons. Some were self-imposed,

---

[110] HC Deb 5 July 1950, vol 477, cols 570–1.
[111] HC Deb 13 September 1956, vol 558, col 326. For comment on public opinion about the Suez crisis, see K Younder, 'Public Opinion and British Foreign Policy' (1964) 40 International Affairs 22, 24, 26, 27.
[112] HC Deb 21 March 2011, vol 525, col 721.
[113] L van Noije, J Kleinnijenhuis, and D Oegena 'Loss of Parliamentary Control Due to Mediatization and Europeanization: A Longitudinal and Cross-Sectional Analysis of Agenda Building in the UK and the Netherlands' (2008) 38 British Journal of Political Science 455.
[114] HC Deb 25 March 1999, vol 328, col 595.

in the form of a general consensus as to what it was proper or improper for MPs to talk about. Some were imposed by the government, for reasons of political expediency, national security, or other. Other limitations were the result of general patterns or trends. These limitations were not strict rules or conventions. They were normally contested, and they were also uncertain and unevenly applied; sometimes these limitations would be used to restrict the purpose and scope of debate in the House, while on other occasions they were ignored or modified.

In this section I identify six limitations on the freedom of speech and debate in the Commons on matters of war and foreign policy:

- the government's exclusive powers over war and foreign policy,
- the need for secrecy,
- the House of Commons' lack of expertise and information,
- the withholding of criticism while the war was ongoing,
- the trend towards bi-partisan foreign policy, and
- the increasing power of the government over the Commons.

Some of the issues raised by these limitations are discussed in more detail in other parts of the book. The discussion here gives a summary of how these limitations affected the purpose and scope of parliamentary debate, and provides some representative examples of their application.

The Government's Exclusive Powers

The assertion of the Crown's exclusive powers to formulate foreign policy and make decisions about war has been used by governments to deny Parliament's right to participate in decision-making or be consulted about matters of war. Government ministers would commonly assert that, although Parliament had a role in the review and scrutiny of governmental decisions, the executive had sole responsibility for making decisions about war: it was 'entirely for the Government to decide when it was proper to make a declaration of war';[115] 'the responsibility of a war lies on the executive Government'.[116]

The denial of Parliament's right to participate or be consulted in decision-making about war had consequences for the content, nature, and timing of parliamentary debate. If the government denies a role for Parliament in the making of decisions about war, it may not inform Parliament or seek its advice in advance of the government actually declaring or waging war. The

---

[115] HL Deb 24 February 1854, vol 130, col 1244.
[116] HL Deb 24 February 1854, vol 130, col 1239.

consequence is that Parliament's debates as to the merits of the decision are inconsequential, and the effective function of parliamentary debate is limited to trying to exert scrutiny of the government's conduct of that war.

The 'exclusive powers' argument has also been used to restrict the scope of parliamentary debate. As during the seventeenth century, the proper scope of parliamentary debate on matters of war was an issue of contestation during the early years of parliamentary government. Some MPs thought that consultation meant participation in decision-making, and advice meant speaking out whenever Parliament thought it fit to speak out.[117] In contrast, governmental ministers tended to define consultation as amounting to little more than asking Parliament to approve a fait accompli, and held that advice meant that Parliament should only speak when it was spoken to.[118] Lord Hawkesbury, for example, in 1803 sought to restrict the proper tendering of advice by MPs to situations of misuse of power:[119]

> for the constitutional right of the House to interpose its advice on the exercise of any branch of the royal prerogative...a good case ought to be made out...As the constitution vested certain powers in the executive government, the inference naturally was, that those powers were not to be restrained or dictated to by any other branch of the legislature, but where they appeared to be abused.

Secrecy

The second limitation on parliamentary debate has been the claimed need for secrecy in matters of war and foreign policy. Certain types of information have been treated by governments as normally requiring secrecy.

Ongoing negotiations—also referred to as affairs or transactions 'upon the anvil'—have normally been regarded as requiring secrecy. In 1714, in response to a request for the release of information about particular engagements, Secretary Stanhope declared it would be 'injurious' to the king's prerogative to release information to Parliament about the nature of those alliances: 'For if the Crown was obliged to impart the secret of affairs to so great a number of persons, the most important negotiations must thereby miscarry.'[120] Robert Walpole in 1739 explained that princes are jealous of 'the punctilio of honour', which made it dangerous to publish the transaction of a negotiation until some time after it had been concluded.[121] Lord Palmerston asserted that to require all confidential communications made by the Foreign

---

[117] Gibbs (n 64) 134. [118] Gibbs (n 64) 133–4.
[119] Parliamentary History, 27 May 1803, vol 36, col 1525.
[120] Parliamentary History, 3 April 1718, vol 7, col 438.
[121] Parliamentary History, 6 February 1739, vol 10, cols 1002–3.

Minister to be laid before Parliament would be 'injurious to the public service' and would defeat the object of his work.[122]

On occasion the content of alliances to which England has already entered has been considered unsuitable for parliamentary debate. Britain's entry into World War One was predicated on secret engagements. In the years leading up to the war, government ministers made several statements to the Commons, denying the existence of any secret agreements or arrangements under which British military forces would be called upon to join in military operations on the Continent.[123] It was subsequently revealed that Britain had entered agreements with France and Russia.[124] The publication of secret diplomatic files by WikiLeaks in late 2010 revealed that agreements and arrangements continue to be withheld from Parliament.[125]

Governments' approach to the release to Parliament of information about engagements, negotiations, and other relations with foreign countries has been shaped by the culture of secrecy prevalent in the Foreign Office. From its establishment in 1832 the Foreign Office has dealt with requests for information about alliances and negotiations with foreign states. Studies of the Foreign Office have found that, wherever possible, the Foreign Office tried to avoid laying papers, being more concerned about the diplomatic repercussions than for the information of Parliament. The attitude of officials in the Foreign Office to MPs tended to be one of contempt: 'What a nuisance they are with their ill-timed questions! they know nothing about foreign affairs: it is our business not theirs.'[126] The responses of the government minister to questions in Parliament were carefully crafted and scrutinized, and often revealed little. A common response was: 'In the opinion of His Majesty's Government any statement or discussion on the subject at the present moment would be inexpedient.'[127] More recently, a report by the Public Administration Select Committee made very similar

---

[122] HC Deb 1 March 1848, vol 97, cols 66–123.

[123] Government ministers made several statements to the House over the course of 1911–14, denying the existence of any secret agreements or arrangements. See, eg, HC Deb 8 March 1911, vol 32, cols 1120, 1191; HC Deb 30 March 1911, vol 33, col 107.

[124] The government's conduct of 'secret diplomacy' was the subject of much debate in the House of Commons in August 1914. See, eg, Molteno, who described the situation in this way: 'This is a continuation of that old and disastrous system where a few men in charge of the State, wielding the whole force of the State, make secret engagements and secret arrangements, carefully veiled from the knowledge of the people, who are as dumb driven cattle without a voice on the question': HC Deb, vol 65, 3 August 1914, col 1851. See also the speech of Ponsonby, HC Deb 3 August 1914, vol 65, cols 2089–90.

[125] R Evans and D Leigh, 'WikiLeaks cables: secret deal let Americans sidestep cluster bomb ban' *The Guardian* (London 1 December 2010) <http://www.guardian.co.uk/world/2010/dec/01/wikileaks-cables-cluster-bombs-britain>.

[126] Quoted in Steiner (n 75) 197. [127] Quoted in Steiner (n 75) 195.

observations. It noted that 'since the inception of Questions in broadly the current form following the Balfour reforms at the beginning of the last century, the Government's approach to answering Questions has, at times, been characterized as minimizing the opportunity for scrutiny of its actions through careful and skilful crafting of answers'.[128]

A third type of information usually considered, for reasons of secrecy, to be unsuitable for parliamentary discussion has been detailed information about military strategy and technical information about weapons, troop numbers, and equipment.[129] In 1710 the Commons wanted information about the number of English troops in Spain and Portugal at the time of the battle of Almanza. Anne said to Parliament that 'in so great and extensive a War, as this is, many things may be usefully undertaken, which are not fit to be communicated beforehand'.[130] Echoing Anne nearly 300 years later, Tony Blair, in a debate on the deployment of UK forces to Kosovo, spoke on the type and extent of information he thought proper to provide to the House: 'It is not possible for us—nor should it be expected of us—to go into every last detail of military tactics, strategy and capability when we are trying to conduct a campaign.'[131] Mr Robertson (the Secretary of State for Defence) in another debate about Kosovo said 'there are many questions to which enormously detailed answers would be of more advantage to the opponents of the alliance than to the House'.[132] A similar approach had been employed during the Suez crisis, when Prime Minister Eden told MPs that he had been compelled 'to take certain precautionary measures of a military nature', including the movement of 'certain' Royal Navy, army, and RAF units.[133]

Secrecy about these matters has not only been imposed by the government: MPs themselves have often been reluctant to debate matters of technical military and strategic information. Pitt told the Commons in July 1794 that the Commons would 'of course' not want a debate on whether allied

---

[128] See Public Administration Select Committee, *Ministerial Accountability and Parliamentary Questions* (Session 2003–04, HC 355) [2].

[129] The types of questions that Ministers of Defence have refused to answer include 'operational matters', accident rates for aircraft, details of arms trades to foreign countries, costs of individual aircraft and other weapons, information about research and development. See, generally, D Leigh, *The Frontiers of Secrecy: Closed Government in Britain* (Junction Books 1980).

[130] Parliamentary History, 6 November 1707, vol 6, col 595.

[131] HC Deb 13 April 1999, vol 329, col 25.

[132] HC Deb 26 May 1999, vol 332, col 359.

[133] HC Deb 2 August 1956, vol 557, col 1606. The lack of information prompted complaints. In the same debate, at cols 1701–7, Desmond Donnelly said: 'I understand that we are talking about commissioning aircraft carriers and putting troops on them, but how many troops? Where are they to go?...At the very moment when the critical situation exists we have no information of anything of this nature.'

troops had been deployed in the most effective theatres.[134] Parliamentarians' reluctance could be attributed to fears of spreading anxiety about military prospects, concern that military secrets (and weaknesses) might be revealed, their lack of expertise, and an unwillingness to second-guess the decisions of military commanders.[135]

The fourth type of information normally kept secret from Parliament has been intelligence information relevant to the government's decision to go to war. For this reason, governments (and often parliamentarians) have argued that Parliament should defer to executive determinations of the threat posed and the response necessary to meet that threat. In a debate in 1717 concerning a grant of supply to maintain a standing army, one MP said Parliament 'must be compelled at last to put an absolute trust in the government because they only know the truth of such matters, and from them we must be content to receive whatsoever account they think fit to give us of them'.[136] Prior to the allied military attack on the Taliban regime in Afghanistan, Tony Blair told the Commons that he would place information in the House library setting out reasons for the conclusion that Osama Bin Laden and al-Qaeda were in close alliance with the Taliban regime, but noted that 'much of the evidence that we have is intelligence and highly sensitive. It is not possible without compromising people or security to release precise details and fresh information that is daily coming in'.[137]

Although certain types of information or subject-matters have consistently been identified as requiring secrecy and therefore being unsuitable for parliamentary debate, governments have often broken their own rules and released such information to Parliament. Parliamentary access to information has frequently been used as a bargaining tool in return for parliamentary support. Most commonly, governments have employed this strategy to persuade a reluctant Commons to support their action or to respond to heavy criticism. For example, when Anne was in pressing need of support, she would voluntarily lay information which was normally kept secret (such as ongoing peace negotiations) with an urgent request that Parliament give its advice.[138] A similar strategy was used during the Hanoverian period. The Crown voluntarily submitted information about war and foreign policy, including treaties, diplomatic records, and other papers, when it needed financial assistance for its projects.[139] Governments have also released information relevant to the government's case for deployment, including information about alliances,

---

[134] Quoted in Towle (n 97) 51.   [135] Towle (n 97) 119–20.
[136] Parliamentary History, 3 May 1717, vol 7, col 519.
[137] HC Deb 4 October 2001, vol 372, col 672.   [138] Turner (n 10) 187.
[139] Turner (n 10) 188.

engagements, and intelligence in attempts to bolster support.[140] Iraq is a good recent example of this tactic.[141]

There has also been a recent pattern of governments releasing detailed military information. For example, governments have presented to the Commons plans as to the number of troops to be deployed[142] and the types of units. During the Falklands war, the government told Parliament which ships and aircraft were being mobilized to overturn the Argentine seizure of the Falkland Islands.[143] In recent debates on force deployment, ministers have seemed much more willing to announce details in the Commons about the number, type, and names of units to be deployed. In the Iraq war of 1990, Margaret Thatcher informed Parliament that the British force being sent to the Gulf included 'a squadron of Tornado F3 air defence aircraft, a squadron of Tornado ground attack aircraft, and a squadron of Jaguar aircraft for ground support.... One Royal Navy destroyer and two frigates ... A second destroyer is on the way there, as are three mine clearance vessels.'[144] In May 1999, the Secretary for Defence identified in the Commons the military units joining the NATO ground force to Kosovo: he announced that three infantry battalion groups, combat support groups, Commando and amphibious brigades, RAF support helicopters and support units were being put on notice, and lay in the House library a full list of the units involved.[145]

Parliamentarians, too, have sometimes bypassed the generally accepted secrecy of matters of military technical information and strategy, particularly in cases of perceived failures of government policy or strategy in the conduct of war. During World War Two, the Commons pushed the government hard on issues of military strategy and equipment. Sometimes it held

---

[140] See, eg, Parliamentary History 11 November 1718, vol 7, cols 557–60, when the King, in a speech to Parliament, stated that he had received intelligence that Spain was planning to attempt an invasion of England and Scotland, and requested a grant of supply to enable adequate preparations to be made; Parliamentary History, 18 May 1803, vol 36, cols 1259 ff, when the Crown directed the laying of copies of papers before Parliament, including internal dispatches, letters from ambassadors, and information about the terminated negotiations with France, in advance of a debate about whether just cause for war against France had been shown; HC Deb 27 March 1854, vol 132, cols 1352–3, when Lord John Russell explained to the House of Commons the circumstances leading to war with Russia, why war was justified and necessary, and the objects and termination of war.

[141] See the government's 'dossiers': 'Iraq's Weapons of Mass Destruction: The Assessment of the British Government' (24 September 2002); 'Iraq: Its Infrastructure of Concealment, Deception and Intimidation' (3 February 2003) <http://webarchive.nationalarchives.gov.uk/+/http://www.number10.gov.uk/>.

[142] See, eg, Parliamentary History, 18 June 1803, vol 36, cols 1602–3, where the Secretary of War presented to the House of Commons the plans for raising and assembling a force.

[143] HC Deb 3 April 1982, vol 21, col 637.

[144] HC Deb 6 September 1990, vol 177, col 738.

[145] HC Deb 26 May 1999, vol 332, cols 355–6.

sessions in secret,[146] but on other occasions it debated such matters in open sessions. A prominent example was a debate in May 1940, in which the government incurred heavy criticism for its conduct of a military operation in Scandinavia. There was detailed scrutiny and questioning of operational and strategic aspects of the military operation, including choices as to modes of transport of the troops, their equipment and uniforms, the time of day of the movement and operation, tactical decisions, and what the next strategic targets should be. The debate went ahead, despite government ministers saying that 'our military advisers have told us in very solemn terms of the dangers of holding such a discussion.'[147] More recently, in relation to the Iraq and Afghanistan wars, Parliament has pressed government for detailed responses to criticisms about the types and availability of specialist equipment for the armed forces.[148]

Lack of Expertise and Information
It has sometimes been asserted that the Commons should not seek to impose its advice or scrutiny on the government because the Commons lacked the necessary expertise and information to do so. One MP thought it would be an 'endless thing', resulting in a 'labyrinth indeed' if MPs sought to involve themselves in matters of state which they knew little about. For that reason, the Commons should put an 'absolute trust in the government because they only know the truth of such matters'.[149] Another thought the House of Commons should refrain from exercising its right to advise the Crown 'except in cases where we have a full information, and are perfectly masters of the affair'.[150] Lord Strange, speaking in the mid-eighteenth century, agreed that it would be improper for Parliament to seek to prescribe binding advice about future treaties and negotiations, on the grounds that 'not only would [it] be unconstitutional', but that it would mean Parliament would be giving its approval without knowing the full information and circumstances—it would be 'a sort of fore-stalling the approbation of parliament, before all the circumstances could be fully known'.[151]

For similar reasons, MPs have often been reluctant to debate matters of military strategy. In November 1915 there were extensive debates in the

---

[146] Finer (n 84) 352. [147] HC Deb 6 May 1940, vol 360, col 1083.
[148] See, eg, the questions asked of government ministers regarding the impact that the alleged lack of helicopters has had on operational effectiveness and success in Afghanistan: HC Deb 13 July 2009, vol 496, cols 1–6, 8–9. See further examples of scrutiny of the conduct of war in citations at nn 76–88.
[149] Parliamentary History, 3 May 1717, vol 7, col 519.
[150] Solicitor General Murray, in the debate in the Commons on continuing the Hanoverian troops in British pay: Parliamentary History, 6 December 1743, vol 13, col 252.
[151] Parliamentary History, 16 November 1749, vol 13, cols 598–9.

Commons after disasters suffered by British forces in the Balkans and the Dardanelles, but comments by MPs indicated their reluctance and sense of incapacity to talk about military problems. George Barns, for example, admitted 'with respect to the conduct of war, I shall say little... I am not a soldier'.[152] Another said 'if private Members begin to discuss questions of high policy, it seems to me that it is extremely dangerous, and that no good can result'.[153] MPs who were former military men often felt more able and justified to speak on matters of military strategy. One asserted that 'nobody who has not fought in a war has much right to talk about what might happen if a war takes place'.[154]

Rallying around the Throne
There has been a general understanding that, once the armed forces have been deployed and the troops are 'in the field', MPs should express their support for the war effort and, in some cases, should refrain from criticizing the government's decision to go to war or their conduct of war. This understanding has been motivated by various factors: patriotism (whether genuine or assumed for appearance's sake), not wanting to undermine the morale of the troops and the nation, and a sense that it would be improper to criticize the government's conduct of war while the war was being waged and people were dying. For these reasons MPs have often spoken of the need to express support for the government during times of crisis and war and to modify the extent of their criticisms.

Various examples can be cited. In 1755, in a debate as to whether England had offended the laws of nations by taking part in naval actions before the declaration of war, one speaker acknowledged the undoubted right of the Commons to 'enquire into, in order to punish or censure the ministers if they have given the King bad advice'. However, those questions should not be enquired into while war was ongoing: 'in my opinion it would be imprudent, as well as improper for us, to enter upon any such enquiry, until peace has been some way or other restored.'[155] Similar sentiment was expressed by Disraeli in 1854. He asserted that, if the Crown informs Parliament that it is necessary to engage in war, then 'it is not an occasion when we are to enter into the policy of impolicy of the advice by which Her Majesty has been guided. It is our duty... to rally around the Throne'.[156] In 1857, one MP recognized 'the wisdom of the policy which proposes to strengthen the hands of the Executive Government whenever a great danger threatens them'.

---

[152] HC Deb 2 November 1915, vol 20, col 551.
[153] HC Deb 2 November 1915, vol 20, cols 571–81. For similar sentiments in WWII, see HC Deb 23 February 1944, vol 397, cols 863, 871, 883, 886.
[154] HC Deb 6 September 1990, vol 177, cols 756 and 762.
[155] Parliamentary History, 2 December 1755, vol 15, col 557.
[156] HC Deb 31 March 1854, vol 132, col 281.

In such circumstances, it was the duty of the House 'not unnecessarily to press upon them'.[157] One MP in a debate during the Boer war invoked the political system of Rome, which deliberately abandoned constitutional government in crisis or war and appointed a dictator who could act with vigour and certainty. He called on the Commons to 'do for the Government just the same as they had to do—namely, we must render the Executive influential, powerful, and capable of rapid and certain action'.[158]

The 'rally around the throne' phenomenon has been generally accepted by participants as necessary for the morale of the armed forces and the nation. Even where England's entry into armed conflict has been controversial, nearly all MPs in parliamentary debate have considered it proper to express support for the war effort. For example, Britain's entry into World War One was the subject of heated debate, but there was a generally shared sentiment, expressed in the speeches on the vote of credit, that it was the duty of the Commons to support the war effort and personal objections should be put aside (at least while the war was being waged). This was not the time for argument, but for unity of purpose.[159] MPs who spoke out against British entry into the war were denounced as 'pacifists' and vilified as traitors.[160] A similar 'rally around the throne' effect was seen in respect of military deployment to Kosovo. Despite serious reservations held by members of both sides of the House, the general sentiment was that the Commons should express its support for the action and for the armed forces.[161] In debate on the controversial military invasion of Iraq in 2003, a number of MPs emphasized the importance of proclaiming support for the armed forces: one considered it vital that the armed forces, who were risking their lives in the national interest, knew that the nation was behind them,[162] while another identified the need to support the armed forces as a clear duty on the House and individual MPs.[163]

Despite the general recognition of the need to express support for the war effort and the armed forces, there are also many examples where MPs have declared themselves unwilling to abdicate their constitutional role as scrutinizer of the executive.[164] In a debate on the Boer war in 1899, one MP spoke of the Commons' predicament:[165]

---

[157] HC Deb 17 July 1857, vol 144, col 1617. [158] HC Deb 5 Feb 1900, vol 78, cols 627–8.
[159] HC Deb 5 August 1914, vol 65, cols 1963–2093.
[160] S Harris, *Out of Control: British Foreign Policy and the Union of Democratic Control, 1914–1918* (University of Hull Press 1996) 41.
[161] HC Deb 24 March 1999, vol 328, col 489.
[162] HC Deb 18 March 2003, vol 401, col 874.
[163] HC Deb 18 March 2003, vol 401, col 901.
[164] See the citations at nn 76–88 for examples of the scrutiny exerted by the House of Commons of governments' conduct of war.
[165] HC Deb 18 October 1899, vol 77, cols 210–11.

It is right that it should be known throughout the country that the conduct of an Opposition in criticising and, if necessary, condemning the policy of a Government which resulted in war is not unpatriotic... Supporting the Government in the carrying out of a war to which the country is committed, an Opposition should not abnegate its duty and its functions of inquiring into the circumstances which have led to war.

The way most MPs got around this bind was to state their support for the war effort and the armed forces, and then launch into their critique. On the outbreak of World War Two, the leader of the opposition asserted the vital scrutinizing task of the Commons. After pledging his party's support for the war effort, he declared: 'But should there be confused councils, inefficiency and wavering, then other men must be called to take their places. We share no responsibilities in the tremendous tasks which confront the government, but we have responsibilities of our own which we shall not shirk.'[166] The opposition employed a similar tactic in respect of the Suez crisis in 1956. The leader of the opposition recognized that in certain moments, particularly in international affairs, it is proper for the opposition to exercise restraint on criticism and debate, '[b]ut restraint of this kind must never be carried so far as to involve the suppression of differences of vital importance. On such occasions it is the duty, not only the right, of the Opposition to speak out loudly and clearly.'[167]

Bipartisan Foreign Policy
Towards the end of the twentieth century, there was an increasing trend towards a bipartisan foreign policy, also known as the 'continuity of foreign policy'. This significantly affected the frequency, intensity, and content of the Commons' debate and scrutiny of the government's conduct of foreign policy. The trend towards bipartisan foreign policy meant parties tended to exclude matters of national security, defence, and foreign affairs from the arena of active debate and the opposition did not closely scrutinize or criticize the government's foreign policies during debate in the House. On issues of foreign policy, the opposition would often refrain from criticism, and extend forbearance and sometimes assistance 'in maintaining the honour of the crown and the just influence of the British government in foreign affairs'.[168] Writing in 1912, one commentator said that the principle of continuity in

---
[166] HC Deb 3 September 1939, vol 351, col 293.
[167] HC Deb 12 September 1956, vol 558, col 16.
[168] A Todd, *On Parliamentary Government in England: Its Origin, Development and Practical Operation* (1887–89) in Hanham (n 70). See also LS Steiner, 'The Foreign Office before 1914: A Study in Resistance' in G Sutherland (ed), *Studies in the Growth of Nineteenth Century Government* (Routledge and Kegan Paul 1972) 161, 167; HN Brailsford, 'The Control of Foreign Affairs: A Proposal' (1909) 4/13 *English Review* 122. For commentary on the continued application

foreign affairs had been carried beyond its proper limits, with the effect that the Foreign Secretary became virtually immune from criticism.[169]

Foreign policy is no longer regarded as bipartisan in the same sense as in the nineteenth century. However, certain actions of government, particularly decisions about war and the interests of national security, are commonly identified as 'beyond party politics'. This sentiment was evident in a debate about the proposed Iraq invasion in 2003. The leader of the opposition stated that where the government acts in the national interest, the opposition should support the government;[170] and another MP said that the decision to commit troops should transcend party politics because the issue was of such importance.[171]

The Increasing Power of the Government over the Commons

In the eighteenth and nineteenth centuries, parliamentary debates regularly took place on issues of foreign policy.[172] By the end of the nineteenth century, however, the prominence and frequency of such debates had markedly declined. Changes in the nature of debate in the Commons, and in the power of the government over the Commons, impacted on the effectiveness and function of parliamentary debate about foreign policy and other governmental business. Many participants observed a shift in the balance of power between the government and the Commons. Parties obtained such a large majority in elections that the party in government had a huge majority in the Commons,[173] and the use of party whips to effect party discipline reinforced the government's effective powers. Although there were frequent parliamentary debates on foreign policy issues, MPs were largely restricted to noisy criticism and censure, and there were few instances of real interference.[174] Adams, a constitutional historian, called such debates 'tactical scrimmages' as the result of the vote was a foregone conclusion, secured by the huge majority.[175] In 1894, Lord Salisbury said 'There is an enormous change in the House of Commons as I recollect it...and we have reached this point—that discussion of a measure is possible in Cabinet,

---

of bipartisan foreign policy in the twentieth century, see D Vital, *The Making of British Foreign Policy* (George Allen and Unwin 1968) 74–6.

[169] S Low, 'The Foreign Office Autocracy' (1912) 91 Fortnightly Review 1, 5.
[170] HC Deb 18 March 2003, vol 401, col 779.
[171] HC Deb 18 March 2003, vol 401, cols 816–17.   [172] Gibbs (n 73) 26.
[173] P Dunleavy and GW Jones, 'Leaders, Politics and Institutional Change: The Decline of Prime Ministerial Accountability to the House of Commons, 1868–1990' (1993) 23 British Journal of Political Science 267. For details of the changes made to the procedures of the House of Commons during the nineteenth century, see P Fraser, 'The Growth of Ministerial Control in the Nineteenth Century House of Commons' (1960) 75 The English Historical Review 444.
[174] Steiner (n 168) 169.   [175] Adams (n 101) 469.

but for any effective or useful purpose, it is rapidly becoming an impossibility in the House of Commons'.[176] In 1911, one MP lamented 'Honourable Members know the conditions under which business is carried on in the house. It is only a form and a name to say that they are left to the house of commons. They are not left to the house at all; they are left to the cabinet'.[177]

Similar concerns continue to be raised. The claimed diminishment of the influence and power of the Commons relative to the government is well documented, in academic research,[178] reports of parliamentary select committees,[179] and government reports.[180]

The Power of Supply

1 Introduction

During the seventeenth and eighteenth centuries, the House of Commons' power of supply enabled the Commons to exert real power and influence over the exercise of the war prerogative. It was also a key mechanism by which the executive and the Commons interacted on issues of war and foreign policy. War forced the Crown to rely on extraordinary supply, granted by the Commons, to fund military requirements. It was standard practice for the Crown, when seeking a grant, to put to the Commons its reasons for going to war and supporting information. In exercising its power of supply the Commons could communicate its opinions on the Crown's policies by granting the whole or part of the supply requested, refusing to grant supply, imposing conditions on its use, or scrutinizing or auditing how the supply

---

[176] Quoted in Adams (n 101) 471–2. [177] Quoted in Adams (n 101) 472.

[178] See, eg, M Russell and A Paun, 'The House Rules? International Lessons for Enhancing the Autonomy of the House of Commons' (The Constitution Unit, UCL 2007), and references listed at 84–9 therein. See also the summary of recent reform proposals in A Tomkins, 'What is Parliament For?' in N Bamforth and P Leyland (eds), *Public Law in a Multi-Layered Constitution* (Hart Publishing 2003) 53.

[179] See, eg, the Reform of the House of Commons Select Committee, *First Report: Rebuilding the House* (HC 2008–09, 1117) ('the Wright Report'), which recommended reforms to procedure in the House of Commons with the objective of increasing its relative power and influence. For reports addressed specifically at the House of Commons' role in foreign policy and war, see House of Lords Select Committee on the Constitution, *Waging War: Parliament's Role and Responsibility. Volume I: Report* (HL 2005–06, 236-I); Public Administration Select Committee, *Taming the Prerogative: Strengthening Ministerial Accountability to Parliament* (HC 2003–04, 422); Joint Committee on the Draft Constitutional Renewal Bill, *Draft Constitutional Renewal Bill* (2007–08, HL 116-I, HC, 551-I); Political and Constitutional Reform Committee, *8th Report—Parliament's Role in Conflict Decisions* (HC 2010–12, 923).

[180] Ministry of Justice, *The Governance of Britain* (Green Paper) (Cm 7170, 2007) 48–56; Ministry of Justice, *War Powers and Treaties: Limiting Executive Powers* (Cm 7239, 2007); Ministry of Justice, *'The Governance of Britain—Constitutional Renewal* (White Paper) (Cm 7342-I, 2008); Ministry of Justice, 'The Governance of Britain. Review of the Executive Royal Prerogative Powers: Final Report' (October 2009).

was spent. During the nineteenth century the ability of the Commons to exert real influence through its power of supply began to wane. Governments with strong majorities were able to obtain majority votes in support of grants of supply without much of the haggling and compromise that were a feature of the seventeenth century. In addition, the rapidly expanding scope of governmental action meant that governments needed supply for a much larger range of purposes and it was no longer practicable for the Commons to exert detailed scrutiny on government spending. The Commons' role in supply evolved to be focused on ensuring effective accountability for government expenditure and scrutinizing the policy choices behind expenditure.

2 The Power of Supply in the 1620s

At the start of the seventeenth century, the Commons accepted constitutional duty was to aid the Crown in wartime with grants of extraordinary supply.[181] It was assumed that the Commons would grant supply, without placing conditions on its use or condemning the purpose for which it was sought.[182] The Commons in the 1620s mostly followed accepted practice, acknowledging that the king should govern and that the Commons should provide him with the money he needed to govern properly. However, on several occasions in the 1620s, the Commons challenged or ignored accepted practice and used its power of the purse to communicate its mistrust of the government's objectives and to influence the king's foreign policy decisions. For example, in 1621 the king requested an immediate grant of £500,000 for the armed forces, but the Commons responded with two subsidies amounting to about £160,000. In the same year, the Commons sent up a petition which implied they would withhold supply until their advice as to foreign policy was accepted.[183]

Several factors probably explain why the Commons employed its power of the purse to attempt to influence the Stuart Kings' foreign policy. The first is the strong ideological and religious differences between the Stuart Kings and the Commons. The majority of MPs supported a pro-protestant, anti-Spain foreign policy, while James and Charles supported alliance with Spain.[184] Another explanation is that the Commons was motivated by discontent with issues relating to domestic affairs.[185] A third possible explanation is that the Commons' ability or willingness to respond to the Crown's demands for military financing was constrained by the need to maintain the support of their

---

[181] D Thomas, 'Financial and Administrative Developments' in Tomlinson (n 29) 103, 115
[182] Keir (n 25) 185.   [183] Tanner (n 37) 276–9.
[184] Mosse (n 48) 116; Kenyon (n 2) 2; S Adams, 'Spain or the Netherlands? The Dilemmas of Early Stuart Foreign Policy' in Tomlinson (n 29) 79, 93.
[185] Keir (n 25) 186.

constituents.[186] The war effort made it increasingly hard for MPs to maintain their dual allegiance to the Crown and to their local communities.[187] Fourthly, on occasion the Crown itself gave the Commons increased control over the use of money allocated for military purposes. In 1621, James authorized the House to appoint a committee to 'see the issuing out of money they give for the recovery of the Palatinate', which gave the House a measure of actual control over the prosecution of the war.[188] Fifthly, the Commons feared that the king would use the supply for improper purposes, such as to fund an army against Parliament.

3 Non-Parliamentary Sources of Revenue

The power of supply could be a potent tool for exerting influence on the foreign policy of the Crown, but that power was negated if the king could bypass the Commons and seek a non-parliamentary source of revenue. This is what happened during the Stuart Kings' reigns, when increasing costs of warfare and the poverty of the Stuart Kings prompted the Crown to exploit other sources of revenue. The sources of the Crown's ordinary revenue (such as Crown lands and customs receipts) were inadequate to support major military operations and, in the absence of extraordinary parliamentary supply, prerogative taxation was the main source of funding. Following the outbreak of war in 1625 and the dissolutions of Parliaments of 1625 and 1626, the emergency powers of the prerogative were employed to justify a number of devices, including the forced loan of 1626, the use of martial law to discipline unpaid soldiers and sailors, and the proposed ship money levy and excise of 1628.[189] These sources of extra-parliamentary revenue enabled Charles to rule without Parliament for ten years.

After the Restoration, the monarch's means of raising revenue were more restricted than they had been before 1641. Legislation in 1641[190] had declared illegal many of Charles I's unpopular fiscal devices, which meant that Charles II was unable to rely on the sources of non-parliamentary revenue that the earlier Stuart Kings had.[191] His dire financial situation was exacerbated by the 1660 and 1661 Parliaments voting to supply an ordinary revenue insufficient to cover the normal costs of administration.[192] Charles' poverty had

---

[186] Thomas (n 181) 117.
[187] C Russell, *Parliaments and English Politics 1621–1629* (Clarendon Press 1979).
[188] SR Gardiner, *History of England under Buckingham and Charles I* vol I (Longmans, Green and Co 1875) 33. See also Russell (n 35); Zaller (n 36) 152; Mosse (n 48) 118.
[189] See citations at nn 49–53, ch 4, for an examination of the courts' consideration of extra-parliamentary revenue.
[190] 16 Car I c 8; 16 Car I c 14.   [191] For more on this issue, see Hart (n 1) 182–8.
[192] Miller (n 57) 30.

fundamental repercussions for his foreign policy. Lacking an adequate army, Charles felt the need for a powerful ally who could support him if his subjects rebelled. He found it in France, with the secret treaty of Dover including a promise that Louis XIV would come to Charles's aid if need arose.[193] Charles II ruled without Parliament in the last four years of his reign, supplementing the ordinary revenue granted by Parliament with French grants.[194] The Commons' use of its power of supply backfired in this situation.

Recourse to non-parliamentary sources of revenue was finally outlawed by the Bill of Rights 1688: Article 4 declares illegal the levying of money for the Crown without grant of Parliament. The executive was rendered dependent upon the Commons for grants of supply, which meant that Parliament was called far more frequently. Since 1688, there has never been a year without a meeting of Parliament.[195]

4 The Power of Supply and Parliamentary Government

In the early years of parliamentary government, the House of Commons' power of supply could still be used as a potent tool to influence decisions about war and foreign policy. Governments knew that war could not be carried on without a grant of supply. Ministers were forced to explain and defend their requests for supply and to offer concessions in return for its grant, while MPs debated and scrutinized carefully the government's requests.[196] MPs would often demand that the government lay relevant information before the Commons before they would agree to support the government's request for money. For example, in 1718, the Commons debated a request for a grant of supply to establish alliances to protect against the threats posed by Sweden. Several members objected, arguing that the threat from Sweden was 'unconsiderable' and such alliances unnecessary. Others thought it 'unparliamentary' to grant supply before detailed information about the engagements and the money required was laid before them.[197] On other occasions, MPs complained they were being asked to vote in favour of supply without being given information about foreign engagements or the government's plans for war or other foreign policies: 'Are we to vote powerful fleets, and numerous armies; are we to lay new and great burthens on the people, and all this without being told any reasons for what we are desired to do?';[198] 'If his Majesty expects the assistance of parliament in the present exigency of affairs, we must be informed how our affairs stand.'[199] MPs also complained about the

---

[193] Miller (n 57) 34–5.   [194] Miller (n 57) 34–5.
[195] Carter (n 69) 44.   [196] Gibbs (n 73) 22–27; Turner (n 10) 191–5.
[197] Parliamentary History, 3 April 1718, vol 7, cols 435, 436, 437.
[198] Parliamentary History, 6 February 1734, vol 9, col 273.
[199] Parliamentary History, 6 February 1734, vol 9, col 226.

granting of significant lump sums for imprecise activities labelled 'extraordinary expenses' and 'secret service'.[200]

As governments grew stronger and their majorities in the Commons larger, votes for grants of supply became increasingly routine. There were still debates on the annual estimates for the army and navy and on votes of supply for war. The House, constituted as the committee for supply, examined the extremely detailed estimates (they itemized, for example, the amount allocated to billiard tables for the military and snuff boxes for foreign ministers), and they were the subject of long debate. However, this detailed consideration of the estimates did not translate into extra control over government spending. By the 1870s it was unusual for even small items of expense to be overturned.[201] Governments were confident they would be able to secure the necessary majority vote at the conclusion of the debates. In 1857, the notion of the Commons being the guardian of the public purse was described by one MP as 'all moonshine'.[202]

The changed nature and scope of the power of supply was the subject of debate in the Commons in July 1857. The issue arose during a debate about whether the government had acted improperly in spending public money to wage war in Persia without Parliament's consent or cognizance. The government had subsequently asked for a grant of supply to cover, retrospectively, the costs of waging war. One MP said 'where large sums of money were to be expended, the representatives of the people should be summoned and consulted on the subject.'[203] Mr Gladstone claimed the vital importance of the Commons' 'control over the Government through the medium of finances.' Without this 'great security', he said, the making of war was at the uncontrolled discretion of ministers and free of the prior and independent judgement of the Commons.[204]

The Commons' capacity to exert influence and control via its power of supply was not only limited in situations where the government did not seek supply in advance of going to war. Its capacity was also limited in the normal situation, in which the government informed the Commons that preparations for war were being taken, or that war had already been declared, and moved for a vote of credit or grant of supply. With their large majorities and strict party discipline, governments could be sure they would win those votes. For example in 1899 the government sought a vote for £10,000,000 to enable

---

[200] eg, Parliamentary History, 13 February 1726, vol 8, cols 549–50.
[201] P Fraser, 'The Growth of Ministerial Control in the Nineteenth Century House of Commons' (1960) 75 The English Historical Review 444, 460.
[202] HC Deb 16 July 1857, vol 146, cols 1577–652.
[203] HC Deb 16 July 1857, vol 146, cols 1608–9.
[204] HC Deb 16 July 1857, vol 146, col 1637.

deployment to South Africa. Despite the long debate in the Commons and MPs' criticism, the vote was 194 in favour, and 42 against.[205] Fifteen years later, as Britain entered World War One, the debate on the 'vote of credit' turned into a debate about the government's decision to enter the war. One MP objected to the voting of such a large sum on the grounds that it divorced Parliament from the control of the war and enabled the government to carry on for at least six months without coming to Parliament for more money: 'I say that a blank cheque for £100,000,000 with no control over the executive, is as undesirable in war as in peace.'[206] Mr Wedgwood was one of the only MPs, however, to raise concern about the grant of supply. Speaking early in the twentieth century, one MP described what he saw as the real nature of the Commons' power of supply: 'I have never believed that discussion in this House on questions of supply really gives us control over the details of expenditure. In prehistoric times there might have been some control over the details of expenditure but there certainly has not been in my parliamentary experience.'[207]

Over the past century, the procedures for scrutinizing and authorizing the government's expenditure proposals have been increasingly stripped to the bare essentials.[208] The Commons has largely abandoned all opportunities for direct control of public expenditure by means of debate and vote on the estimates presented to the House.[209] The annual spending round has been replaced by major three-year plans. Estimates for the maximum number of service personnel to be retained in the navy, army, and air force are presented just before the start of the financial year to which they relate, and are put without debate. The research, development, and procurement of new weapons or equipment and the recruitment, pay, and accommodation of the armed forces involves authorization of expenditure, but such authorization is treated with a broad brush.[210] For example, for several years, no mention was made in Parliament of the decision to develop an atomic bomb—the necessary

---

[205] HC Deb 20 October 1899, vol 77, cols 405–84.
[206] HC Deb 5 August 1914, vol 65, cols 2092–3.
[207] HC Deb 30 July 1908, vol 193, col 1784.
[208] A Robinson, *Parliament and Public Spending: The Expenditure Committee of the House of Commons, 1970–76* (Heinemann 1978); Blackburn and Kennon (n 71) [6-176]. See also House of Commons Select Committee on Procedure, *Scrutiny of Public Expenditure and Administration* (HC 1968–69, 410); discussed in E McGovern, 'The Report of the House of Commons Select Committee on Procedure: Scrutiny of Public Expenditure and Administration' (1970) 33 Modern Law Review 190.
[209] Compare this with the practice in the United States, where Congress uses its power of the purse and restrictive appropriations as a tool to participate in national security decision-making. For a good overview of the position in the US, see P Raven-Hansen and WC Banks, 'Pulling the Purse Strings of the Commander in Chief' (1994) 80 Virginia Law Review 833.
[210] See further Blackburn and Kennon (n 71) [6-176]–[6-188].

expenditure was buried under the broad headings of weapons research and development.

The funding of wars also passes the Commons with a minimum of consideration. Supply for these purposes may be obtained from within the ordinary defence appropriation or from the contingency fund in an emergency. Otherwise, it is an item in the Budget, sometimes subject to special funding arrangements.

5 Appropriation and Audit

Appropriation was first used by the Commons towards the end of James I's reign. During Charles II's reign, the Commons increasingly imposed conditions and audited the government's use of supply. The use of appropriation and audit did not follow a linear pattern, but varied between and within reigns, depending on factors such as whether politicians were suspicious or fearful of the Crown, how much money was available, and whether the Commons was successful in obtaining the Crown's compliance with appropriation or audit conditions. When successfully employed, appropriation and audit were potent tools. They enabled the Commons to exert real influence on the formulation of policy by restricting the uses to which supply could be applied, or by imposing conditions on its use. The very act of appropriating specific sums to a particular need of government involved a decision upon the question of which need was more pressing or which objective preferable, and enabled control over the conduct of government.[211]

The Commons of the early Stuart Kings used the tools of appropriation and audit of supply to try to pressure James I and Charles I into abandoning their pro-Spanish foreign policies. In 1624 the Commons granted supply with the condition it be used to fit out the fleet and defend the English coast, Ireland, and the United Provinces: preparations for the defensive war it wanted.[212] Its aim was to pressure James to break off negotiations with Spain. On that occasion, the Commons' attempts to impose conditions on the use of the grant were unsuccessful as James spent the money for his own project. Despite attempts to scrutinize the Crown's use of the subsidy (including scrutiny of the accounts of the Council and Treasury and summoning the Council of War to explain its use of the funds), the Commons was unable to bring the Crown to account for the misuse.[213] Similar conditions were placed

---

[211] Maitland (n 26) 385.

[212] ME Kennedy 'Legislation, Foreign Policy, and the "Proper Business" of the Parliament of 1624' (1991) 23 Albion: A Quarterly Journal Concerned with British Studies 41, 55.

[213] P Seaward, 'The Cavalier Parliament, the 1667 Accounts Commission and the Idea of Accountability' in Kyle and Peacey (n 6) 149, 150.

on supply of subsidies in 1640 and 1641, with Parliament demanding direct involvement in the administration and oversight of the money it had voted.

The Restoration Parliaments continued the practices of appropriation and audit. For example, the supply legislation of 1666 directed that £380,000 of the money voted be applied to the payment of seamen's wages.[214] They also took up the practice from the revolutionary period of parliamentary committees, divided along departmental lines, conducting inquiries into the conduct and administration of wars.[215] Concerned about the honesty of the Crown's claims about revenue, and the heavy expenditure associated with the Dutch war, the Commons also sought to scrutinize the accounts of the money given for the war. In the supply legislation of 1665, the Commons ordered a register to be kept in the Exchequer of the receipts from the taxes voted and the nature of the disbursements.[216] In 1667 the Commons established (eventually with the king's consent) a commission for the taking of public accounts, after the Crown used taxes appropriated by statute to militia use for purposes not related to the militia.[217] The commission was established to ensure that the money raised for war was used for the purposes for which it was raised, and with 'such care, fidelity and good husbandry' as expected.[218] The commission had the power to subpoena officials of the army, navy, and ordnance, and any others employed in the management of the war, to conduct examinations under oath, and to access financial records. The Commons' intent to enforce appropriation clauses was made clear when it impeached Danby (a key royal official) on a charge that he breached an appropriation clause.[219] The commission was appointed for only three years, but it was an important precedent taken up again after the Revolution.[220]

By 1678, the practice of appropriation was used more frequently. When the Commons was asked to vote money for the disbandment of the army the king had raised for the Flanders campaign, it took stringent precautions to ensure that it was used for that purpose and no other. It even wrote into the Act the date of demobilization.[221]

After the Revolution, systems of appropriation and audit were revived as part of the new system of financial management. The Commons granted supplies more readily to William III, but insisted that the Crown present estimations and planned expenditures and carefully scrutinized the spending of the unprecedented sums voted for the Nine Years' war with France. In 1690, the

---

[214] 18 & 19 Car II c 13.
[215] B Chubb, *The Control of Public Expenditure: Financial Committees of the House of Commons* (Clarendon Press 1952) 14–15.
[216] 17 Car II c I.   [217] Western (n 20) 47; Seaward (n 213) 149.
[218] 19 & 20 Car II c I.   [219] Maitland (n 26) 310.
[220] Kenyon (n 2) 389.   [221] 30 Car II c I.

creation of a Commission of Public Accounts enabled more detailed scrutiny of estimates and expenditures, although the commission was short-lived.[222] Various other parliamentary committees were established on an ad hoc basis throughout the eighteenth century in response to particular events or concerns, but they tended to be hindered by a lack of information and expertise, and their impact was limited.

The Commons' tactics in the seventeenth and eighteenth centuries represented a slow but spasmodic drift towards the assumption that Parliament should play a role in ensuring the effective accountability for government expenditure.[223] The development of parliamentary government negated the ability of the Commons to decide how to spend money. Decisions on the use of public money are decisions of policy, and they came to be initiated and controlled by responsible ministers. By the end of Anne's reign, the direction of the government over matters of finance had been accepted. Standing Order No 66 (adopted in 1713) provided that no money could be voted for any purpose except on the motion of a minister of the Crown.

The economical movement of the 1780s reinforced the increased focus on audit and accounting, directing greater attention towards government spending and the reorganization of the civil administration. An aspect of these reforms was requiring the defence departments to provide a more detailed classification of expenditure and estimates. From 1688, supply for the defence services was voted annually on the presentation of estimates to the Commons. However, the estimates were not detailed, and were not published until 1800.[224] In addition to the requirement for more detailed estimates, Parliament established special commissions and committees of account to examine and audit accounts, and, in 1785, established a statutory Audit Board.[225] Parliamentary committees were very industrious during this time also. The 1797 Finance Committee, for example, issued thirty-six reports identifying administrative and financial deficiencies of the French wars, and the Select Committee on Public Expenditure of 1807–12 issued thirteen follow-up reports.[226]

The same pattern continued during the twentieth century, with the Commons delegating detailed audit and scrutiny tasks to committees and departments. MPs became less interested in the minutiae of government finance as government spending mushroomed and the estimates became

---

[222] Black (n 98) 16.   [223] Seaward (n 213) 149.
[224] Chubb (n 215) 6, 10–11, 14–15.   [225] Chubb (n 215) 18–19.
[226] P Harling and P Mandler, 'From "Fiscal-Military" State to Lassez-Faire State, 1760–1850' (1993) 32 Journal of British Studies 44, 55; see also V Cromwell, 'The Losing of Initiative by the House of Commons, 1780–1914' (1968) 18 Transactions of the Royal History Society 1, 20.

increasingly complex. Debates in the committee of supply centred on general policy rather than financial details.[227]

Various parliamentary committees conducted (and continue to conduct) in-depth examinations into the administration and conduct of war. They have revealed some major flaws. For example, the Public Accounts Committee's inquiry into the South African war revealed incompetence and foolish extravagance in its administration and various deficiencies in defence departments' systems, such as poor stock-taking, chaotic accounting, expensive delays, and wasteful shipping.[228] The Public Accounts Committee continues to investigate and report on various aspects of policy, administration, and expenditure connected with war; for example, it has recently issued reports on support to high intensity operations,[229] the failures of the government's provision of Type 45 destroyers,[230] the UK's future nuclear deterrent capability,[231] the Chinook Mk 3,[232] and treating injury and illness arising on military operations.[233]

Retrospective Scrutiny

1 Introduction

From at least the beginning of the seventeenth century, Parliament has claimed powers of retrospective scrutiny over the government's conduct of war and foreign policy. During the age of monarchical government the Commons focused its attentions on the monarch's officials and advisers, and sought to censure and punish those it judged to have made poor decisions contrary to the interests of the kingdom.[234] Impeachments, committees of inquiry, and requests for information were all employed to exert retrospective scrutiny. With the development of parliamentary government the Commons' scrutinizing focus turned to using parliamentary debate and other procedural mechanisms to question and criticize governments' conduct. During the eighteenth and nineteenth centuries, votes of no confidence and censure were a very real check on governmental conduct, and several ministries fell on issues of war and foreign policy. By the start of the twentieth century,

---

[227] Cromwell (n 226) 21.
[228] Chubb (n 215) 72–3.
[229] Public Accounts Committee, *Ministry of Defence: Support to High Intensity Operations* (HC 2008–09, 895).
[230] Public Accounts Committee, *Ministry of Defence: Type 45 Destroyer* (HC 2008–09, 372).
[231] Public Accounts Committee, *The UK's Future Nuclear Deterrent Capability* (HC 2008–09, 250).
[232] Public Accounts Committee, *Ministry of Defence: Chinook Mk 3* (HC 2008–09, 247).
[233] Public Accounts Committee, *Ministry of Defence: Treating Injury and Illness Arising on Military Operations* (HC 2009–10, 427).
[234] Turner (n 10) 186.

however, strong governments have been able to control and marginalize the Commons' attempts to exert scrutiny.

2 Impeachment

In the seventeenth century impeachment was regarded as the ultimate safeguard of public liberty. The Commons in 1626 declared its 'antient, constant, and undoubted right and usage of parliaments' to question officials accused of abusing their powers, whatever their position.[235] Blackstone recognized impeachment as the only constitutional check on the exclusive prerogatives of the Crown to enter war and to make treaties. Parliaments, he said, could impeach ministers who had advised policies subsequently held by Parliament to derogate from the honour and interest of the nation or 'for improper or inglorious conduct, in beginning, conducting, or concluding a national war'.[236] Despite its theoretical importance, however, the number of successful impeachments has been relatively small, as evidenced by statistics: in the whole of English history there have been only seventy impeachments and a quarter of those were in 1640–42, in the pre-Civil war period.[237]

In the seventeenth century, Parliaments used impeachments (or attempted impeachments) of royal officials to express disapproval of the Crown's foreign policies. Impeachment was usually motivated by dissatisfaction with the content or outcome of a particular war or foreign policy, but the articles of impeachment were normally framed as criticizing the procedure by which the foreign policy was made. The two key parliamentary gripes were failing to communicate treaties to Parliament and waging war without consulting Parliament. In the 1670s the Commons conducted in-depth examinations of Charles II's foreign policies, motivated by (accurate) suspicions that key treaties contained secret clauses and by disappointment with the results of war. The Commons targeted the second Duke of Buckingham, one of Charles' top advisers, and cross-examined him on the circumstances leading to the war and the making of particular treaties. The Commons asked Buckingham: 'By whose Counsel and Ministry the Triple League was made. And the Second Treaty with the French King at Utrecht, and the Articles thereof. And by whose Counsels the War was made, without Advice of Parliament; and the Parliament thereupon prorogued.'[238] In 1685, the Earl of Danby, another royal official, was impeached on the charge that he 'traitorously encroached to himself the regal power by treating in matters of peace and war with foreign

---

[235] Parliamentary History, 5 April 1626, vol 2, cols 69–70.
[236] Sir William Blackstone, *Commentaries on the Laws of England, in Four Books* vol 1, 13th edn (E Christian ed, Strahan 1800) 256–8.
[237] Maitland (n 26) 317.
[238] Parliamentary History, 14 January 1674, vol 4, cols 644–5.

ministers and ambassadors, and giving instructions to His Majesty's ambassadors abroad without communicating the same to the Secretaries of State and the rest of His Majesty's Council'.[239]

Impeachments were also attempted during William's reign. They were motivated by parliamentarians' anger with William's informal and secret conduct of foreign relations. When war threatened in 1700, the parliamentary majority resolved not to be dragged into war and investigated and attacked the procedure by which the Partition Treaties had been made and the policy they embodied. Attempts were made to impeach key governmental officials when it was admitted that the first treaty had been concluded on oral instructions from the king and without consultation with other members of the Privy Council.[240] Another impeachment was sought on similar grounds in 1715 in the wake of an unpopular treaty and unsuccessful war. The Whigs in the Commons declared that they would inquire into the miscarriage and unsuitable conclusion of the war and asked the Queen for all papers relating to the negotiations. After investigation the Commons impeached Oxford on the grounds that he had misrepresented negotiations to the Queen, and therefore to Parliament, and concealed information from council and Parliament, and so 'prevented the just Advice of the Parliament to her Majesty'.[241]

Impeachments were a particularly useful tool for parliamentarians, because impeachment enabled them to maintain the fiction that 'kings can do no wrong': by persecuting the advisers of the monarch for alleged wrongdoing or maladministration, the king's honour and dignity were left untouched. The articles of impeachment were usually drafted in a way that portrayed the monarch as a victim of his or her official. For example, the articles of impeachment against the Earl of Oxford in 1715 stated that he 'did most wickedly betray the honour of her late majesty and the imperial crown of these realms in advising her…without the advice of her council or her parliament.'[242]

From the mid-eighteenth century, the uses and frequency of impeachment changed. The last case of impeachment on purely political-policy grounds was in 1715. Impeachment charges from thereon focused on issues of competence and truthfulness, rather than being used as a political tool.[243] It came to be recognized that an impeachment is a criminal process and that a mistake in policy is not a criminal offence.[244] The last recorded case of impeachment was in 1806.[245]

---

[239] *R v Earl of Danby* (1685) 11 State Tr 600, 621–2.
[240] Turner (n 10) 182–3; Keir (n 25) 279.
[241] Parliamentary History, 17 June–21 September 1715, vol 7, cols 68–219.
[242] Parliamentary History, 2 August 1715, vol 7, col 122.
[243] House of Commons Library, 'Impeachment' (Research Briefing, SN/PC/2666, 2004).
[244] W Holdsworth, *A History of English Law* vol 10 (Methuen and Co 1938) 367.
[245] CE Nicholson and G Carnall (eds), *The Impeachment of Warren Hastings* (Edinburgh University Press 1989).

In 1848, private members attempted (unsuccessfully) to persuade the Commons to bring an impeachment against Palmerston as Foreign Secretary, for allegedly making a secret treaty with Russia.[246] Even though impeachment is now largely obsolete in practice, Parliament retains formal powers of impeachment. In 2004, a small group of MPs attempted to bring impeachment proceedings against Blair for his conduct in the war against Iraq. The motion for impeachment was drafted and tabled for debate in November 2004, but the three main parties forbade their MPs from signing the motion and it was never selected for debate.

3 Committees

In addition to the use of impeachment, Parliament in the seventeenth and eighteenth centuries used ad hoc committees of inquiry to scrutinize foreign policy decisions. These committees investigated such allegations as failing to consult Parliament before entry into a treaty or a war, improper use of finances, and acting on incorrect information or advice. In the twentieth and twenty-first centuries, these ad hoc committees have been replaced by permanent subject select committees and by commissions of inquiry.

Starting in the second half of the seventeenth century, Parliament established various committees and inquiries to investigate the government's conduct of war and foreign policy. During the 1670s, Parliament conducted in-depth examinations of Charles II's foreign policy, establishing inquiries and calling for information relating to the preparations for war, the administration of finances, the conduct of the fleet, and general policy.[247] Further inquiries were conducted in 1689, into the miscarriages of war in Ireland; and in 1694, into the policy of the admiralty.

In 1715, the Commons investigated the unpopular treaty of Utrecht, establishing a committee to 'inquire into the late Peace, and the Management of the late Queen's Ministry'. Established by a motion of the Commons, the committee examined the instructions, papers, and despatches relating to the negotiations leading up to the treaty. The papers were of such a volume and type to be unsuitable for examination by the whole House, so a sub-committee was established by ballot of MPs as a committee of secrecy. The committee reported back to the House, with the reading of their report taking seven hours. It concluded that proceedings of impeachment be initiated against the officials who negotiated an 'unsafe and dishonourable' peace.[248]

---

[246] HC Deb 23 February 1848, vol 96, cols 1132–242. For Lord Palmerston's response, see HC Deb 1 March 1848, vol 97, cols 66–23.
[247] J Milward, *The Diary of John Milward, Esq, Member of Parliament for Derbyshire September, 1666 to May, 1668* (C Robbins ed, CUP 1938) 97, 109.
[248] Parliamentary History, 2 August 1715, vol 7, col 122.

In addition to inquiries by ad hoc parliamentary committees, the Commons could constitute itself as a committee to investigate a particular incident. This occurred in 1757, when the Committee of the Whole House conducted an inquiry into the loss of Minorca. The committee considered papers and accounts documenting intelligence as to the designs of the French, the preparations made for war, the orders made during war, and the conduct of the defence of the dominions in the Mediterranean in 1755–56.[249]

Committees of inquiry were not restricted only to the age of monarchical government. When political power transferred from the monarch to responsible ministers, the Commons still possessed inquisitorial power through committees of the House or parliamentary commissions.[250] However, a majority vote was required to establish a committee of inquiry. As parliamentary majorities got larger and party discipline stronger it became increasingly difficult to summon the necessary support, except where there was widespread criticism of the government's conduct. This was the problem faced by Mr Burdett in 1802, when he brought a motion for an inquiry into the conduct of the late administration in the pursuit of the war against France.[251]

From the end of the nineteenth century onwards, there were regular calls for the establishment of a permanent parliamentary committee to scrutinize foreign policy.[252] It was not until 1979, however, that a select committee on foreign affairs was established as part of a comprehensive move towards the monitoring of all governmental departments by 'functional' select committees.[253] The committee's function is to scrutinize the policy, administration, and expenditure of the Foreign Office. It has no input into policy formulation. Other parliamentary committees with a remit over war and national security include the House of Commons Defence Committee and a joint committee of the Houses (the Intelligence and Security Committee), which has responsibility for the scrutiny of the intelligence agencies.[254] The departmental select committees conduct inquiries into the policy, administration, and expenditure of the departments within their remit.[255]

---

[249] Parliamentary History, 3 May 1757, vol 15 cols 822–7.
[250] Maitland (n 26) 380–1.
[251] Parliamentary History, 12 April 1802, vol 36, col 492.
[252] See, eg, S Low, 'A Foreign Affairs Committee' (1895) 38 The Nineteenth Century: A Monthly Review 506.
[253] JM Lee, 'Parliament and Foreign Policy: Some Reflections on Westminster and Congressional Experience' (1988) 2 Irish Studies in International Affairs 1, 12.
[254] See citations at nn 59–61 in ch 6 for more on the Intelligence and Security Committee.
[255] Recent inquiries conducted by the Defence Committee include inquiries into operations in Afghanistan, the prospects for political settlement in Afghanistan, and intervention in Libya. Recent inquiries by the Foreign Affairs Committee include UK foreign policy towards Afghanistan and Pakistan. For more, see the UK Parliament website: <http://www.parliament.uk/business/committees/>.

Governments have on occasion initiated commissions of inquiry, independent of the government and of Parliament, into their conduct of a particular war. For example, Thatcher's government established a royal commission of inquiry into the government's conduct leading up to the Falklands crisis,[256] and various inquiries have been conducted into the conduct of the Iraq war.[257]

4 Requests for Information

Requests for information relevant to the conduct of war and foreign policy have been an important aspect of the Commons' scrutinizing function. Since the late-seventeenth century, parliamentarians have requested information be laid before the House about treaties, negotiations, intelligence, and despatches and the conduct of war. In the 1670s, the Commons made a request for intelligence information about the movements of the Dutch fleet. It recognized the need to maintain the secrecy of some information, requesting 'an account to the House of Commons as to matters of fact, but not to publish and reveal the secrets of Council.'[258] In 1727, the Commons asked for copies of memorials and letters which had recently passed between the courts of Britain, France, and Spain. It wanted to obtain additional evidence to assess the validity of statements made in ministers' speeches about the recent deterioration in Anglo-Spanish relations. The government granted Parliament's requests, and laid the correspondence before the Houses, consisting of about a dozen letters.[259]

Parliament's requests, however, were not always so easily met. In 1729, Parliament determined to examine the state of Anglo-Spanish trade, particularly the activities of the naval squadrons which had been sent to the West Indies and Spain to intercept the Spanish galleon fleet. Requests were made for the release of the instructions of the squadron commanders, the correspondence between the commanders and the secretaries of state, the details of Spanish attacks made upon British ships since 1725, the correspondence relating to measures taken against piracy, and the copies of all the memorials, petitions, and representations made to George I and George II about the captures of British ships. The copying of over 500 documents, more than half of them in duplicate, severely strained the administrative machine.[260]

---

[256] Report of a Committee of Privy Counsellors, *Falklands Island Review* (Cmnd 8787, 1983).
[257] Report of a Committee of Privy Counsellors, *Review of Intelligence on Weapons of Mass Destruction* (HC 898, 2004) ('Butler Report'); Lord Hutton, *Report of the Inquiry into the Circumstances Surrounding the Death of Dr David Kelly CMG* (HC 247, 2004) ('Hutton Inquiry'); the ongoing Iraq Inquiry (the 'Chilcot Inquiry'), which was launched on 30 July 2009.
[258] Milward (n 247) 97, 109.
[259] Gibbs (n 73) 31.   [260] Gibbs (n 73) 32–3.

During the Hanoverian period the practice of 'calling' for papers developed as a potent political tool.[261] It became an established political tactic for the opposition to request that all correspondence relating to a particular negotiation or diplomatic crisis be laid before the House. The release of information was also used as a bargaining tool by the government, given in return for receiving necessary financial support.[262]

Although governments recognized Parliament's right to call for diplomatic papers and other relevant information, they usually regarded such requests as troublesome, because they exposed sources and angered foreign powers.[263] Governments did not always accede to parliamentary requests, and, sometimes, released information which was not the complete truth.[264] Information was redacted or its release delayed where judged necessary for the interests of security or political expediency.[265]

MPs' access to information is very similar today. Ministers give additional information as they choose in the course of debates on bills or motions. They might also respond to information specifically requested by MPs in the course of debate or by means of parliamentary questions.[266] There is some information that the government will not or cannot readily give in general debate or in answer to questions, because the information is voluminous and complex, secret, or ministers are simply reluctant to release it. In practice, it can be easy for a minister to avoid giving information if he or she wishes to do so.[267]

5 Votes of Censure and No Confidence

The advent of parliamentary government and the evolution of the doctrine of collective ministerial responsibility led to the development of other forms of retrospective scrutiny of governments' conduct of war and foreign policy.[268] In the eighteenth and nineteenth centuries, votes of censure and

---

[261] PDG Thomas, *The House of Commons in the Eighteenth Century* (OUP 1971) 24–5, 38–9.
[262] Turner (n 10) 188.
[263] J Black, *A System of Ambition? British Foreign Policy 1660–1793* (Longman 1991) 47–49. See, more generally, J Black, 'Parliament, the Press, and Foreign Policy' (2006) 25 Parliamentary History 9, 14.
[264] Black, *A System of Ambition?* (n 263) 48.
[265] Gibbs (n 73) 32–3; FR Flournoy, *Parliament and War* (PS King and Son, 1927) 20.
[266] R Brazier, *Ministers of the Crown* (Clarendon Press 1997) 245–56; Blackburn and Kennon (n 71) [1-027]–[1-030].
[267] DC Watt, 'Foreign Affairs, the Public Interest and the Right to Know' (1963) 34 The Political Quarterly 124. The judicial inquiry report in the 'Arms to Iraq' affair identified how deliberately misleading information about arms sales to Iraq was given to Parliament by ministers and officials: see Lord Justice Scott, *Report of the Inquiry into the Export of Defence Equipment and Dual-Use Goods to Iraq and Related Prosecutions* (HC 115, 1996).
[268] Erskine May, *Parliamentary Practice*, 20th edn (Butterworth 1983) 65–6; AV Dicey and ECS Wade (eds), *Introduction to the Study of the Law of the Constitution,* 10th edn (Macmillan 1959) 441.

no confidence were powerful tools for the House of Commons. There are many examples of ministers and governments resigning or being defeated on an issue of foreign policy.[269] In 1839, Lord Melbourne resigned after his Jamaica Bill carried by only five votes. In 1840, the government's handling of Anglo-Chinese relations prompted a motion of no confidence in the government, alleging that it had involved the country in a needless and unjust war. The motion was defeated, but not until after three nights of debate.[270] In 1852, Lord Palmerston resigned after a defeat on an amendment to the Militia Bill, which was designed by the government as a measure of protection against supposed French aggression. In 1855, Lord Aberdeen resigned after a motion of inquiry was brought into his handling of the Crimean war. Later in 1855, Lord John Russell resigned the office of Colonial Secretary before a vote could be taken on the motion 'That the conduct of our Minister in the recent negotiations at Vienna has, in the opinion of this House, shaken the confidence of this country in those to whom its affairs are entrusted'.[271] In 1863, a motion of censure was brought over the government's inept handling of the Schleswig-Holstein crisis.[272] In 1898, the government's policy on China dominated debate, and even members of the government's party were openly critical of the government's conduct.[273]

By the early-twentieth century, however, it was very rare for the fate of ministers or governments to turn on an issue of foreign policy. This was due to a combination of factors. It reflected the general trend of the increasing power of the government relative to the Commons. Individual MPs were unable to scrutinize effectively or intervene in foreign policy matters. Although the Commons still had the power to censure, any attempts to do so would be resisted by the strength of the government and its majority.[274] It also, in part, reflected a change in the interests and motivations of MPs, who were increasingly concerned with wooing voters. Issues of foreign policy were perceived as not of interest to average voters, at least compared with their interest in matters of domestic policy.[275] Further, from the latter part of the nineteenth century, it became to be regarded as 'unethical' to turn out a ministry on a question of foreign policy due to the development of a bipartisan foreign

---

[269] P Langford, 'Prime Ministers and Parliaments: The Long View, Walpole to Blair' (2006) 25 Parliamentary History 382.

[270] G Melanson, 'Honour in Opium? The British Declaration of War on China, 1839–40' (1999) 21 The International History Review 855.

[271] HJ Hanham, 'Cabinet Government: The Cabinet and the Ministry' in Hanham, *The Nineteenth-Century Constitution 1815–1914* (n 70) 75, 78–9.

[272] HC Deb 7 July 1864, vol 176, cols 952–1073.

[273] HC Deb 29 April 1898, vol 56, cols 1580–3.   [274] Low (n 169).

[275] cf Ottee (n 107).

policy and a hesitation to turn out a government on the basis of disagreement with just one aspect of its policies.[276]

It would be extraordinary but not inconceivable for a government today to be turned out or resign on an issue of foreign policy. There are more recent examples where governments have been defeated on a particular proposal in the Commons. For example, in 1978 on the issue of Rhodesia, 116 Conservative MPs defied the leadership's directions to abstain, and voted against the Sanctions Renewal Order. In 2003, 122 Labour MPs defied the whip and voted against the substantive motion on intervention in Iraq. In neither of these examples did the government lose office, but it does indicate that, in an extreme situation, a government could lose the confidence of the Commons on a matter of foreign policy or war. It would be difficult for a government to remain in office if it were defeated on a substantive motion concerning the deployment of force.

Consultation with Parliament about War

1 Introduction

For over four hundred years, the questions of whether the government must or should consult with Parliament about the decision to declare war or deploy the armed forces have been the subject of contestation between Parliament and the government. A dichotomy between the orthodox constitutional theory and the practice characterizes the approaches of both governments and parliaments to this issue. Governments have normally (consistent with constitutional orthodoxy) asserted their exclusive power over war and denied a role for Parliament in its exercise. But through practice, they have implicitly recognized that they must exercise the power in conjunction with Parliament. This dichotomy between the assertion of constitutional orthodoxy and the reality of practice is evident throughout the time period under consideration, and is still evident today. The approach of Parliaments has generally been similar: parliamentarians have paid proper lip-service to the executive's exclusive prerogatives, but have vehemently opposed the executive's exercise of these powers without adequate involvement on their part.

2 Theory and Practice

In the early-seventeenth century it was general understanding that a parliament should always be called at the beginning of a war. Speaking in the Commons in 1641, one MP observed 'how many of our parliament rolls do

---

[276] Flournoy (n 265) 10–11; Low (n 252) 508.

record that the king advised with his parliament about his foreign wars, and could not undertake them without the advice and supplies of the parliament?'[277] That understanding is backed up by statistics: from 1323 to 1639, only one significant war started without the meeting of a Parliament, and that was because the king had promised not to ask for a subsidy for one year.[278] The key pragmatic motivation for the monarch to call Parliament was the need for a grant of supply. A war necessitated an extraordinary grant of taxation, and the Crown reasoned that the grant was more likely to be forthcoming if Parliament had already been a party to the decision to go to war. In addition to the financial imperatives, there was another less pragmatic reason why a monarch was expected to consult with Parliament about the waging of war. Since medieval times, the conception of a just and wise ruler implied that he would seek counsel on important matters.[279] On a matter as important as the decision to go to war, a monarch was expected to consult with his 'great council'. Two pamphleteers, writing in 1730, suggested that although the powers of war and peace were undeniably held by the king, he should not exercise those powers without first consulting Parliament:[280]

As to the right of making peace and war, the same is allowed and granted to be part of the King's high prerogative, tho' we find that the wisest of our monarchs have very rarely enter'd into any war without the approbation and consent of their parliaments: for who can give better and more wholesome advice and counsel in such arduous affairs?

The practice through the reign of the early Stuarts demonstrated the dichotomy, already identified, between the orthodox assertion of the king's exclusive powers over war and the exercise of those powers. There was shared consensus that, in theory, the king had the sole and exclusive power to make and wage war. However, in practice, the Crown's approach to parliamentary involvement in issues of war was not nearly as clear-cut. On some occasions, the Crown denied Parliament's competence on matters of war, while on others it actively sought parliamentary input. On several occasions the king's officials briefed the Commons on current issues in foreign affairs and sought their advice.[281] At the opening of Parliament in 1624, James asked the Commons' advice on relations with Spain and on the proposed match of the prince.[282] James said to the House that although war and peace were the prerogatives of

---

[277] Parliamentary History, 7 February 1641, vol 2, cols 1078–9.
[278] Russell (n 29) 129; see also Russell (n 187) 82.
[279] See the discussion in J Waldron, *Law and Disagreement* (Clarendon Press 1999) 56–60.
[280] Quoted in Black (n 70) 76–7. See further Black (n 98) 4–5.
[281] See, eg, in 1621 when Lord Digby submitted to the Commons an outline of the king's foreign policies and told the House that his master's peaceful policies had failed and that war was now a last resort: Mosse (n 48) 113. See further examples, in citations at nn 34–54.
[282] Mosse (n 48) 116.

the king, he would not make decisions on these matters without first informing the House and hearing their advice.[283] The House of Commons' actions, also, did not comply with the constitutional orthodoxy. On several occasions the Commons gave very detailed guidance and instructions to the king as to matters of war and foreign policy.[284]

In the post-revolutionary period some MPs suggested the existence of a convention that the Crown must seek Parliament's consent before going to war. The context for this development was the Third Dutch war, which was declared in May 1672 when Parliament was not sitting. When Parliament next met in February 1673 there was a decided shift in the attitude of the Commons towards the king's foreign commitments and an assertion of the parliamentary role in advising the king.[285] In the opening session one MP reminded the king that historically, war was undertaken after the advice of Parliament: 'not that the King is obliged, but de facto had done it'.[286] There were many intense speeches against the war.[287] MPs' major grievance was that the war had been entered into without parliamentary consent, and for that reason Parliament would not pay to continue it. Rumours spread that a bill was being prepared to regulate the deployment of men and ships so that it would not be possible for the king to make war without the consent of Parliament.[288] Charles II responded by inviting more active parliamentary participation, and he ordered the Speaker to read the terms of peace and sought Parliament's advice on them.[289] A few years later, Sir William Coventry reiterated the position that had been taken in the Commons in 1677, declaring that 'there is no precedent spoken of, when money has been given for a war or alliances before they have been declared in parliament'.[290]

Not all parliamentarians were in favour of the practice of seeking parliamentary consultation and approval of war. Some expressed reluctance about giving their sanction to a war without having full knowledge of what it was about. Without having access to all the relevant information, Parliament was approving and assuming responsibility for something before it knew what it was. For example, Robert Walpole, speaking in a debate about an address to the king expressing the Commons' approval for naval action taken against Spain, said 'the giving sanction, in the manner proposed to the late measures,

---

[283] 'The King's Answer, 8 March 1624' in Tanner (n 37) 296, 299.
[284] See discussion in citations at nn 34–54.
[285] PS Lachs, 'Advise and Consent: Parliament and Foreign Policy under the Later Stuarts' (1975) 7 Albion: A Quarterly Journal Concerned with British Studies 45.
[286] Quoted in Lachs (n 285) 44.   [287] Lachs (n 285) 45.
[288] Lachs (n 285) 47.   [289] Lachs (n 285) 47.
[290] Parliamentary History, May 25 1677, vol 5, col 385, in a debate on the Address to the King, declining further supply 'till his Majesty's Alliances are made known'. For commentary, see Gibbs (n 60) 67.

could have no other view, than to screen ministers, who were conscious of having done something amiss, and, who having begun a war against Spain, would now make it parliament's war'.[291] These concerns were echoed by parliamentarians eighty-five years later, when the king sent a message to the Commons informing it he was making preparations to respond to a threat posed by France and Holland, and stating that he should 'rely with perfect confidence on their public spirit and liberality'. The Commons passed a motion expressing its support for the king, but not without a couple of MPs pointing out the difficulty for the Commons of being asked to support something they knew nothing about.[292]

During the nineteenth century, there are further examples where the government's manner of exercise of the war prerogative indicated an implicit recognition of the importance of parliamentary consultation and consent in decision-making about war. For example, in 1803, the king informed the Commons that he had determined it necessary for the defence of the UK to raise and assemble a large additional force. The statement read: 'His majesty recommends this subject to the consideration of his faithful Commons; and relies with confidence on their zeal and public spirit, that they will adopt such measures necessary for carrying this into execution.'[293] Similarly, in 1854, an address from the Queen stated that negotiations with Russia had been terminated and the deployment of armed forces deemed necessary. The Queen sought the 'loyal devotion and zeal' of the Commons in the pursuance of war.[294] In debate on the Queen's address, a minister explained the circumstances leading to war, why the war was justified and necessary, and laid relevant papers before the House.[295]

By the nineteenth century, the increasing influence of democratic thought and the changing conceptions of Parliament's functions modified the justifications advanced for why Parliament—and in particular the Commons—should be consulted by the executive over matters of war. The representative nature of the Commons replaced the justification based on the idea of Parliament as the 'great council' of the nation. Writing in the early-nineteenth century, George Canning (the Tory Foreign Secretary) argued consultation with the Commons was a source of strength: the Commons represented the people, and therefore consultation with it signalled sympathy between the people and the government and the confidence and cooperation of the

---

[291] Parliamentary History, 11 November 1718, vol 7, col 564.
[292] Parliamentary History, 9 March 1803, vol 36, cols 1162–6.
[293] 'King's Message Relative to the Defence of the Country', Parliamentary History, 18 June 1803, vol 36, cols 1602–3.
[294] HC Deb 27 March 1854, vol 132, cols 1352–3.
[295] HC Deb 31 March 1854, vol 132, cols 198–308.

Commons and the Crown. He rejected the contentions that the Commons was merely an impediment to the free action of the Crown, and that it was to be managed, but not consulted. He stated:[296]

> It [the Commons] is as essential a part of the national council as it is of the national authority; and woe be to the Minister who should undertake to conduct the affairs of this country upon the principle of settling the course of its foreign policy with a Grand Alliance, and should rely upon carrying their decisions into effect by throwing a little dust in the eyes of the House of Commons.

The dichotomy between theory and practice continued through the nineteenth century, despite the recognition of the desirability and, sometimes, the necessity of parliamentary consultation. While governments informed Parliaments of their plans for war and asked for their support, they continued to claim exclusive powers over war and to deny the existence of a constitutional requirement of consultation. The existence (or not) of such a constitutional requirement was the subject of heated debate in the Commons in 1857. The issue arose when the government waged war against Persia without informing Parliament or seeking its consent. Some MPs vigorously protested the government's disregard of what they identified as the constitutional right of Parliament to be consulted about the initiation of war and moved motions of censure of the government. Roebuck's motion stated that '[t]he war was carried on without information of such transaction being communicated to Parliament, while expensive armaments were equipped without the sanction of the vote of the House of Commons.'[297] Grey's motion censured ministers on the ground that when 'they advised her Majesty to give orders for the invasion of Persia' they did not 'at the same time advise her Majesty to call Parliament together so that Parliament might have learned without delay that the nation was about to be involved in war, and might have had an opportunity of submitting to her Majesty any advice it might have judged such an occasion to require'.[298] Gladstone went further than most other MPs when he asserted that Parliament should have been called before the declaration of war was made or Britain got involved.[299]

Prime Minister Palmerston rejected that Parliament had a constitutional right to be consulted before the government commenced war. However, he conceded that when England becomes involved in a war with one of the 'great powers', involving 'serious consequences', then 'it is the duty of the Government to call parliament together to state the grounds of the quarrel,

---

[296] Quoted in Low (n 169) 3. [297] HC Deb 16 July 1857, vol 146, cols 1582–3.
[298] HC Deb 3 February 1857, vol 144, cols 75.
[299] HC Deb 16 July 1857, vol 146, col 1637.

Interactions

and to ask for the means of carrying on the contest'. He rejected the assertion, however, that the government must consult with Parliament with regard to every war. For instance, he rejected any need to call Parliament in respect of the war against Persia, 'a remote country, a conflict with which is not likely to entail upon us any considerable efforts'. In such a situation, he thought, 'to call Parliament specially together would only be a burlesque on our constitutional forms'.[300]

The issue arose again a couple of decades later. In 1880, in a debate about the Egyptian war, one MP asked for the government to 'undertake, before committing the country to warlike measures, that Parliament should have the opportunity of considering whether the object was one for which the blood and treasure of this country ought to be expended'.[301] The Prime Minister responded:[302]

> Parliament puts into the hands of the Executive Government the use of the military and naval power within certain limits; and though we should be the first to assert that such military and naval power ought never to be used except under the gravest necessity, and with the clearest proof of right, yet we are not prepared to say, and, indeed, we might sacrifice the honour of the country if we were prepared to say, that on no condition should it be exercised and no measure should be taken that could even so remotely result in its exercise until Parliament had been called together and consulted at the very outset as to the origin of the measure.

The governments of the early-twentieth century continued the practice established in the earlier centuries of calling Parliament together to inform them about war and to seek their support. In most cases, however, they had already committed Britain to war before Parliament got involved. For example, in the case of the Boer war, by the time that Parliament was assembled the question of Britain's involvement was no longer an open one. It would have been virtually impracticable for the government to have reversed its policy or the entry into war.

The situation in World War One was similar. Britain's entry into World War One was controversial, with a small but vocal number of MPs focusing their criticism on the government's conduct of 'secret diplomacy'.[303]

---

[300] HC Deb 3 February 1857, vol 144, cols 167–8.
[301] HC Deb 4 September 1880, vol 256, col 1314–15. See also a debate on a similar motion in 1886: HC Deb 19 March 1886, vol 303, cols 1386–423.
[302] HC Deb 4 September 1880, vol 256, col 1326.
[303] An organization called the Union of Democratic Control was active during and immediately following the WWI period. It called for reform to the processes by which foreign policy was made, and in particular was concerned to secure real parliamentary control over foreign policy and prevent it being made in secret. See the book by one of its leading members (and an MP), Arthur Ponsonby, *Democracy and Diplomacy* (Methuen 1915).

On 3 August 1914, Foreign Secretary Grey explained to the Commons the government's determination that it should support France, but asserted that the Commons was free to give or withhold its support for the policy. It had before it 'the issue and the choice', and the government might presume only 'to advise the House of Commons what to do'.[304] Despite Grey's assurances that it was for the Commons to determine whether to support the government's policy, in reality the government's consultation with the Commons was a matter of form only.[305] The government had already, on the previous day, pledged to guarantee the protection of the French coast and shipping—although Grey stated in the Commons that the government had made this assurance 'subject to the policy of His Majesty's Government receiving the support of Parliament'.[306] Deployment was also already under way: the navy had been mobilized and the mobilization of the army was taking place. Further, as was subsequently revealed, Grey did not disclose all the conditions which tied England to France when seeking Parliament's support. The government had entered secret arrangements with France and Russia which created ties that were specifically denied in the Commons.[307]

MPs contributing to the debate observed that the government had essentially placed a fait accompli before them. One noted that, although the Foreign Secretary claimed they were free to come to a decision as to whether to support the plans for military action, he had also informed the Commons that the country was under obligations which it could not turn back on.[308] Another said that, despite the Foreign Secretary saying the Commons had the opportunity of saying 'Yea or Nay' to any proposition made, it seemed that he had already pledged support by the answer he gave to the French Ambassador.[309]

In the case of World War Two, the government informed the Commons, two days before it formally declared war, of the preparations being made, which included complete mobilization of the navy, army, and air force, and 'a number of other measures, both at home and abroad, which the House will not perhaps expect me to specify in detail.'[310] The government had made regular statements to the Commons in the lead-up to the outbreak of war, with

---

[304] HC Deb 3 August 1914, vol 65, col 1826.
[305] Although see Flournoy (n 265) 238–9, who observes that it has been suggested that the consultation with Parliament was more than a matter of form, and that the government's policy was at certain times directly influenced by the movement of opinion in Parliament.
[306] HC Deb 3 August 1914, vol 65, col 1817.
[307] M Pugh, *The Making of Modern British Politics 1867–1939* (Basil Blackwell 1982) 162.
[308] HC Deb 3 August 1914, vol 65, col 1851.
[309] HC Deb 3 August 1914, vol 65, col 1847.
[310] HC Deb 1 September 1939, vol 351, cols 125–39.

Interactions 103

updates of events in Europe and attempts to broker peace.[311] The Prime Minister explained that 'in times like these we have felt that it was right that the House should be kept as far as possible continuously informed of all the developments in the situation as they took place.'[312]

In the Korean and Suez wars, the governments marginalized Parliament's involvement in the decision-making process. On 28 June 1950, Prime Minster Attlee informed the Commons that 'we [Her Majesty's Government] have decided to support the United States action in Korea'.[313] No further information was given. Debate did not take place until 5 July, when the Prime Minister moved a motion in support of the action taken by the government. He said 'the only question before the House today is as to whether or not the Government are right in the action which they have taken in the circumstances which have arisen in Korea'.[314] The motion was passed, after a six-hour debate, with all but one or two MPs speaking in favour of the government's action.[315]

The Suez war was more controversial, and Parliament's input was even more restricted than it had been in respect to the Korean war. On 2 August 1956, the Prime Minister announced that the government had thought it necessary to take military action as a precautionary step in response to President Nassar's nationalization of the Suez Canal.[316] The issue was not debated in the Commons until 12 September, and on 13 September the government moved a motion to adjourn the sitting of the House. Some MPs spoke vehemently against the proposed adjournment. One said it was a 'negation of democracy, for the House to adjourn at a time like this'.[317] Another noted that '[i]f the House is not in session when great issues of foreign policy are occupying the attention of the country and the world, there is no democratic life within Britain.'[318]

In the cases of the Falklands, Kosovo, and Afghanistan conflicts, Parliament's participation in the decision-making process was essentially restricted to a right to be informed in a general sense about the conflict and a right to debate and scrutinize the government's conduct of war. Prior to the outbreak of each conflict, the government gave regular updates to the Commons about the escalating

---

[311] eg, there were debates in the Commons on the 'European situation' on HC Deb 26 April 1939, vol 346, cols 1109–14; 31 July 1939, vol 350, cols 1992–2103; 24 August 1939, vol 351, cols 2–63. The government's conduct of foreign relations was the subject of intense criticism in the House of Commons for the eighteen months preceding England's declaration of war on Germany.
[312] HC Deb 29 August 1939, vol 351, col 111.
[313] HC Deb 28 June 1950, vol 476, cols 2319–20.
[314] HC Deb 5 July 1950, vol 477, col 485.
[315] HC Deb 5 July 1950, vol 477, cols 485–596.
[316] HC Deb 2 August 1956, vol 557, col 1602–43.
[317] HC Deb 13 September 1956, vol 558, cols 321–2.
[318] HC Deb 13 September 1956, vol 558, cols 325–6.

situation. For example, in the Falklands crisis, the Commons was recalled on a Saturday for the purpose of informing it that the situation in the Falklands had become 'increasingly grave', and that an Argentine attack was expected soon.[319] The crisis and subsequent NATO military action in Kosovo were the subject of many statements and debates in the Commons during early 1999.[320] In respect of Afghanistan, Parliament was recalled from summer adjournment after the 9/11 terrorist attacks, and there were regular updates and debates on the attacks and subsequent events.

Although Parliament was kept informed in a general sense, in respect of each conflict the House was told that the government had decided to deploy the armed forces after the decision had already been made. In a debate regarding the negotiations taking place for the settlement of the Falklands conflict, the leader of the Opposition opined that 'the House of Commons has the right to make judgment on this matter before any decision is taken by the Government that would enlarge the conflict'. In response, the Prime Minister stated: 'It is an inherent jurisdiction of the Government to negotiate and reach decisions. Afterwards the House of Commons can pass judgment on the Government.'[321] In the case of Kosovo, on 11 February the Secretary of State for Defence informed the House that the government had decided to prepare the British forces for immediate deployment should a NATO force be sent to Kosovo.[322] When one MP asked whether Parliament would be given an opportunity to give its judgement before British forces were committed, the Secretary fudged the response, saying 'I have already made it clear that I will expect to keep Parliament informed of any decision that is taken about using the troops'.[323] The government also repeatedly refused to address directly questions about the legal basis for intervention—an issue which was far from clear.[324] On 24 March, the Deputy Prime Minister announced that, earlier that evening, British aircraft attacked targets in Yugoslavia.[325] In respect of Afghanistan, the Commons was again informed, after the fact, that military action had been taken.[326]

---

[319] HC Deb 2 April 1982, vol 21, cols 571–7.
[320] HC Deb 18 January 1999, vol 323, cols 565–78; 1 February 1999, vol 324, cols 597–608; 11 February 1999, vol 325, cols 565–76; 24 February 1999, vol 326, cols 404–14; 23 March 1999, vol 328, cols 161–74.
[321] HC Deb 11 May 1982, vol 23, cols 597–8.
[322] HC Deb 11 February 1999, vol 325, cols 565–6.
[323] HC Deb 11 February 1999, vol 325, col 568.
[324] HC Deb 11 February 1999, vol 325, col 568.
[325] HC Deb 24 March 1999, vol 328, col 483. Further statements were made to the House during the conflict, updating the Commons as to the progress of military operations, refugee and humanitarian efforts, and further deployments. See HC Deb 29 March 1999, vol 328, col 731; 31 March 1999, vol 328, cols 1088–204; 13 April 1999, vol 329, cols 19–33; 20 May 1999, vol 331, col 21; 26 May 1999, vol 332, cols 355–72; 8 June 1999, vol 332, cols 463–79; 9 June 1999, vol 332, cols 744–57.
[326] HC Deb 8 October 2001, vol 372, cols 811–902.

Interactions   105

The government claimed that the decision-making processes leading up to the British invasion of Iraq in 2003 were unprecedented in their extent of parliamentary involvement. However, the effectiveness of that involvement is questionable. First, although the government provided Parliament with certain information relevant to the government's case for deployment, much of that information has subsequently been revealed as selective and misleading. For example, on 17 March 2003, Jack Straw circulated several documents to all MPs, including a copy of the Attorney General's response to a written question in the House of Lords setting out the legal basis for the use of force against Iraq, a briefing paper summarizing the legal background, a note summarizing Iraq's record of non-compliance with resolution 1441, and a compilation of key recent United Nations documents.[327] The briefing paper summarizing the legal basis of the planned invasion was subsequently revealed to be a selective and misleading summary of the Attorney General's full opinion.[328] The 'dossier' of intelligence information purportedly showing Iraqi possession of weapons of mass destruction has since been discredited. Secondly, the timing of the Commons' debate and vote on a substantive motion of support for the deployment reduced the Commons' input to essentially a rubber stamp of a fait accompli: 40,000 British troops had already mobilized into the region. Britain could not withdraw without a massive loss of credibility and authority, a factor which influenced many of the MPs speaking in the debate.[329] In addition to these two major limitations there had been uncertainty as to Parliament even being in session at the critical time. During late 2002, when it was clear that the UK and US were close to engaging in military action in Iraq, Parliament was in recess and the government initially refused to recall it. Only after MPs organized an informal recall did the government back down and reconvene Parliament.[330]

Events in Libya in 2011 brought to the forefront once again the issue of parliamentary consultation before war. This time, the current government acknowledged the existence of a constitutional convention in favour of parliamentary debate before deployment. In response to an oral question about whether or not the Commons would have a vote before there was any military action in Libya, the government said:[331]

[327] HC Deb 17 March 2003, vol 401, col 704.
[328] R Norton-Taylor, 'Revealed: the government's secret legal advice on Iraq war' *The Guardian* (London 28 April 2005) <http://www.guardian.co.uk/politics/2005/apr/28/uk.world3>.
[329] HC Deb 18 March 2003, vol 401, cols 829, 840–1.
[330] S Burall, B Donnelly, and S Weir, *Not In Our Name: Democracy and Foreign Policy in the UK* (Politico's 2006) 29.
[331] HC Deb 10 March 2011, vol 524, col 1066. This response reiterated a prior statement of the government's position. In written evidence to the Committee on Political and Constitutional Reform, the Cabinet Secretary, Sir Gus O'Donnell, stated that 'the Government believes that it is

A convention has developed in the House that before troops are committed, the House should be given the opportunity to debate the matter. We propose to observe that convention except where there is an emergency and such action would not be appropriate.

The *Cabinet Manual*, which is a guide to the laws, conventions, and rules on the operation of government, references this statement in the Commons as evidence of the existence of a convention in favour of parliamentary consultation about deployment.[332]

Despite the government's statement, however, the Commons was not given the opportunity to debate on a substantive motion the deployment of British forces to Libya until three days after the government had taken the decision to act.[333] The Prime Minister said that there was no time for consultation before military action: 'We were in a race against time to avoid the slaughter of civilians.'[334]

Legislation

By the enactment of various statutes, Parliament has imposed restrictions on the Crown's raising, keeping, and discipline of an armed force. However, these statutes have not restricted or limited the Crown's prerogative to deploy the armed forces (with one exception), but affirmed the Crown's war prerogative. A statute passed by the Restoration Parliament in 1661 affirmed that the Crown had the sole powers of government, command, and disposition of the armed forces. It provided: 'within all his Majesty's realms and dominions, the sole supreme government, command and disposition of the militia, and of all forces by sea and land, and of all forts and places of strength, is, and by the laws of England ever was, the undoubted rights of his majesty, and his Royal predecessors, Kings and Queens of England.'[335] The Act of Settlement

---

apparent that since the events leading up to the deployment of troops in Iraq, a convention exists that Parliament will be given the opportunity to debate the decision to commit troops to armed conflict and, except in emergency situations, that debate would take place before they are committed' (*Written Evidence to the Committee's Inquiry into the Role and Powers of the Prime Minister*, 17 May 2011, (2010–12) <http://www.publications.parliament.uk/pa/cm201011/cmselect/cmpolcon/writev/842/m11.htm>).

[332] Cabinet Office, *The Cabinet Manual*, 1st edn (October 2011) 44, [5.36]–[5.38].

[333] UN Security Council Resolution 1973 authorizing military intervention in Libya was made on 17 March 2011; on 18 March the government issued a statement that it would deploy British forces to Libya; and on 19 March, British forces were deployed. The House of Commons debate on the deployment took place on 21 March.

[334] HC Deb 21 March 2003, vol 525, col 705.

[335] Preamble of the statute 13 Car 2 st 1 c 6. The preamble was repealed by the Statute Law (Repeals) Act 1969, s 1, sch, pt I. See citations at nn 18–24 in ch 4.

of 1701 was the key exception to the unrestricted legal powers of the Crown to deploy the armed forces. It declared that upon the accession of the House of Hanover, Britain would not be obliged to engage in any war for the defence of the Crown's foreign possessions without the consent of Parliament.[336] This statutory limitation was directed at William III, for having used British military power to advance Dutch interests.

Since 1688, legislation has been used by Parliament to impart some measure of control over the presence and size of a standing army in peacetime. The key statutory provision is article 4 of the Bill of Rights 1688, which prohibits the maintenance of a standing army in peacetime without the consent of Parliament.[337] Since then, Parliament has each year given its sanction for the standing army and its code of discipline. Various statutes provide for the existence, organization, and discipline of the armed forces.[338] The Defence (Transfer of Functions) Act 1964 provides for a Secretary of State to have general responsibility for defence and for the establishment of a Defence Council with powers of command and administration of the armed forces.

Part IV Conclusion

This chapter has traced the interactions of the executive and the Commons in the exercise and scrutiny of the war prerogative. It has demonstrated that the Commons has played a varying, but influential, role in the exercise and scrutiny of the war prerogative. It has also highlighted the disparity between orthodox political and constitutional discourses, which assert the executive's exclusive power over war, and how the war prerogative is exercised in practice.

The current role of the House of Commons in the exercise and scrutiny of the war prerogative fulfils four functions. First, the Commons performs a legitimation function in respect of the exercise of the war prerogative. A legitimation function is a legislative 'stamp of approval' of initiatives taken elsewhere.[339] The Commons performs an overt and conscious action of legitimation of the government's decision to go to war when MPs express in debate their support for the action, vote in favour of a substantive motion of support, or grant supply for the war effort.

---

[336] For more, see Gibbs (n 60) 66–7.   [337] 1 Wm & Mary 2 c 2.
[338] The law relating to the armed forces was consolidated by the Armed Forces Act 2006. See further *Halsbury's Laws of England*, 'Armed Forces', vol 3, 5th edn (2011) [312]–[318] and AW Bradley and KD Ewing, *Constitutional and Administrative Law*, 14th edn (Pearson Education 2007) 343–4.
[339] Packenham (n 71) 88.

Secondly, the Commons performs a mobilizing consent function in respect of the exercise of the war prerogative. Political scientist Samuel H Beer, writing in the 1960s, identified the 'mobilizing consent' function of legislatures as involving the building of consent for government policy.[340] Legislatures assist in the building of consent through a continual process of communication with the community, with the objective of winning acceptance of the coercions placed on the citizen by the government. Public processes of policy and decision-making can be shaped as a means of winning consent to those policies and decisions.[341] In the case of the war prerogative, public debate in the Commons and interactions between MPs and their constituents can help to build support amongst citizens for the war effort.

Thirdly, the Commons performs a scrutinizing function in respect of the exercise of the war prerogative. This scrutiny is exerted through debate and other parliamentary procedural mechanisms, committees of inquiry and select committees, and scrutiny of expenditure policy. Sometimes the scrutiny function is exerted retrospectively, meaning that it can only ever potentially influence future conduct. However, sometimes the scrutinizing function enables the Commons to exert an influence or decisional function, meaning it gets somebody to do something he or she otherwise would not do.[342] A decisional function is evidenced by a capacity to modify, delay, or defeat legislative and policy proposals, to influence policy formulation and implementation, and to alter departmental budgets and personnel.[343] The Commons is a 'policy influencing' legislature, meaning it can modify or reject measures put forward by government, but cannot substitute a policy of its own.[344] In the case of the war prerogative, the Commons can exert influence on policy and decisions through its scrutiny of the government's conduct of an ongoing war.

Fourthly, the Commons performs an expressive function in respect of the exercise of the war prerogative, by expressing public opinion and sentiment on government policies and actions. Philip Norton has identified this as a 'tension-release' function of Parliament,[345] because it provides an outlet for the expression of different views in society and thus plays an important part in the dissipation of tension.

---

[340] SH Beer, 'The British Legislature and the Problem of Mobilising Consent' in E Frank (ed), *Lawmakers in a Changing World* (Englewood Cliffs 1966) 30, reprinted in Norton, *Legislatures* (n 71) 62, 65.

[341] Beer (n 340) 77–80.   [342] Packenham (n 71) 90.

[343] These indicators of a legislature's ability to exert a 'decisional' role are drawn from M Weinbaum, 'Classification and Change in Legislative Systems' in CL Kim and GR Boynton (eds), *Legislative Systems in Developing Countries* (Duke University Press 1975) 43.

[344] Norton, 'Parliament and Policy in Britain: The House of Commons as a Policy Influencer' (n 71) 178.

[345] P Norton, 'Introduction' in P Norton (ed), *Parliament in the 1980s* (Basil Blackwell 1985) 5.

The Commons' capacity to effectuate these functions is influenced by three key factors. The first is access to information. If the Commons has access to limited or inaccurate information, its ability to fulfil effectively these functions is restricted. The second is the timing of parliamentary involvement. The Commons is less able to fulfil effectively certain of these functions if its participation is delayed until the government has already committed the country to war. Thirdly, the Commons' capability is limited by the executive's dominance in the initiation, formulation, and implementation of policies and decisions about war. The executive is the policy and decision-making body. Parliament's participation is limited to trying to influence those policies and decisions.

4

Judicial Treatment of the War Prerogative

Part I Introduction

An unbroken line of judicial authority affirms that the Crown possesses, by virtue of the prerogative, exclusive power over the making of war and the deployment of the armed forces (the 'war prerogative'). This line of judicial authority also establishes that the courts cannot or will not interfere in its exercise. The courts have consistently found that attempted challenges to the manner of exercise of the war prerogative either fall outside their jurisdiction or are inappropriate for judicial consideration and determination. This has remained the position for over four centuries, although the reasoning applied by the courts has changed fundamentally over that period, in response to the influence of different political theories and evolving conceptions of judicial responsibility and function.

For most of the period under consideration, the courts' refusal to intervene in issues connected with the war prerogative entailed a bare assertion of the executive's exclusive power over war, defence, and foreign policy. There were changes over time in the underlying values and justifications, but the general approach—an assertion of the executive's exclusive powers—remained the same. However, the past fifty years has seen a shift in the courts' reasoning to justify their inability or unwillingness to review executive powers associated with war. They have engaged more closely with the issues raised by judicial consideration of these powers. This deeper engagement has involved consideration of the theoretical nature of a decision to abstain from determining issues intimately connected with the war prerogative. I argue in this chapter that the decision not to intervene is a matter of justiciability, not of jurisdiction.

Part II of this chapter examines the handful of cases where the courts have considered the existence and scope of the war prerogative and the greater number of cases where the courts have considered the existence and scope of the 'incidental' war powers. Part III evaluates the courts' approach to the justiciability of issues connected with the war prerogative. The final three parts examine three situations in which the courts do or might consider the exercise of the war prerogative: judicial review of the exercise of the war prerogative on established grounds, judicial review of the war prerogative under the Human Rights Act 1998 ('HRA'), and tort actions based on the conduct of war.

Part II The War Prerogative: Existence and Scope

Introduction

The courts have long asserted their jurisdiction to determine the existence and scope of the prerogative.[1] In relation to the war prerogative, however, the courts have tended to limit their consideration of its existence and scope to a broad assertion of the Crown's undoubted and exclusive prerogative to declare war and deploy the armed forces. They have not considered in depth or detail its precise existence or scope, as these have been taken as axiomatic, and matters over which the courts should properly defer to the Crown.

This part first provides a representative sample of judicial descriptions of the war prerogative. These judicial descriptions are mostly sourced from cases not dealing with the war prerogative specifically, but with related subject-matters. Secondly, I examine the handful of cases where the courts have directly addressed the existence and scope of the war prerogative strictly defined (the prerogative power to declare war and to deploy the armed forces). Thirdly, I consider the courts' treatment of the 'incidental' war powers, which are those powers sourced in the prerogative that enable the government to conduct war.

Judicial Descriptions of the War Prerogative

In the seventeenth century, the war prerogative's 'absolute' nature was the dominating theme in judicial descriptions of the prerogative. The courts identified the war prerogative as the subject of the king's absolute discretion and exclusive competence, unfit to be discussed in the courts of common law. The courts accepted the king's assertions of the existence and scope of the war prerogative and did not question what was done in its name.[2]

---

[1] The prerogative is part of the common law. It is the function of the courts to declare what the common law is, and therefore it is for the courts to define the existence and scope of the prerogative: *Case of Proclamations* (1611) 12 Co Rep 74; *AG v De Keyser's Royal Hotel* [1920] AC 508; *Burmah Oil Co Ltd v Lord Advocate* [1965] AC 75.

[2] *Weymberg v Touch* (1669) Ch Cas 123; *Troner v Hassold* (1670) 1 Ch Cas 173; *Blad v Bamfield* (1674) 3 Swanst 604.

Statements to this effect can be seen in the seventeenth century case law. In a 1682 decision concerning letters of marque, the court declared: 'the king's prerogative in matters of peace and war is absolute and unlimited'.[3] In *Calvin's Case*, Chief Baron Sir Thomas Fleming (a prominent proponent of absolute monarchy) quoted with approval a passage from Bracton identifying the King's absolute discretion over war and peace: 'his absolute power hathe no lawe to dyrecte him: he is absolute in warre & peace, & maye Commaunde the subjecte to goe whither he pleasethe.'[4] In another case, Sir Thomas Fleming identified the divine origin of the king's prerogatives: the king was answerable only to God, not the court.[5]

In *Bate's Case*[6] (a case concerning Bate's refusal to pay an import duty on currants) the court expanded on the concept of the 'absolute' prerogative. The court described the king's powers as being of two types: ordinary and absolute. Ordinary powers were those applied for the benefit of particular subjects, exercised by the king's judges for dispensing justice under the common law. Absolute powers were those exercised for the general benefit of the people and the common good, encapsulated in the maxim *salus populi suprema lex* (the welfare of the people is the supreme law). Absolute powers were unlimited and not subject to legal control. In *Hampden's Case* (a case concerning Hampden's refusal to pay Charles I's ship money levy), Hutton J described the absolute and inseparable nature of the king's prerogative over defence:[7]

There are some inseparable prerogatives belonging to the Crown, such as the Parliament cannot sever from it. The care for the defence of the kingdom belongeth inseparably to the Crown, as head and supreme protector of the kingdom.

As the guardian of the kingdom, the king was the sole judge of the threat posed to the realm and the response necessary to meet that threat. The courts would not question what was done by the king in the exercise of his prerogative powers over defence and war. The court's opinion in favour of Charles I's 1636 ship money levy stated that 'we are...of the opinion that in such case your majesty is the sole judge both of the danger, and when and how the same is to be prevented and avoided'.[8] In *Hampden's Case*,[9] the same was

---

[3] *R v Carew Ct of Chancery* (1682) 3 Swanst 669, 36 ER 1016.
[4] (1608) 7 Co Rep 1a, 77 ER 377.   [5] *Bate's Case* (1606) 2 St Tr 371, 389.
[6] *Bate's Case* (n 5).   [7] *R v Hampden* (1637) 3 St Tr 825, 1194 ('*Hampden's Case*').
[8] 3 St Tr 844, quoted in W Holdsworth, *A History of English Law* vol VI, 7th rev edn (Sweet and Maxwell 1956) 51.
[9] *Hampden's Case* (n 7). For differing interpretations of this decision, see DL Keir, 'The Case of Ship-Money' (1936) 52 Law Quarterly Review 546; Holdsworth (n 8) (addenda et corrigenda).

expressed: the king was the guardian of the kingdom's safety and the sole judge as to the best manner of providing such defence. Therefore, the court did not have the jurisdiction to adjudge whether there existed an emergency or what steps might be necessary to meet it: these matters fell to the king's absolute discretion and were beyond the cognizance of his judges.

The use of the concept of absolute prerogative died out in the second half of the seventeenth century, and the courts stopped describing the war prerogative as 'absolute'. However, they continued to treat the Crown's war prerogative as a special and unique power and the subject of the Crown's exclusive discretion. For example, in *Rustomjee*, the court stated: 'The making of peace and the making of war, as they are the undoubted, so they are, perhaps, the highest, acts of the prerogative of the Crown.'[10] Similarly: 'His Majesty's pleasure supersedes all enquiry, as he has absolute direction and command of the army.'[11]

The courts have also continued to describe the Crown's war prerogative as stemming from the Crown's guardianship role and its responsibility for the general welfare. One court said: '[T]here is a duty on the King, by reason of his being King, to defend the realm, and therefore of course all his realm and every part of his realm.'[12] In *De Keyser*, Lord Dunedin identified it as a 'right' and 'duty' to protect the realm.[13] More recently, it has been termed 'the Crown's first duty'[14] and 'one of the cardinal features of government'.[15] In *Belmarsh*, Lord Nicholls observed that '[a]ll courts are very much aware of the heavy burden, resting on the elected government... to protect the security of this country and all who live here.'[16]

Existence and Scope of the War Prerogative

1 Introduction

This section examines the judicial authorities establishing the existence and scope of the war prerogative, strictly defined. I first discuss the Court of Appeal's decision in *China Navigation v AG*,[17] which affirmed the existence of the war prerogative. I then examine the handful of cases dealing with the scope of the war prerogative.

---

[10] *Rustomjee v R* (1876) 2 QBD 69, 73.   [11] *MacDonald v Steele* (1793) Peake 175.
[12] *Attorney General v Tomline* (1880) 14 Ch D 58, 66.   [13] *De Keyser* (n 1) 524.
[14] *Marchoiri v Environment Agency* [2002] EWCA Civ 03, (2002) 127 LR 574 [38].
[15] *R v Spear* [2002] UKHL 31, [2003] 1 AC 734 [3] (Lord Bingham).
[16] *A v Secretary of State for the Home Department* [2004] UKHL 56, [2005] 2 AC 68 [39] ('*Belmarsh*') [79].
[17] [1932] 2 KB 197.

2 Existence

In *China Navigation*,[18] the Court of Appeal confirmed that the prerogative was the source of the government's powers over the government, command, and deployment of the armed forces. The appellants had argued that the army had become a purely statutory body after 1689 and that the Crown's prerogative to raise and deploy an army no longer existed. The court rejected the argument. It found that the prerogative was the source of the Crown's powers over the government, command, and deployment of the armed forces. The preamble to a 1661 statute[19] was material to the finding. It declared that 'within all his Majesty's realms and dominions, the sole supreme government, command and disposition of the militia, and of all forces by sea and land, and of all forts and places of strength, is, and by the laws of England ever was, the undoubted rights of his majesty, and his Royal predecessors, Kings and Queens of England'. The judges regarded this preamble as key evidence affirming the existence of the war prerogative.[20] It was material that the rest of the Act had been repealed in 1863,[21] leaving just the preamble remaining in force.

While affirming the existence of the war prerogative, the court acknowledged that the existence and discipline of the armed forces was sourced in statute. Since the Bill of Rights 1688, the court noted, the army may properly be said to be a statutory and not a prerogative force. However, as the court observed, Parliament has never purported expressly to confer upon the Crown any powers of disposing or using the army or administering its affairs:[22]

When Parliament has given its consent to the raising and keeping of the army for the year, it leaves the Crown to exercise its prerogative powers as to the manner in which the army is to be raised and kept and in respect to the disposition and use of the army and the administration of its affairs.

China Navigation is the most recent authority dealing directly with the existence of the war prerogative. In *Chandler*, the court identified *China Navigation* as affirming the existence of the war prerogative and its unsuitability for judicial consideration.[23] The preamble of the statute 13 Car 2 st 1 c 6 (which the court relied on heavily in *China Navigation*) was repealed in 1969. However, the existence of the war prerogative continues to be assumed, though no recent authority explicitly addresses the issue. In a 1988 decision dealing with the existence of a prerogative of keeping the peace within the

---

[18] *China Navigation* (n 17). [19] 13 Car 2 st 1 c 6.
[20] *China Navigation* (n 17) 227–8 (Lawrence LJ); 215 (Scrutton LJ).
[21] Statute Law Revision Act 1863 (26 & 27 Vict c 125).
[22] *China Navigation* (n 17) 228; see also 239 (Slesser LJ).
[23] *Chandler (Terence Norman) v DPP* [1964] AC 763, 782, 791, 800, 814 (HL).

realm, the Court of Appeal commented that '[t]he Crown's prerogative of making war and peace, the war prerogative, has never been doubted'.[24]

3 Scope

A Hazy Outline

A hazy outline of the scope of the war prerogative can be discerned from a small number of key cases. For two general reasons it is difficult to develop a definitive picture of its scope. First, the courts have very rarely addressed directly issues as to the war prerogative's scope, on the grounds of lack of jurisdiction or non-justiciability. There are very few cases examining specifically the extent of the Crown's prerogative to declare war or deploy the armed forces, because the courts have uniformly held these subject-matters to be outside their purview.[25]

Secondly, there is a long history in English judicial decision-making of a presumption that the government is acting in good faith. The presumption of good faith in executive motives has an especially entrenched history in the national security sphere, and it has conditioned the courts to accept executive assertions as to what was done in the name of the war prerogative. In the seventeenth century it was reflected in an underlying assumption about the benevolent nature of the king and the way in which he exercised his powers. The king's duty was to defend the realm, and it would be disrespectful for the courts to suppose that he would abuse his discretionary powers in the exercise of that duty. In *Godden v Hales*,[26] a case concerning the king's dispensing power, Herbert CJ said that no one would deny that the king has power to proclaim war when he pleases, and yet it could also be said that he could keep the nation always in war and so ruin his subjects. His response was: 'We should not suppose that the King would use his powers for anything but the benefit and protection of his subjects, and not to their damage.'[27] Later, the presumptive faith in a benevolent king morphed into the courts placing a 'faithful trust in government motives'[28] in the national security sphere. Simpson labels this 'the Reading Presumption of Executive Innocence', so named for Lord Reading's comment in a World War One internment case: 'It

---

[24] *R v Secretary of State for Home Department, ex parte Northumbria Police Authority* [1989] QB 26, 56.
[25] There are, however, a larger number of cases examining the scope of the Crown's 'incidental' war powers: see citations at nn 44–88 for judicial treatment of the incidental war powers.
[26] *Godden v Hales* (1686) 11 St Tr 1165.
[27] *Godden v Hales* (n 26).
[28] L Lustgarten and I Leigh, *In from the Cold: National Security and Parliamentary Democracy* (Clarendon Press 1994) 332.

is of course always to be assumed that the executive will act honestly and that its powers will be reasonably exercised.'[29]

Today, the courts continue to defer to the government's special competence over matters intimately connected with war and the deployment of force, but they do so for reasons stronger and more legitimate than a blind faith in government motives and actions.[30] Judges are also much more ready to criticize measures taken by the executive, and their underlying motives. In *Belmarsh*, for example, Lord Rodger warned that '[t]here is always a danger that, by its very nature, those concerned with national security may bring forth measures that are not objectively justified.'[31]

Scope

It is not possible to define with certainty the precise scope of the war prerogative. However, on existing case law it can be said that the war prerogative extends, at least, to the powers to (1) declare war, (2) deploy the armed forces, (3) determine when to deploy the armed forces, (4) determine the objectives of the deployment, (5) determine the armament of the armed forces, and (6) conduct the operations of war.

The courts have long recognized that by virtue of the prerogative the Crown makes and conducts war. In a case decided in 1793 the court declared: 'His Majesty's pleasure supersedes all enquiry, as he has absolute direction and command of the army.'[32] The prerogative is vested in the Crown, even though it is now exercised by ministers responsible to the Commons. In *R v Bottrill, ex parte Kuechenmeister*, the court asserted that '[i]n the British Constitution, which is binding on all British courts, the King makes both war and peace, and none the less so, in the eyes of the law, that he does so as a constitutional monarch upon the advice of his democratic Cabinet.'[33] In *Chandler (Terence Norman) v DPP*,[34] each judge made clear the executive's sole power and exclusive discretion over the government, disposition, and command of the armed forces. Lord Reid said: 'It is in my opinion clear that the disposition and armament of the armed forces are and for centuries have been within the exclusive discretion of the Crown'.[35] Viscount Radcliffe stated: 'The disposition, armament and direction of the defence forces of the State are matters decided upon by the Crown and are within its jurisdiction as the executive power of the State.'[36] Likewise, Lord Hodson: 'The Crown has, and this is not disputed, the right as head of

---

[29] *R v Governor of Wormwood Scrubs Prison* [1920] 2 KB 305; AWB Simpson, *In the Highest Degree Odious: Detention without Trial in Wartime Britain* (OUP 1992) 29.
[30] See the discussion in citations at nn 89–190 on the courts' approach to jurisdiction and justiciability.
[31] *Belmarsh* (n 16) [177].   [32] *MacDonald v Steele* (n 11).
[33] [1947] 1 KB 41, 50.   [34] *Chandler* (n 23).
[35] *Chandler* (n 23) 791.   [36] *Chandler* (n 23) 796.

the State to decide in peace and war the disposition of its armed forces';[37] and Lord Devlin: 'It is by virtue of the prerogative that the Crown is the head of the armed forces and responsible for their operation.'[38]

By virtue of its war prerogative, the Crown has exclusive power to determine the timing and objectives of a deployment of armed force. In *R (on the application of Campaign for Nuclear Disarmament) v Prime Minister*[39] (hereafter '*CND*'), the Divisional Court identified the determination and evaluation of the purposes of military action as an aspect of the executive's war prerogative.[40]

The court in *CND* might also be construed as treating the interpretation of the UK's obligations under international law (as relevant to a proposed military action) to be an aspect of the war prerogative. *CND* dealt with an application for a declaratory judgment that an invasion of Iraq without UN Security Council approval would be unlawful under international law. The court dismissed the application on the grounds that the questions raised were non-justiciable (and, in any case, the court lacked jurisdiction to interpret the relevant international resolution). The court said that it was for the government to determine the legal basis of its proposed military action. Although the court did not explicitly identify this power as an aspect of the war prerogative, presumably it must fall under either the war prerogative or the prerogative to conduct foreign relations. In *Gentle*, Lord Hope identified the issue of legality as an issue of international law belonging to the area of relations between states and a matter of political judgement.[41]

Finally, a series of cases affirm that the war prerogative extends to the armament of the armed forces. The leading decision on this point is *Chandler*,[42] where the court identified the power to determine the armed forces' methods and types of armament and equipment as coming within the scope of the war prerogative. It followed that it was for the exclusive discretion of the Crown to determine whether or not to use nuclear armaments. Similar findings have been made in respect of the Trident missile system.[43]

'Incidental' War Powers

1 Introduction

In addition to the powers to declare war and deploy the armed forces, the courts recognized that the Crown possessed (and maybe still does possess)

---

[37] *Chandler* (n 23) 800.　[38] *Chandler* (n 23) 807.
[39] [2002] EWHC 2777 (Admin).　[40] *CND* (n 39) [36]–[44], [59].
[41] *R (on the application of Gentle) v Prime Minister* [2008] UKHL 20, [2008] 1 AC 1356 [24]. See further citations at nn 200–203.　[42] *Chandler* (n 23).
[43] *Lord Advocate's Reference (No 1 of 2000)* 2001 JC 143 (Scotland), applying *Chandler* (n 23); *Hutchinson v Newbury Magistrates* (2000) 122 ILR 499.

prerogative powers necessary for the carrying out of war. These powers have been given various labels, including 'incidental war powers', 'war prerogative', and 'defence of the realm prerogative'. Whatever the label, it refers to an amorphous and uncertain collection of discretionary powers exercised by the government and subject to limited, if any, judicial control. Chitty described them thus: 'As the constitution of the country has vested in the King the right to make war or peace, it has necessarily and incidentally assigned to him on the same principles the management of the war; together with various prerogatives which may enable His Majesty to carry it on with effect.'[44]

At their broadest conception, the courts held that the incidental war powers based on the prerogative empowered the Crown to do anything it deemed necessary for the defence of the realm. The exercise of these incidental powers was for the exclusive determination and control of the king, and the courts would not interfere in their exercise. They included the enforced billeting of soldiers, imposition of blockades and embargoes, acquisition of private property, taxation and levies, and making and strengthening fortifications. Although the king's defence prerogative in the seventeenth century was virtually unlimited, by the time that Chitty wrote his treatise (in 1820), these incidental powers were restricted to those thought necessary to conduct war, which meant that they were tied tightly to the actual conduct or preparation for armed conflict.[45] The House of Lords in 1965 confirmed the incidental war powers as the powers which the Crown is armed with in times of war or imminent threat of invasion or attack.[46] Lord Reid thought 'the prerogative certainly covers doing all those things in an emergency which are necessary for the conduct of war'.[47] Their lawful exercise was therefore dependent on the existence of a state of war. The courts have taken as conclusive the executive's position on the existence or not of a state of war.[48]

The following discussion outlines the types of incidental war powers identified by the courts, and evaluates their potential relevance today.

---

[44] J Chitty, *A Treatise on the Law of the Prerogatives of the Crown: And the Relative Duties and Rights of the Subject* (Butterworth 1820) 44.

[45] Chitty (n 44) 42–8. For comment see Lustgarten and Leigh (n 28) 324.

[46] *Burmah Oil* (n 1) 115–116 (Viscount Radcliffe); 145 (Lord Pearce); 166 (Lord Upjohn).

[47] *Burmah Oil* (n 1) (Lord Reid).

[48] Sir Arnold McNair and Sir Arthur Watts, *Legal Effects of War*, 4th edn (CUP 1966) 34–6; *ex parte Kuechenmeister* (n 33) 50. In the last fifty years, the determination of the existence or not of a state of war has become less certain and more contested. See *Amin v Brown* [2005] EWHC 1670 (Ch), [2006] IL Pr 5 for a summary of recent practice as to the determination of a state of war and the legal consequences which flow from it.

2 Prerogative Taxation

The early Stuart Kings, in their efforts to secure alternative sources of funding and avoid recourse to Parliament, imposed indirect taxation under pretence of the prerogative through various duties, levies, and forced loans. These revenue-gathering efforts were challenged in the courts on several occasions but the judges uniformly held for the king. Berkeley J declared that the king possessed extra-legal powers: 'There was a rule of law and a rule of government, and many things which might not be done by the rule of law might be done by the rule of government.'[49] An opinion of the judges in favour of the legality of the 1636 ship money levy stated:[50]

We are of the opinion that when the good and safety of the kingdom in general is concerned, and the whole kingdom is in danger, your Majesty may by writ under the great seal of England, command all the subjects of this your kingdom, at their charge to provide and furnish such number of ships, with men, munition, and victuals, and for such time as your majesty may think fit, for the defence and safeguard of the kingdom from such danger and peril.

In *Hampden's Case*,[51] Charles I persuaded his judges that under the prerogative he could levy his subjects to furnish ships to defend the kingdom in time of danger. The majority of the Court of Exchequer held that the king was the sole judge of the existence of the danger to the realm and the steps necessary to avert it. The king was entrusted with the defence of the country, and in an emergency he had an absolute prerogative, inseparable from his person, to act as he pleased for the preservation of the safety of the nation.[52]

The cases holding that the Crown has the power to impose indirect taxation by virtue of its war prerogative can be confined to the particular circumstances of the early-seventeenth century. Prerogative taxation was subsequently outlawed, first by specific legislation in 1641[53] and then by a general prohibition in the Bill of Rights 1688 of the raising and spending of public moneys without the consent of Parliament.

---

[49] SR Gardiner (ed), *The Constitutional Documents of the Puritan Revolution, 1625–1660* vol 8, 3rd edn (OUP 1906) 103.

[50] 3 St Tr 844, quoted in Holdsworth (n 8) 51.

[51] *Hampden's Case* (n 7).

[52] See the discussion in citations at nn 8–10. For comment, see Keir (n 9); Holdsworth (n 8); P Craig, 'Prerogative, Precedent and Power' in C Forsyth and I Hare (eds), *The Golden Metwand and the Crooked Cord: Essays on Public Law in Honour of Sir William Wade QC* (Clarendon Press 1998) 65, 70. See also ES Cope, *Politics without Parliaments: 1629–40* (Allen and Unwin 1987) 116; JS Hart Jnr, *The Rule of Law 1603–1660* (Pearson Education 2003) 182–8.

[53] 17 Car 1 c 14 declared that the levy of ship money, the writs by which it was ordered, the extra-judicial opinions of the judges approving its legality, and the judgment against Hampden 'were and are contrary to the laws and statutes of the realm'.

3 Requisition and Acquisition of Property

The courts have recognized the Crown's right, by virtue of its prerogative, to make use of a subject's property during war. *The King's Prerogative in Saltpetre*,[54] *Hampden's Case*,[55] and *Hole v Barlow*,[56] affirmed the king's power to acquisition land or premises, based on his right and duty to protect the realm.

A series of cases during the two world wars confirmed that the Crown, pursuant to its prerogative, has the power to requisition in times of war property owned by subjects or by neutrals who enjoyed its use subject to British law.[57] On the day before Britain's entry into World War One, the Crown issued a proclamation by prerogative authorizing the Admiralty to requisition British ships for war purposes. In *The Broadmayne*[58] and *Crown of Leon*,[59] it was accepted as an act of prerogative power.[60] The courts recognized an inherent right in the Crown to take the property of individuals, and in case of grave emergency, to destroy it. It was not for the courts to inquire into the degree of necessity: they inferred that the requisition was in the public interest.[61]

While upholding the Crown's right to acquisition property by virtue of its war prerogative, the courts have recognized certain conditions upon its lawful exercise. In *Re a Petition of Right*,[62] the court held that the king is not entitled under his prerogative to take a man's fee simple estate: the extent of the king's right was to 'take and use the lands for so long and in such manner as may be necessary for securing the public safety and the defence of the realm during the present war'.[63] Further, the power to requisition may be exercised in times of war only. The Crown has not claimed or sought to exercise in peacetime a right to take land, except by agreement or under statutory powers; most likely because, according to Viscount Radcliffe in *Burmah Oil*, in peacetime Parliament was accessible and there could be no sufficient 'necessity'.[64]

The courts have also insisted on the payment of fair compensation for the Crown's use or acquisition of land and property. In *De Keyser*,[65] the court held that the Crown is not entitled, by virtue of its prerogative, to take possession of property and use it for defence purposes without paying compensation. The court based its decision on an analysis of past practice where land had

---

[54] (1606) 12 Rep 12.   [55] *Hampden's Case* (n 7).
[56] (1858) 4 CB (NS) 334, 345.
[57] *The Zamora* [1916] 2 AC 77; *Re a Petition of Right* [1915] 3 KB 649; *The Broadmayne* [1916] P 64.
[58] [1916] P 64.   [59] *Crown of Leon v Admiralty Commissioners* [1921] 1 KB 595.
[60] *Burmah Oil* (n 1) 115–16 (Viscount Radcliffe).   [61] *The Canton* [1917] AC 102.
[62] [1915] 3 KB 649.   [63] *Re a Petition of Right* (n 57) 665.
[64] *Burmah Oil* (n 1) 115–16 (Viscount Radcliffe).   [65] *De Keyser* (n 1).

been acquired for the purposes of defence. It found that, since 1788, statutes authorizing the acquisition of land had included provision for compensation. *Burmah Oil*[66] affirmed this approach in 1965 when it found that where the Crown requisitions or destroys a subject's property under its war prerogative, it must also make good the loss. Compensation was not payable, however, where the destruction of property occurred in the course of actually fighting the enemy.

4 Restrictions on Trade and Other Relations

A long line of authority holds that when Britain is at war, it is unlawful for a British subject to have any relations, commercial or otherwise, with an enemy except by the permission of the Crown. In *The Hoop*, Lord Stowell declared that 'trading with an enemy without the King's licence was illegal in British subjects'.[67] *Esposito v Bowden*[68] held that the declaration of war imports a prohibition of commercial intercourse and correspondence with the inhabitants of an enemy's country: 'The force of a declaration of war is equal to that of an Act of Parliament prohibiting intercourse with the enemy except by the Queen's licence. As an Act of State, done by virtue of the prerogative exclusively belonging to the Crown, such a declaration carries with it all the force of law.'[69] The courts affirmed this approach during World War One, in cases such as *Horlick v Beal*[70] and *Tingle v Mueller*.[71] A declaration of war was also held to have legal effects in respect of contracts: contracts made before the declaration of war that had not yet been executed at the time of declaration were dissolved if the execution of that contract would be unlawful or impossible as involving intercourse with the enemy.[72]

The courts articulated two justifications for the prohibition of trading or other relations with the enemy. The first, based on *Calvin's Case*, was that war declared by one sovereign against another involved all the subjects of both: 'a war declared against him who has the supreme authority in a population is considered to be declared against all his subjects.'[73] The second justification

---

[66] *Burmah Oil* (n 1). However, the appellant was denied its victory in this case by the War Damage Act 1965, which relieved the Crown of its obligation to make the reparations. The Act is limited to acts of the Crown that destroyed property during or in contemplation of war, and does not affect the Crown's obligation to compensate for loss incurred through requisitioning property under the prerogative. See *AG v Nissan* [1970] AC 179, 229 (Lord Pearce) (HL).
[67] (1799) 1 C Rob 196. Confirmed in *Potts v Bell* (1800) 8 TR 548, 561.
[68] (1855) 4 El & Bl 963; (1857) 7 El & Bl 763.   [69] (1857) 7 El & Bl 763, 781.
[70] [1916] 1 AC 486 (HL).   [71] [1917] 2 Ch 144 (CA).
[72] *Ertel Bieber & Co v Rio Tinto Ltd* [1918] AC 260 (HL); *Robson v Premier Oil and Pipe Line Co* [1915] Ch 136. For a recent authority, see *Amin v Brown* (n 48). For comment, see AH Hudson, 'Effect on Commercial Law of Non-Declaration of War' in P Rowe (ed), *The Gulf War 1990–91 in International and English Law* (Routledge 1993) 333.
[73] (1608) 7 Rep 1a.

was based on public policy, the aim of the prohibition being to forbid acts that might be of advantage to the enemy and increase its capacity to prolong hostilities.

Restrictions on relations with the enemy imposed by the prerogative have probably been replaced by statutory provisions of similar effect. A statute passed in 1939 restricting trade with enemies is still in force,[74] and specific trade restrictions are made by orders pursuant to the Export Control Act 2002 and the United Nations Act 1946.[75]

5 Imprisonment and Deportation

The courts have held that the government can imprison and deport British subjects and aliens in the exercise of its prerogative. In World War One the executive relied mainly upon statutory powers for executive imprisonment and internment,[76] but in World War Two the Crown relied on the prerogative to detain aliens. The courts held that this was a lawful exercise of the prerogative and beyond the purview of the courts. *R v Bottrill, ex parte Kuechenmeister*[77] concerned the executive detention of a German man who had lived in England for many years and had an English wife. The court declared that by virtue of the prerogative, the Crown had the right to intern, expel, or otherwise control an alien enemy according to its discretion, and that right could not be questioned in or controlled by the courts. The prerogative was relied upon as recently as the first Gulf war (1990–91) to detain thirty-five Iraqis in the UK who were classified as prisoners of war.[78]

Today, it seems unlikely that the government would rely on prerogative power to imprison individuals. Governments have instead relied on broad statutory powers enabling detention and control, although not without controversy.[79]

6 Other Incidental War Powers

In addition to the incidental war powers outlined already, there are several other more obscure and probably obsolete powers sourced in the war prerogative. These include the powers to impress subjects for the navy, issue letters

---

[74] Trading with the Enemy Act 1939.

[75] Orders made under the United Nations Export Act 1946 were considered by the Supreme Court in *A v HM Treasury* [2010] 2 AC 534; *R v Forsyth* [2011] UKSC 9.

[76] See the Alien Restriction Act 1914 and regulations made under the Defence of the Realm Consolidation Act 1914.

[77] *Kuechenmeister* (n 33). See also *R v Commandant of Knockaloe Camp* (1917) 117 LT 627; *R v Vine Street Police Station Superintendent, ex parte Liebmann* [1916] 1 KB 268.

[78] G Risius, 'Prisoners of War in the United Kingdom' in Rowe (n 72) 289.

[79] See, eg, ss 22 and 23 of the Terrorism Act 2006.

of marque, issue letters of safe conduct, prohibit subjects from leaving the realm, order subjects to return to the realm, and to dig for saltpetre.[80]

7 Incidental War Powers Today

It is unclear exactly what incidental war powers the executive today possesses by virtue of its prerogative. The difficulty is that there are many prerogative powers for which there is no recent judicial authority or no judicial authority at all. I make three observations as to their potential continued application.

First, statute has replaced prerogative as the source of many of the executive's incidental war powers.[81] Where a statute confers similar powers on the Crown as previously enjoyed under the prerogative, the Crown is bound to exercise its statutory power.[82] In *Burmah Oil*, the House of Lords observed that the Crown has increasingly relied upon statutory powers to found its incidental powers of war, rendering the use of the prerogative mainly of theoretical or historical importance.[83] Lord Reid observed: 'There is difficulty in relating the prerogative to modern conditions. In fact no war which has put this country in real peril has been waged in modern times without statutory powers of an emergency character.'[84] He explained that it would be impracticable to wage a modern war by use of the prerogative alone, because the mobilization of the industrial and financial resources of the country could not be done without statutory emergency powers.

Recent enactments have made reliance on the prerogative unnecessary, if not impossible. The Civil Contingencies Act 2004 establishes a broad and flexible framework for dealing with emergency situations. A recent government review reported that the Civil Contingencies Act probably 'covers the field', leaving no room for the continuation of the prerogative. It suggested, however, that action might still be taken in reliance on the prerogative in the 'particularly extreme' case when immediate action is required to combat an urgent threat and the emergency regulations procedure is unavailable.[85]

Secondly, the prerogative is capable of adapting to new situations, but new prerogatives cannot be created. Warrington LJ explained that the war

---

[80] For more detailed consideration of these obscure incidental war powers, see G McBain, 'Abolishing Crown Prerogatives Relating to the Military' (2011) 20 Nottingham Law Journal 14.

[81] See, eg, statutes enacted during the Napoleonic Wars, which regulated or conferred executive powers in times of emergency: 38 Geo 3 c 27, 43 Geo 3 c 55; Defence of the Realm Act 1914; Emergency Power (Defence) Acts 1939 and 1940. More recent statutes conferring executive powers in times of emergency and in the combat of terrorism include: Terrorism Acts 2000 and 2006; Anti-Terrorism, Crime and Security Act 2001; Civil Contingencies Act 2004; Prevention of Terrorism Act 2005; Counter-Terrorism Act 2008.

[82] *De Keyser* (n 1). [83] *Burmah Oil* (n 1) 101 (Lord Reid), 115–16 (Viscount Radcliffe).

[84] *Burmah Oil* (n 1) 101 (Lord Reid).

[85] Ministry of Justice, 'The Governance of Britain. Review of the Executive Royal Prerogative Powers: Final Report' (October 2009) [66]–[76].

prerogative 'must of necessity vary with the times and the advance of military service'.[86] However, new prerogatives cannot be created: 'It is 350 years and a civil war too late for the Queen's Courts to broaden the prerogative.'[87] It follows, as Lord Bingham observed in the *Bancoult* case, that whenever 'the existence or effect of the royal prerogative is in question the courts must conduct an historical inquiry to ascertain whether there is any precedent for the exercise of the power in the given circumstances'.[88]

Thirdly, whether or not the government today possesses incidental war powers by virtue of its prerogative, whenever possible the government will rely on statutory powers in times of emergency. It is politically safer for the government to rely on statutory powers, rather than prerogative powers, particularly if it is taking controversial action or action which has severe or wide-ranging effects.

Part III Jurisdiction and Justiciability

Introduction

An unbroken line of judicial authority holds that the courts will not review the exercise of the war prerogative. The theoretical basis of this judicial abstention poses interesting and unexplored questions. Until *CCSU v Minister for the Civil Service* ('*GCHQ*'),[89] in 1985, the courts disclaimed jurisdiction to examine the manner of exercise of prerogative powers. Now, the courts claim such jurisdiction, but have continued to treat the exercise of the war prerogative as beyond their purview. This part considers the basis of the judicial abstention. It argues that

(1) the courts possess jurisdiction to review the exercise of the war prerogative; and
(2) in determining whether or not to abstain from review of the exercise of the war prerogative, the courts are determining whether or not the particular issue is justiciable. In determining whether or not a particular issue is justiciable, the courts will evaluate various criteria which compare relative institutional competence and legitimacy to determine that issue.

Jurisdiction

The High Court possesses jurisdiction to review all exercises of governmental power. This was not always true. Until *GCHQ*,[90] the courts' examination

---

[86] *Re a Petition of Right* (n 57) 666.   [87] *BBC v Jones* [1965] Ch 32, 79 (Diplock LJ).
[88] *Bancoult (No 2)* [2008] UKHL 61, [2009] 1 AC 453 [69].   [89] [1985] AC 374.
[90] *GCHQ* (n 89).

of the prerogative was limited to an inquiry of its existence and scope; the courts would determine whether an asserted exercise of the prerogative was one properly recognized by law, but hold that they lacked jurisdiction to question the manner of its exercise.[91] The character of the war prerogative bolstered this position: as one of the paradigm royal prerogatives, the courts strongly disclaimed their competence over its subject-matter and identified it as falling within the exclusive discretion of the Crown. In *China Navigation* the court held it could not review or control the Crown's discretion to deploy the armed forces. It was for the 'uncontrolled discretion of the King as head of the army, both as to whether he shall afford such protection against such anticipated, not actual danger, and as to the terms on which he should afford it'.[92] In *Chandler*, Viscount Radcliffe proffered:[93]

> If the methods of arming the defence forces and the disposition of those forces are at the decision of Her Majesty's Ministers for the time being, as we know that they are, it is not within the competence of a court of law to try the issue whether it would be better for the country that that armament or those dispositions should be different.

The courts also employed the concept of an act of state to identify executive acts in external affairs as beyond the purview of judicial review.[94] In *Johnson v Pedlar*[95] it was said: 'Municipal Courts do not take it upon themselves to review the dealings of State with State or of Sovereign with Sovereign.' An act of state was used in two senses: as a defence to an action in tort and as a principle of justiciability or jurisdictional rule.[96] In the latter sense, it was indistinguishable from the rule that the exercise of prerogative power was unreviewable.

GCHQ[97] opened prerogative powers to judicial review. The majority judgments of Lords Scarman, Diplock, and Roskill found that the prerogative is reviewable on the same grounds as those applying to statutory powers (illegality, irrationality, and procedural impropriety), subject to an important qualification: that the particular prerogative is susceptible to judicial review. Lord

---

[91] *Prohibitions del Roy* (1607) 12 Co Rep 63, 77 ER 1342; *Case of Proclamations* (n 1); *Rustomjee* (n 10); *Chandler* (n 23).
[92] *China Navigation* (n 17) 218.   [93] *Chandler* (n 23) 788.
[94] ECS Wade, 'Act of State in English Law' (1934) 15 British Yearbook of International Law 98; P Cane 'Prerogative Acts, Acts of State and Justiciability' (1980) 29 International and Comparative Law Quarterly 680.
[95] [1921] 2 AC 262, 290 (HL).
[96] *Nissan* (n 66) 231; *Kuwait Airways Corp v Iraq Airways Corp* [2002] 2 AC 883 [265]: 'the non-justiciability principle can only be understood in relation to earlier authority on the act of state doctrine, to which it is related.' See also Cane (n 94) 680; A Perreau-Saussine, 'British Acts of State in English Courts' [2007] British Yearbook of International Law 176.
[97] *GCHQ* (n 89).

Scarman concluded: 'Today... the controlling factor in determining whether the exercise of prerogative power is subject to judicial review is not its source but its subject-matter.'[98] Subject-matter goes to justiciability, not jurisdiction. If a question arises as to the legality of an action taken by the executive, the court has jurisdiction to entertain the question unless the court's powers have been expressly removed or restricted by Parliament.[99] The editors of *De Smith's Judicial Review* declare: 'Judicial review has developed to the point where it is possible to say that no power—whether statutory or under the prerogative—is any longer inherently unreviewable.'[100]

Justiciability

1 Introduction

Post-*GCHQ*, the starting point is that the courts possess jurisdiction to review all exercises of governmental power. However, the fact that a court possesses jurisdiction does not necessarily mean that it should decide the issue raised in the particular case, or that it can provide an effective remedy: these matters go to the justiciability of the particular issue. In determining whether or not a particular issue is justiciable, the courts will evaluate various criteria which compare relative institutional competence and legitimacy to determine that issue. In the *CND* case, Maurice Kay J described justiciability as rules 'the courts have imposed upon themselves in recognition of the limits of judicial expertise and of the proper demarcation between the role of the courts and the responsibilities of the executive under our constitutional settlement'.[101]

Justiciability is a judicial doctrine, which means that its content and application evolve over time. In *Al Rawi*, Laws LJ summarized the changed approach to jurisdiction and justiciability in a case reviewing the exercise of the foreign policy prerogative:[102]

> A generation or more ago the courts would, we think, have said there was no jurisdiction to conduct such a review. More recently the line would have been—has been—that the conduct of foreign relations is so particularly the responsibility of government that it would be wrong for the courts to tread such ground; and aside from the division of constitutional territory, the courts have not the competence to pass objective judgment, hardening into law, in so intricate an area of state practice.

---

[98] *GCHQ* (n 89) 407.
[99] *R v Criminal Injuries Compensation Board, ex parte P* [1995] 1 All ER 845, 855.
[100] J Jowell, A Le Sueur, H Woolf, *De Smith's Judicial Review*, 6th edn (Sweet and Maxwell 2007) 15.
[101] *CND* (n 39) [50].
[102] *R (on the application of Al Rawi) v Secretary of State for Foreign and Commonwealth Affairs* [2006] EWCA Civ 1279, [2008] QB 289 [2].

There are various definitions and uses of the term 'justiciability'.[103] Here, I use the term to mean the aptness of a question for judicial solution. In this sense, a 'non-justiciable issue is one in respect of which there is no satisfactory legal yardstick by which the issue can be resolved'.[104] The proper focus of justiciability should be the discrete issue or question in its particular context. I reject the broader concept of justiciability, which has been employed to identify certain zones of decision-making (including national security) immune from judicial review.[105] The focus on subject-matter and context was emphasized in *Abbasi*: justiciability depends 'not on general principle, but on subject-matter and suitability in the particular case'.[106]

Justiciability is usually decided at the striking out stage or determined as a preliminary issue. When the court finds an issue to be non-justiciable, the court will not make a determination on that issue. The effect of a finding of non-justiciability will depend upon the particular case; the court might find the whole case cannot be determined at all because the central issues are non-justiciable, or it might be that only certain issues in the case are non-justiciable.

The following discussion evaluates the justiciability of the war prerogative. The first section reviews the development of justiciability in this context. It will draw where appropriate on case law in related subject-matters, in particular national security and foreign relations. The second section evaluates the use of justiciability in war prerogative cases. It argues that the continued use of justiciability is useful and justified in this context and identifies the criteria that the court should evaluate when determining the justiciability of an issue.

2 Development of Justiciability

Since *GCHQ*, justiciability has been the determining factor in deciding whether or not the exercise of a particular executive power is susceptible to judicial review.[107] However, even before *GCHQ* opened the exercise of prerogative

---

[103] For comment, see G Marshall, 'Justiciability' in AG Guest (ed), *Oxford Essays in Jurisprudence* (OUP 1961) 265; B Harris, 'Judicial Review, Justiciability and the Prerogative of Mercy' (2003) 62 Cambridge Law Journal 631, 644; JA King, 'Institutional Approaches to Judicial Restraint' (2008) 28 Oxford Journal of Legal Studies 409, 420–2; P Daly, 'Justiciability and the "Political Question Doctrine" '[2010] Public Law 160–78.

[104] *Curtis v Minister of Defence* [2002] 2 NZLR 744, 752 (NZ), in which the NZ Court of Appeal held that whether the minister's decision to disband the air combat force of the Royal NZ Air Force had left the the air force insufficiently armed was a non-justiciable question.

[105] This broader concept of justiciability has sometimes been labelled 'primary justiciability': see Harris (n 103) 644; Daly (n 103).

[106] *R (on the application of Abbasi) v Secretary of State for Foreign and Commonwealth Affairs* [2002] EWCA Civ 1598, [2003] UKHRR 76 [85].

[107] *GCHQ* (n 89) 407 (Lord Scarman); 411 (Lord Diplock); 418 (Lord Roskill).

power to judicial review, the courts justified their refusal to review exercises of the war prerogative with justiciability-type arguments.[108] Although the exercise of prerogative power was patently non-reviewable, in cases such as *China Navigation*[109] and *Chandler*,[110] the courts identified the exercise of the war prerogative as unsuitable for judicial consideration for reasons of institutional competence and legitimacy. In *China Navigation*, for example, the judges identified the Crown's 'imperfect obligation' of protection as non-justiciable and legally unenforceable because there were no legal rules or standards that could be applied in situations where the Crown had allegedly failed to perform its obligation.[111] Likewise, in *Chandler* the judges went into detail as to why decisions concerning the disposition and armament of the armed forces were unsuitable for judicial determination.

In *GCHQ*, their Lordships continued this line of reasoning by identifying certain powers as non-justiciable on account of their subject-matter. They classified certain executive functions to be matters of 'high policy' and non-justiciable, and included the powers of making war and deploying the armed forces. Lord Fraser declared that 'many of the most important prerogative powers concerned with control of the armed forces and with foreign policy are matters which are unsuitable for discussion or review in the Law Court'.[112]

In addition to the justiciability test based on the subject-matter of the particular power, *GCHQ* created a second potential barrier to review of certain prerogatives: the 'national security trump'.[113] In *GCHQ*, the House of Lords held that it could not review the factual finding that the Prime Minister had acted in the interests of national security in prohibiting GCHQ employees from belonging to a union. The Prime Minister was the sole judge of what the interests of national security required.

The effect of this 'national security trump' was that, if an exercise of a prerogative (or statutory) power had national security implications, the courts would find the issues raised non-justiciable. This meant that (1) prerogative powers concerned with foreign policy and the control of the armed forces were non-justiciable, and (2) the 'national security trump' established 'no-go' zones for the courts. The total effect rendered matters falling within either (1) or (2) beyond the purview of the courts. Writing extra-judicially in 1995,

---

[108] D McGoldrick, 'The Boundaries of Justiciability' (2010) 59 International and Comparative Law Quarterly 981, 983 comments that the terms 'justiciability' and 'jurisdiction' also appear to have been used interchangeably.
[109] *China Navigation* (n 17).   [110] *Chandler* (n 23).
[111] *China Navigation* (n 17) 211–13.   [112] *GCHQ* (n 89) 398.
[113] C Forsyth, 'Judicial Review, the Royal Prerogative and National Security' [1985] 36 Northern Ireland Legal Quarterly 25.

Jurisdiction and Justiciability 129

Simon Brown LJ observed how the words 'national security' had acquired 'an almost mystical significance. The mere incantation of the phrase of itself instantly discourages the court from satisfactorily fulfilling its normal role of deciding where the balance of public interest lies.'[114]

Since *GCHQ*, the courts have softened their approach to both (1) and (2). An increasing range of prerogative powers which touch upon foreign policy or war have been rendered subject to judicial review, and the fact that a case has national security implications no longer renders it non-justiciable. An early demonstration of the first point was *R v Secretary of State for Foreign and Commonwealth Affairs, ex parte Everett*.[115] It held that the decision whether or not to issue a passport to a citizen under the prerogative was reviewable, because it was an administrative decision which affected the rights of the individual and was unlikely to have foreign policy implications. Twenty years later, an Order of Council made under prerogative power in respect of a British Overseas Territory was justiciable;[116] and the Divisional Court suggested that a decision to ratify a treaty was not altogether outside the scope of judicial review.[117]

Although a broader range of prerogative powers are now considered apt for judicial consideration, the courts have repeatedly held that decisions taken by the executive in its dealings with foreign states are non-justiciable.[118] Matters of 'high policy', including the deployment of the armed forces and the conduct of foreign policy, continue to be treated as beyond judicial purview on account of their non-justiciability. In *CND*, Maurice Kay J observed that the areas Lord Roskill identified in *GCHQ* as non-justiciable have reduced, but the 'authorities provide no hint of retreat in relation to the subject-matter of the present case...Foreign policy and the deployment of the armed forces remain non-justiciable'.[119] In the same case, Richards J declared: 'In my view it is unthinkable that the national courts would entertain a challenge to a government decision to declare war or to authorise the use of armed force against a third country. That is a classic example of a non-justiciable decision.'[120] In another case, Laws LJ described as a hopeless proposition the suggestion that

---

[114] S Brown LJ, 'Public Interest Immunity' [1994] Public Law 579, 589.
[115] [1989] QB 811 (CA). [116] *Bancoult* (n 88).
[117] *R (on the application of Wheeler) v Prime Minister* [2008] EWHC 1409 (Admin) [55]. The court however considered that the subject-matter, nature, and context of the issue in this case placed it in the realm of politics, not the courts, and it was therefore non-justiciable.
[118] *R v Secretary of State for Foreign and Commonwealth Affairs, ex parte Pirbhai* (1985) 107 ILR 462, 479; *R v Secretary of State for Foreign and Commonwealth Affairs, ex parte Ferhut Butt* (1999) 116 ILR 607, 615, and 622; *R (on the application of Suresh and Manickavasagam) v Secretary of State for the Home Department* [2001] EWHC Admin 1028.
[119] *CND* (n 39) [50]. [120] *CND* (n 39) [59].

'the court should dictate to the executive government steps that it should take in the course of executing foreign policy'.[121]

In *Abbasi*, the Court of Appeal considered these issues in depth.[122] The court held there was no scope for judicial review of a refusal to render diplomatic assistance to Mr Abbasi (a British national imprisoned in Guantanamo Bay), who was suffering violation of a fundamental human right by the actions of a foreign state. Relying on *GCHQ*, the court said that the 'issue of justiciability depends, not on general principle, but on subject matter and suitability in the particular case'.[123] The court held that the decision whether or not to make diplomatic representations, and if so in what form, was for the discretion of the Secretary of State, who must be free to give full weight to foreign policy considerations. Such considerations were non-justiciable: 'the courts cannot enter the forbidden areas, including decisions affecting foreign policy'.[124] However, that does not mean, the court said, that the whole process is immune from judicial scrutiny: the citizen has a legitimate expectation that his or her request will be 'considered' (as consistent with published policy) and that all relevant factors will be thrown into the balance.[125] The court left open the possibility for judicial review in the 'extreme case', where (contrary to its stated practice) the Foreign and Commonwealth Office were to refuse even to consider whether to make diplomatic representations on behalf of a subject whose fundamental rights were being violated. In such a case, the court hypothesized, it would be appropriate for the court to make a mandatory order to the Foreign Secretary to give appropriate consideration to the applicant's case.[126] The court stressed that the context and circumstances of the particular case were key. The court's determination of whether a particular issue was justiciable, and if so, the nature and extent of the court's intervention, must be made within the circumstances of each case.[127]

The Supreme Court's decision in *Rahmatullah*[128] is a good example of the application of the specific and nuanced approach advocated in *Abbasi*. *Rahmatullah* concerned a Pakistani national who had been taken into custody by British forces before being transferred to US forces in accordance with the terms of a memorandum of understanding between the two countries. Mr Rahmatullah was taken by US forces to Afghanistan and kept in detention. The Supreme Court commented on the obligations of the UK government under international law as relevant to Mr Rahmatullah's entitlement to habeas corpus. Lord Kerr (with whom Lord Dyson and Lord Wilson agreed) said that 'the UK

---

[121] *Foday Saybana Sankoh* (2000) 119 ILR 389, 396.   [122] *Abbasi* (n 106).
[123] *Abbasi* (n 106) [85].   [124] *Abbasi* (n 106) [106].
[125] *Abbasi* (n 106) [99].   [126] *Abbasi* (n 106) [104].   [127] *Abbasi* (n 106) [105].
[128] *Secretary of State for Foreign and Commonwealth Affairs v Rahmatullah* [2012] UKSC 48.

government was under a clear obligation, on becoming aware of any failure on the part of the US to comply with any provisions of [the Geneva Convention IV], to correct the situation or to request the return of Mr Rahmatullah'.[129] This required the UK government to 'take effective measures' to correct the breaches of the Geneva Convention by, for instance, questioning the transfer of Mr Rahmatullah at the time he was removed and making representations at the time that the authorities became aware of it.[130] The majority rejected the submission that requiring the government to seek Mr Rahmatullah's return was an inappropriate intrusion into the affairs of state or an attempt to 'dictate to the executive government steps that it should take in the course of executing Government foreign policy'.[131] Lord Kerr said that the Court of Appeal's decision requiring the Secretaries of State to make a return to the writ did not amount to an instruction to the government to demand Mr Rahmatullah's release. Instead, he said, it requires the government to test whether it has the control that it appeared to have over his custody and to exercise the control it appears to have or explain why it is not possible to do so.[132] Lord Kerr was careful, however, to distinguish the claim to habeas corpus (a remedy which must be granted as a matter of automatic entitlement if the conditions for its issue are satisfied) from a claim of judicial review (which can be withheld on a discretionary basis). Lord Carnwath and Lady Hale went further and said that the UK government's actions (in particular, its letter to the USA government) were inadequate, and rejected the Court of Appeal's finding that the court should not go behind the 'language of diplomacy' for reasons of potential sensitivity.[133] Lord Carnwath and Lady Hale asserted: 'Where liberty is at stake, it is not the court's job to speculate as to the political sensitivities which may be in play.'[134]

Recent cases indicate a softening of the courts' approach to the justiciability of the government's prerogatives over war and foreign affairs. Although the courts have stressed they will be 'very slow' to intervene in the exercise of these prerogatives, they have not absolutely ruled out judicial scrutiny. The judicial attitude is one of caution and reticence—but, unlike in earlier precedents, appears to leave open the possibility for review in the extreme case. In *R v Jones (Margaret)*, Lord Bingham summarized the position thus:[135]

there are well established rules that the courts will be very slow to review the exercise of prerogative powers in relation to the conduct of foreign affairs and the deployment of the armed services, and are very slow to adjudicate upon rights arising out of transactions entered into by sovereign states on the plane of international law.

---

[129] *Rahmatullah* (n 128) [38]. [130] *Rahmatullah* (n 128) [39].
[131] Quoting Laws LJ in *Foday Saybana Sankoh* (n 121) [9]. [132] *Rahmatullah* (n 128) [60].
[133] *Rahmatullah* (n 128) [125]–[130]. [134] *Rahmatullah* (n 128) [129].
[135] *R v Jones (Margaret)* [2006] UKHL 16, [2007] 1 AC 136, [30].

The second obstacle to review identified in *GCHQ*—the 'national security trump'—has also been significantly modified. The fact that a case touches upon national security no longer renders it non-justiciable. An early indication of this point was *ex parte Smith*,[136] where the Court of Appeal accepted without argument the justiciability of the legality of the policy banning homosexuals from serving in the military. In the judgment of the Divisional Court, Simon Brown LJ considered that only true questions of national security, over which the courts really do lack the expertise or material to form a judgment, would be non-justiciable.[137] In *ex parte Smith*, the issue was justiciable, even though it touched on national security, because it involved individual human rights and did not involve operational considerations.[138]

The cases dealing with recent legislative and executive measures in the 'war on terror' confirm the justiciability of issues of national security. The national security context of decision-making is now mostly regarded as going to the proper extent of judicial deference to the executive rather than to the issue of justiciability.[139] Lord Steyn in *Rehman* declared that it was 'well established in the case law that issues of national security do not fall beyond the competence of the courts'.[140] However, his Lordship added that this must be read subject to the proviso that: 'It is, however, self-evidently right that national courts must give great weight to the views of the executive on matters of national security.'[141] The courts may find it appropriate to defer to the executive in relation to specific issues relating to national security, but they no longer treat national security implications as a trump which places the case outside the purview of the courts.

3 Continued Relevance and Utility of Justiciability

Some have critiqued the use of justiciability on the grounds that it amounts to unjustified judicial abstention.[142] The main critiques are that the use of justiciability 'insulates' certain types of governmental action by declaring those actions to be inherently unreviewable;[143] and is an invalid and unjustified

---

[136] *R v Ministry of Defence, ex parte Smith* [1996] QB 517.
[137] *ex parte Smith* (n 135).   [138] *ex parte Smith* (n 135) 539 (Simon Brown LJ).
[139] A Kavanagh, 'Defending Deference in Public Law and Constitutional Theory' (2010) 126 Law Quarterly Review 222, 241–2; 'Constitutionalism, Counterterrorism, and the Courts: Changes in the British Constitutional Landscape' (2011) 9 International Journal of Constitutional Law 172.
[140] *Secretary of State for the Home Department v Rehman* [2001] UKHL 47, [2003] 1 AC 153 [31].
[141] *Rehman* (n 140) [31].
[142] Kavanagh, 'Defending Deference' (n 139) 240–2. See also TRS Allan, 'Human Rights and Judicial Review: A Critique of Due Deference' [2006] Cambridge Law Journal 671, 671–2, 688–9; J King, 'The Justiciability of Resource Allocation' (2007) 70 Modern Law Review 197, 198; King (n 103) 412–3, 421–4; Kavanagh, 'Constitutionalism, Counterterrorism, and the Courts' (n 139).
[143] Kavanagh, 'Defending Deference' (n 139) 240–2; Allan (n 143) 680–1, 683, 688–9, 692, 694–5.

abdication of the courts' role of protecting human rights and/or upholding the rule of law. Some commentators advocate abandoning the use of justiciability in favour of applying normal principles of deference because deference is a 'less drastic judicial option' than non-justiciability.[144]

I have three responses to those who advocate abandoning justiciability in favour of deference. First, the commentators who advocate abandoning justiciability tend to focus their objections to justiciability on its blunt use to insulate entire subject-matters from judicial review. I also object to justiciability being used in this way: in the past justiciability was too frequently and too broadly employed by the courts, with the effect of insulating from judicial review wide swathes of governmental decision-making and action. However, I argue that a narrower and more nuanced concept of justiciability has continued relevance and utility in the context of potential review of the war prerogative. Secondly, the commentators who advocate abandoning justiciability tend to use HRA cases to support their arguments. They have not addressed their arguments to the potential judicial review of the war prerogative or considered whether even the most deferential review would be appropriate in this context.[145] Judicial review of governmental action which impinges upon an individual's rights raises very different issues from judicial review of the government's exercise of its war prerogative. Thirdly, I agree with David Dyzenhaus' argument that 'grey' holes can be more pernicious than 'black' holes: half-hearted judicial oversight might be worse than no judicial oversight at all. Half-hearted or 'light touch' judicial review might mean that all that judges are doing is plastering a 'veneer of legality' over the exercise of exceptional powers.[146]

The use of justiciability is justified in the context of judicial review of the war prerogative. The nature of issues connected with the exercise of the war prerogative means that they are likely, in all but the most extraordinary case, to be more suitable for determination by the political branches than the courts. The identification and evaluation of the criteria relevant to assessing the justiciability of an issue highlights why the war prerogative is unlikely to be suitable for judicial consideration and determination.[147] Further, the

---

[144] Kavanagh, 'Defending Deference' (n 139) 241. Although, in a later article, Kavanagh concedes that justiciability is justified in some contexts: 'Constitutionalism, Counterterrorism, and the Courts' (n 139) 174. See also King (n 103) 421–2, who describes non-justiciability as 'a rather nuclear option' that 'creates zones of legal unaccountability'.

[145] For a useful examination of the application of justiciability and deference principles in the context of the war prerogative, see D Jenkins, 'Judicial Review under a British War Powers Act' (2010) 43 Vanderbilt Journal of Transnational Law 611. Jenkins argues that justiciability has continued utility in this context.

[146] D Dyzenhaus, *The Constitution of Law: Legality in a Time of Emergency* (CUP 2006) 3.

[147] See the discussion and the citations at nn 154–190.

discussion of hypothetical challenges to the war prerogative later in this chapter shows that it is difficult to see how an attempted challenge could be viable or successful.[148]

The Evaluation of Justiciability

1 Introduction

Justiciability and deference are different facets of the 'ordinary respect which the courts show to the substantive decisions of the political branches'.[149] Each concept has continued relevance and utility. When a court decides that an issue falling within its jurisdiction is non-justiciable, it is exercising its discretion to determine whether it is appropriate to exercise the court's powers. A determination of justiciability is based upon the court's assessment of the relative institutional competence and legitimacy of the courts and the political branches to consider and determine an issue.[150] On this analysis, justiciability and deference are not wholly distinct concepts.[151] When deciding to abstain from judicial review, or when according deference to the decision of another governmental institution, the court is making an assessment of relative institutional competence and legitimacy.[152]

The court will consider certain criteria to assess the justiciability of an issue. The criteria are guidelines for assessing a court's competency and legitimacy to consider and determine a particular issue rather than for generally classifying subject-matter as permanently justiciable or not. A court's assessment of justiciability is a contextual, case-by-case analysis of its own institutional competency and legitimacy to adjudicate the particular issue in question, relative to the competency and legitimacy of other governmental institutions.[153] It is important that the court flesh out its reasoning for its assessment of the justiciability of an issue: it is not enough simply to state that a matter is unsuitable for judicial resolution.

---

[148] See the discussion and citations at nn 191–218.

[149] L Henkin, 'Is There a "Political Question" Doctrine?' (1976) 85 Yale Law Journal 597, 605. See also the discussion of these issues in Jenkins (n 144) esp 645–6.

[150] See Lord Steyn's analysis of the courts' discretion to defer to the determinations of other governmental institutions: 'Deference: A Tangled Story' [2005] Public Law 346, 352.

[151] See the discussion in M Elliot, 'Judicial Review's Scope, Foundations and Purposes: Joining the Dots' [2012] New Zealand Law Review 75.

[152] See McGoldrick (n 108) esp pt III for an examination of the rationales for the principle of justiciability.

[153] See Neil Komesar, who emphasizes that the evaluation of institutional competence must be based upon a comparative evaluation of which institution is the best among the available alternatives for resolving a given problem: N Komesar, *Imperfect Alternatives: Choosing Institutions in Law, Economics and Public Policy* (University of Chicago Press 1997).

Jurisdiction and Justiciability 135

The following criteria are relevant to a court's evaluation of the justiciability of an issue:

- the constitutional allocation of functions and powers,
- the contention that certain types of decisions should be made by democratically elected or responsible institutions,
- relative expertise and competence over the subject-matter of the issue in question, and
- the potential impact of the courts intervening in a political decision which has already been made.

2 Constitutional Allocation

The courts have placed significant weight on the constitutional allocation of functions and powers amongst governmental institutions when assessing the justiciability of an issue connected with the war prerogative. The courts have held that the exercise of the war prerogative is not subject to judicial review because, according to the constitutional allocation of powers and functions, its exercise is for the executive alone.[154] Lord Radcliffe in *Chandler* said:[155]

If the methods of arming the defence forces and the disposition of those forces are at the decision of Her Majesty's Ministers for the time being, as we know that they are, it is not within the competence of a court of law to try the issue whether it would be better for the country that that armament or those dispositions should be different.

The English courts cannot point to a written constitution which explicitly identifies and allocates governmental functions and powers. Instead, the courts have relied on a long history of executive responsibility for war, national security, and foreign policy.[156] More recently judges have referred to the 'separation of powers' as determining the powers and functions of governmental institutions.[157] According to the separation of powers, '[a]s a matter

---

[154] *Chandler* (n 23) 791 (Lord Reid); 796 (Lord Radcliffe); 800 (Lord Hodson). See also the cases cited in the earlier section of this chapter, including *China Navigation* (n 17); *CND* (n 39).

[155] *Chandler* (n 23) 796.

[156] For statements as to the executive's responsibility for national security and foreign affairs see *Rehman* (n 140) [50]–[53] (Lord Hoffmann); *Al Rawi* (n 102) [2] (Laws LJ); *R (on the application of Corner House Research) v Director of the Serious Fraud Office* [2009] 1 AC 756, [2008] UKHL 60; *R (on the application of Al-Haq) v Secretary of State for Foreign and Commonwealth Affairs* [2009] EWHC 1910 (Admin); *R (on the application of Mohamed) v Foreign Secretary (No 2)* [2010] EWCA Civ 65, [2010] EWCA Civ 158, [2010] 3 WLR 554 [131] (Lord Neuberger MR), [44] (Lord Judge CJ).

[157] See, eg, Lord Hoffmann in *R (on the application of ProLife) v British Broadcasting Corporation* [2003] UKHL 23, [2004] 1 AC 185 [75]: 'In a society based upon the rule of law and the separation of powers, it is necessary to decide which branch of government has in any particular instance the decision-making power and what the legal limits of that power are.' See further Lord Hoffmann, 'The COMBAR Lecture 2001: Separation of Powers' [2002] Judicial Review 137.

of principle, decisions in connection with national security are primarily entrusted to the executive, ultimately to Government Ministers, and not to the judiciary'.[158]

In two further respects, arguments based on the constitutional allocation of functions are relevant to the evaluation of justiciability. First, the courts have emphasized Parliament's constitutional role as the primary scrutinizer of the executive when finding the exercise of the war prerogative unsuitable for judicial consideration and determination. In several of the cases dealing directly with the exercise of the war prerogative, judges have observed that the way in which the Crown deploys the armed forces may 'form the subject of just criticism in the House of Commons'.[159] In *ex parte Smith* the Divisional Court considered it highly relevant that Parliament and a select committee had recently debated the policy regarding homosexuals in the military.[160] In *Gentle*, Lord Hope identified questions about the legality of a military action to be a matter of political judgement, for the conduct of which ministers are answerable to Parliament, and ultimately to the electorate.[161] In *Smith*, Lord Rodger identified Parliament as the appropriate forum for raising and debating choices about matters such as the armament and transport of the armed forces because these are issues 'which are essentially political rather than legal'.[162] The courts have also pointed to the Commons' financial controls over the executive's maintenance and deployment of the armed forces.[163] In these cases, the courts are using arguments based on the constitutional allocation of powers to identify Parliament (not the courts) as holding primary responsibility for scrutinizing the exercise of the war prerogative. It is an implicit recognition that the political branches ought to take responsibility for such decisions and that it is normally outside the courts' institutional competence and legitimacy to intervene.

Secondly, arguments based on the constitutional allocation of functions are also relevant when individual rights are in play. The courts have long claimed their responsibility to protect individual rights against executive action. Their

---

[158] *Mohamed* (n 156) [131].

[159] *China Navigation* (n 17) 230. Some judges have also pointed to the ability of individuals to express their disagreement with government policy through lawful protests or at the ballot box. See, eg, *Chandler* (n 23) 791; *Marchoiri* (n 14) [30].

[160] *ex parte Smith* (n 136) 540 and 545. See also the statements by Sir Thomas Bingham MR on the appeal to the Court of Appeal, where he observed that the policy 'was supported by both Houses of Parliament' (558).

[161] *Gentle* (n 41) [24].

[162] *R (on the application of Smith) v Oxfordshire Assistant Deputy Coroner* [2010] UKSC 29, [2010] 3 WLR 223 [127].

[163] *China Navigation* (n 17) 234.

constitutional function as the guardian of individual rights will be relevant in assessing justiciability: a strong human rights dimension will count in favour of the courts' intervention, including in subject areas, such as national security, where the courts may be otherwise reluctant to intervene.[164]

By our unwritten constitution, the executive possesses primary responsibility and decision-making power for matters of war, national security, and foreign policy. However, the courts should not overplay arguments as to constitutional allocations of functions and powers. In the absence of a written constitution demarcating strict lines of authority and responsibility, the courts should not employ an assertion of executive responsibility for national security on its own to find that prerogative powers over war and foreign policy are non-justiciable.[165] To do so would be to apply an inappropriately strict and formalist conception of separation of powers—a conception which has no relevance to English constitutional arrangements, where powers, functions, and institutions are fused and not separated along strict lines. A healthier approach to the constitutional allocation of governmental powers and functions is to recognize the potential for all governmental institutions to contribute to their exercise, control, or scrutiny. The executive has primary responsibility for the initiation, formulation, and implementation of policies and actions concerning war, national security, and foreign policy; but Parliament and the courts can and should, with proper regard to their institutional competencies and legitimacies, participate in the execution and scrutiny of those policies and actions. This approach is founded on principles of comity and respect, rather than artificial and formalist attempts to carve out areas of exclusive power. A strong factor in the evaluation of the justiciability of an issue connected with the war prerogative will be the executive's primary responsibility for war and national security. It should not, however, be the sole factor in that evaluation.

3 Democratic Arguments

The second relevant factor in the justiciability calculation is 'democratic arguments': the contention that certain types of decisions should be made by democratically elected or responsible institutions. The types of decisions commonly identified as decisions that should be made by democratically elected or responsible institutions include decisions made in the national interest, 'policy'[166] or

---

[164] See, eg, the comments of Lord Nicholls in *Belmarsh* (n 16) [79].
[165] For support for this view, see, eg, Steyn (n 149); D Feldman, 'Human Rights, Terrorism and Risk: The Roles of Politicians and Judges' [2006] Public Law 364, 375–7; D Dyzenhaus, 'Deference, Security and Human Rights' in BJ Goold and L Lazarus (eds), *Security and Human Rights* (Hart Publishing 2007) 125, 136–7.
[166] Most definitions of 'policy' decisions refer to Ronald Dworkin's work. Dworkin defines a policy as something that sets out a goal to be reached—generally an improvement in some economic,

'political' decisions,[167] and decisions that have widespread effects on the community. A decision to deploy the armed forces could fall under each of these types of decisions.

The courts have used democratic arguments to explain why primary responsibility for war and national security is vested in the executive and why the courts should accord appropriate deference to the executive's decisions on these subjects. Much has been written on the relevance of democratic arguments to determining the appropriate level of deference owed by the courts to the elected branches.[168] Lord Hoffmann, in a postscript to *Rehman*, declared that decisions about national security are decisions which have 'serious potential results for the community' and 'require a legitimacy which can be conferred only by entrusting them to persons responsible to the community through the democratic process'.[169] In *Marchoiri* Laws LJ identified the executive's democratic mandate and accountability as justifying the allocation of responsibility for national security and defence to the executive: 'There is not, and cannot be, any expectation that the unelected judiciary play any role in such questions, remotely comparable to that of government.'[170]

The relevance and strength of the 'democratic arguments' in the justiciability calculation will depend upon the particular power and issue in question. The courts now tend to reject the argument that they should defer automatically to the elected branches based on democratic arguments. The courts draw on their own, separate legitimacy in the conduct of their functions.[171] In a comment about the appropriate extent of deference owed by the court to the executive, Lord Bingham, in *Belmarsh*, said: 'While any decision made

---

political, or social feature of the community. Determinations of policy involve utilitarian calculations of the public good. See, eg, *Taking Rights Seriously* (Harvard University Press 1978) 22.

[167] In *Chandler* (n 23) 791, Lord Reid identified the question of whether it is beneficial to use the armed forces in a particular situation as a 'political question', meaning 'a question of opinion on which anyone actively interested in politics, including jurymen, might consider his own opinion as good as that of anyone else'. Sandra Fredman defines a political question as one which 'can only be made by weighing up different interests according to political criteria': S Fredman, 'From Deference to Democracy: The Role of Equality under the Human Rights Act 1998' [2006] 122 Law Quarterly Review 53, 56.

[168] See, eg, the difference of opinion between Jeffrey Jowell and Murray Hunt on the appropriateness of judicial reliance on democratic legitimacy as a ground for deference: J Jowell, 'Judicial Deference: Civility, Servility or Institutional Capacity?' [2003] Public Law 601; M Hunt, 'Sovereignty's Blight: Why Contemporary Public Law Needs the Concept of "Due Deference"' in N Bamforth and P Leyland (eds), *Public Law in a Multi-Layered Constitution* (Hart 2003) 349.

[169] See Lord Hoffmann, postscript to *Rehman* (n 140) [62]. See also Lord Hoffmann's judgment in *Huang v Secretary of State for the Home Department* [2005] EWCA Civ 105, [2006] QB 1 [53]; and Lord Hoffmann, 'The COMBAR Lecture 2001: Separation of Powers' (n 157).

[170] *Marchoiri* (n 14) [38].

[171] See further Feldman, 'Human Rights, Terrorism and Risk' (n 165) 374–5 on the different sources of legitimacy for governmental institutions and decision-making.

by a representative democratic body must of course command respect, the degree of respect will be conditioned by the nature of the decision.'[172] The nature and consequences of the decision to deploy the armed forces strengthens the argument that its exercise and scrutiny should be left primarily to the elected branches. The decision to deploy the armed forces is a complex decision of wide-ranging effect. It should be made by institutions with a diverse and representative composition that can reflect community opinion and evaluate and balance competing public interests.[173] In the evaluation of justiciability, democratic arguments will be highly relevant, but should not be determinative.

4 Institutional Competence and Expertise

Relative institutional competence and expertise is a crucial criterion in evaluating the justiciability of an issue. The focus is the court's competence and expertise to determine a particular issue relative to the competence and expertise of the other governmental institutions. Issues of war, national security, and foreign policy raise special practical difficulties for the courts. Lord Diplock in *GCHQ* explained why certain prerogatives (including the prerogatives over the deployment of the armed forces and the conduct of foreign relations) remained unsuitable for review:[174]

> Such decisions will generally involve the application of Government policy. The reasons for the decision-maker taking one course rather than another do not normally involve questions to which, if disputed, the judicial process is adapted to provide the right answer, by which I mean that the kind of evidence that is admissible under judicial procedures and the way in which it has to be adduced tend to exclude from the attention of the court competing policy considerations which, if the Executive discretion is to be wisely exercised, need to be weighed against one another—a balancing exercise which judges by their upbringing and experience are ill-qualified to perform.

Issues concerning the conduct of war, foreign policy, and the armed forces are typically identified as axiomatically unsuitable for determination by judicial methods of information-gathering and decision-making. Compared with the government and Parliament, judicial decision-making procedures and methods make the courts ill-equipped to make judgements on these matters. A decision to deploy the armed forces is a paradigm example of a 'polycentric' issue: it involves the interlocking of many related interests.[175] Sandra Fredman explains

---

[172] *Belmarsh* (n 16) [39].
[173] For more on the inherent and instrumental value of democratic decision-making in the context of the war prerogative, see the citations at nn 46–100 in ch 5.
[174] *GCHQ* (n 89) 411.
[175] On polycentricity, see L Fuller, 'The Forms and Limits of Adjudication' (1978–79) 92 Harvard Law Review 353. For more general discussion of the courts' capacity to handle complex policy issues

that '[t]he bipolar, reactive, dispute-based nature of judicial processes means that judges cannot achieve the wide lens necessary to make polycentric decisions'.[176] In *Chandler*, Viscount Radcliffe summed up why issues connected to the war prerogative are inherently unsuitable for judicial determination. He identified the issue in that case ('is it prejudicial to the interests of the State to include nuclear armament in its apparatus of defence?') as exemplifying one of the least triable issues, because its determination depended on numerous and varied considerations:[177]

The question whether it is in the true interests of this country to eclair, retain or house nuclear armaments depends upon an infinity of considerations, military and diplomatic, technical, psychological and moral, and of decisions, tentative or final, which are themselves part assessments of fact and part expectations and hopes.

The decision to deploy the armed forces is a decision 'where there are no predefined legal standards and opinions might reasonably differ on the outcome'.[178] Judicial decision-making typically involves evaluating divergent evidence and opinions and balancing competing interests. Judges come to decisions by applying legal rules and tests to the evidence. However, the decision to deploy is a decision which, in nearly every instance, is unable to be assessed according to legal standards. The decision to deploy armed forces to country X might be one on which individuals reasonably disagree, but it is difficult to see how that decision could be assessed according to existing legal rules and standards.[179] The character of decisions made in the national security context reinforces the inapplicability of legal standards. Decisions about threats to national security and the responses necessary to avert them are often anticipatory, based on risk assessments and factual predictions about what might occur and what people might or might not do.[180] Legal standards and rules are inept to deal with decisions of such an evaluative and tentative nature.

The myriad of types and sources of information relevant to a decision to deploy the armed forces pose practical difficulties for the courts. Relevant information

---

and evidence, see D Butt, 'The Capacity of Courts to Handle Complexity: Report and Analysis of a Workshop Held at St Hugh's College, Oxford' (Foundation for Law, Justice and Society, 5 December 2008) <http://www.fljs.org>.

[176] Fredman (n 167) 56.
[177] *Chandler* (n 23) 799. cf the opinion expressed in C Walker, 'Review of the Prerogative: The Remaining Issues' [1987] Public Law 62.
[178] Fredman (n 167) 56.
[179] See the discussion and citations at nn 191–218, identifying possible challenges to the exercise of the war prerogative on existing grounds of review.
[180] For discussion on the role of uncertainty and risk in national security cases, see T Poole, 'Courts and Conditions of Uncertainty in "Times of Crisis"' [2008] Public Law 234. See also Lord Bingham in *Belmarsh* (n 16) [29] on the 'problematical' nature of predicting the future behaviour of human beings, and how people may reasonably disagree on such predictions.

includes information about weapons capabilities, threats to national security, anticipated responses, international negotiations and diplomacy, international law and politics, and military strategy. Judges are experienced in processing large amounts of complex information and conflicting opinions, and make decisions in areas in which others are more expert than they by assimilating the relevant facts and the opinions of experts.[181] However, the types and sources of information relevant to an assessment of the exercise of the war prerogative would pose particular problems for judges. Some of the information relevant to the assessment may not be admissible according to strict judicial rules of evidence. There would be considerable practical difficulties with attempting to prove, with admissible evidence, issues or questions which would arise in litigation concerning the war prerogative. Even if the information meets the admissibility rules, it might be contrary to national security to consider it in open court. For example in *CND* the court recognized that requiring the government to explain its interpretation of the international instrument in question (relevant to opinions as to the legality of a military invasion of Iraq) would be seriously detrimental to the national interest and conduct of international relations.[182] The courts have options available in some situations to deal with such information privately, either by proceedings *in camera* or through the use of 'special advocates'.[183] However, neither option provides an optimal solution to the problem.[184] The recently enacted Justice and Security Act 2013 provides for a 'closed material procedure' in all civil proceedings, in which sensitive information is concealed from the other party and disclosed only to a special advocate.[185] The Supreme Court has commented that a closed procedure is

---

[181] See JH Ely, 'Suppose Congress Wanted a War Powers Act That Worked' [1988] 88 Columbia Law Review 1379, 1408 for comment on how the nature of the courts' decision-making processes affects their ability to determine issues relating to the exercise of the war power.

[182] *CND* (n 39) [43].

[183] The Anti-Terrorism, Crime and Security Act 2001 and the Prevention of Terrorism Act 2005 allow the appointment of special advocates who may have access to 'closed material' in control order proceedings and Special Immigration Appeals Commission proceedings.

[184] Gus Van Harten identifies some of the weaknesses of the use of secret evidence in judicial decision-making, including the fact that the courts are uniquely reliant on the executive to be fair and forthcoming about confidential information, the dynamic or atmosphere of closed proceedings may condition a judge to favour the security interest over other interests, and the judge is precluded from hearing additional information that can come to light only if the individual or the public is aware of the executive's claims. See G Van Harten, 'Weaknesses of Adjudication in the Face of Secret Evidence' (2009) 19 International Journal of Evidence and Proof 1.

[185] See the concerns about the closed material procedure expressed by the Joint Committee on Human Rights, The Justice and Security Green Paper (2010–12, HL 286, HC 1777). The Intelligence and Security Committee also expressed concern with the overly broad scope of the Act. The Committee thought that only two types of information should be protected by closed hearings: UK intelligence material which might compromise operations, individuals involved, or techniques used; and foreign intelligence material provided by another country on the strict promise of confidentiality. Press release, 27 March 2012 <http://isc.independent.gov.uk/news-archive/27march2012>.

inconsistent with the fundamental common law right to natural justice and is only permissible under statutory authority.[186]

5 Impact of a Judicial Decision

In evaluating justiciability, the court should consider the potential impact that judicial intervention could have for a political determination which has already been made. Some commentators have suggested that, in cases concerning foreign affairs, the courts should be aware of the potential for damage or embarrassment to the national interest from multiple or varying pronouncements by different governmental institutions on a particular issue.[187] I do not think that potential 'embarrassment' should be a relevant consideration in the courts' evaluations of justiciability. However, the courts should be sensitive to the intended and potential unintended effects of their decisions.[188] This concern should make the courts reluctant to intervene in a decision to deploy. It is unlikely that in such a dynamic and complex context, the courts will be able to anticipate accurately all the potential consequences of their intervention. The courts' scrutiny will, in nearly all cases, be retrospective. The decision to deploy will already have been taken and troops will probably be in the field. It could be very detrimental to the national interest (and, potentially, to the safety of the armed forces) for the courts to intervene in a decision to deploy.

6 Availability of a Suitable Remedy

The final criterion in the evaluation of justiciability is the availability of a suitable remedy. Again, this criterion is likely to point in favour of a finding of non-justiciability, particularly in cases of an attempted challenge to a decision to deploy. As noted earlier, the courts should be aware of the potential intended and unintended consequences of their intervention. In the case of a challenge to a decision to deploy, the decision will already have been made and deployment underway. In this situation, it is difficult to see what a suitable remedy could be. Different considerations would apply if an attempted challenge were made before deployment has actually taken place; however, even in this situation, it is difficult to conceive of an appropriate remedy. A suitable remedy might be for the court, as in the *Abbasi* case (discussed earlier in the chapter),[189] to make a mandatory order that the government

---

[186] *Al Rawi v Security Service* [2011] UKSC 34 [69].
[187] See L Collins, 'Foreign Relations and the Judiciary' (2002) 51 International and Comparative Law Quarterly 485, 487–94 for a good discussion of the development of the 'one voice' principle, which holds that the executive and judiciary should speak with one voice in foreign affairs.
[188] CR Sustein, *Legal Reasoning and Political Conflict* (OUP 1996) 45.
[189] *Abbasi* (n 106). See the citations at nn 122–127.

give appropriate consideration to a particular matter when making a decision regarding deployment; for example, the court might make an order that the government consider, in its decision-making process, a UN resolution concerning the planned deployment or the likely impact the decision would have on specific identified individual(s).

7 Conclusion

The evaluation of the justiciability of an issue requires the courts to consider several criteria which go to the relative legitimacy and competence of governmental institutions to determine the particular issue. Some have suggested that justiciability should be replaced by a flexible application of deference principles, which would enable the courts to exercise some degree of review over all governmental decisions or actions. These suggestions have not, however, addressed directly whether or not even the most deferential review would be appropriate for the war prerogative. Judicial review may be appropriate for more peripheral or incidental exercises of power connected with the war prerogative, particularly when individual rights are in play—for example, the policy of homosexuals in the military or the requisition of private property under the prerogative. However, issues as to the manner of exercise of the power to deploy the armed forces are likely, in nearly all cases, to be inappropriate for judicial determination. As Timothy Endicott has written:[190]

> While every public decision ought to be reasonable, *not* every decision can be made more reasonable by judicial review: sometimes because judges cannot be expected to come up with a better conclusion, and sometimes because there are political reasons for someone else to be responsible for it.

In most cases involving the war prerogative, the court is likely to exercise its discretion to find the issue non-justiciable and abstain from review. In an exceptional case the court might find the issue justiciable and entertain a challenge to the exercise of the war prerogative or to some aspect of it. However, even if the court finds that it is appropriate to consider and determine the issue, it will still have to consider the appropriate extent of deference to give to the government's decision. In these exceptional cases the court will most likely accord significant deference to the political branches for reasons of institutional competence and legitimacy. In practice, this means that even if a court found an issue connected with the exercise of the war prerogative to be justiciable it will exert a light standard of review, according significant weight to the judgements of the government.

---

[190] T Endicott, 'The Reason of Law' (2003) 48 American Journal of Jurisprudence 83, 89.

Part IV Review on Established Grounds

Introduction

Putting to one side arguments as to justiciability, it is interesting to hypothesize the likely judicial response to challenges to the exercise of the war prerogative (strictly defined) under the established grounds of review. How would the courts respond to arguments that the exercise of the war prerogative was irrational, or made for improper purpose, or that the decision-maker took into account an irrelevant consideration? In all but the most extraordinary (and probably hypothetical) case, it will be extremely difficult for an applicant to make out a ground of review under the established heads in respect of a decision to deploy the armed forces.[191] Even if he or she were able to, and the court found the issue justiciable, the court would accord such a high degree of deference to the government that it would exert the very lightest of reviews.

The following discussion identifies potential claims and the likely judicial response. Its focus is arguments under the heads of illegality and irrationality. It is difficult to conceive of review on procedural grounds. Rights-based claims are dealt with in a separate section later in the chapter.[192]

Standing

The first hurdle for an applicant is to show that the decision to deploy affected him or her in the sense necessary to establish standing. The test for standing in judicial review proceedings is that the applicant must show 'sufficient interest in the matter to which the application relates'.[193] The question of sufficient interest presents little problem in most applications for judicial review today. There is a trend for standing to be considered as part of the legal and factual context of the whole case.[194] However, difficulties may arise where the applicant is not personally affected and is acting in the public interest.[195] The merit of the case will also likely be taken into account in determining

---

[191] See the brief discussion of these issues in I Leigh, 'The Security Service: The Press and the Courts' [1987] Public Law 12, 17.
[192] See the citations at nn 219–250.   [193] Supreme Court Act 1981, s 31(3).
[194] *Al-Haq* (n 156) [47]–[48], [61]–[62].
[195] In *Al-Haq* (n 156) a foreign NGO was denied standing. In *R (on the application of Evans) v Secretary of State for Defence* [2010] EWHC 1445 (Admin) standing was granted to a peace activist opposed to the wider presence of UK and US armed forces in Afghanistan on the ground that the claim was brought in the public interest. For further on standing in public interest challenges, see D Feldman (ed), *English Public Law*, 2nd edn (Oxford 2009) [17.43]–[17.44].

whether the test for standing is met,[196] which could be a significant hurdle for an applicant seeking to challenge the exercise of the war prerogative.

Illegality

A decision-maker must understand correctly and give effect to the law that regulates its decision-making power.[197] I will consider two types of potential challenge on the ground of illegality: abuse of discretionary power and error of law.

A decision-maker abuses his or her discretionary power by exercising a power for an improper purpose or by taking into account irrelevant considerations. The typical case concerns abuse of a statutory power, but the courts have applied the principles of illegality to review the exercise of certain prerogative powers; most notably, the prerogatives of mercy[198] and stay of proceedings.[199]

A potential claim on the irrelevant consideration ground could be that, in deciding to deploy the armed forces, the government took into account the expected boost in domestic political support the decision would elicit. A potential claim on the improper purpose ground could be that the government exercised its war prerogative for the purpose of obtaining control over oil reserves, not in response to a threat to national security. The courts' likely response to the first claim would be that it is for the government to determine what factors are relevant or irrelevant to a decision to deploy and their relative weight. The decision involves a myriad of considerations. It would be inappropriate, for reasons of legitimacy and institutional competence, for the courts to intervene and find that the government relied on irrelevant factors in the exercise of its war prerogative. There would—in any event—be insurmountable evidential hurdles for the applicant to prove such a claim. The response to the claim based on improper purpose is likely to be the same: it is for the executive to determine the purpose of a deployment. Presumably, the war prerogative must be exercised in the defence of the realm: the Crown is the guardian of the general welfare and its paramount duty is to protect the community. However, it is very unlikely that the courts would enter into detailed consideration of purpose.

A second potential claim under the head of illegality is that the decision-maker made an 'error of law'. On this ground, a possible argument could be that the

---

[196] Feldman (n 195) [17.36]–[17.37].
[197] *GCHQ* (n 89) 408 (Lord Diplock).
[198] *R v Secretary of State for the Home Department, ex parte Bentley* [1994] QB 349.
[199] *R v DPP, ex parte Kebilene* [2000] 2 AC 326; *R (on the application of Pretty) v DPP* [2001] UKHL 20, [2002] 1 AC 800.

government made an error of law by undertaking military action which was illegal in international law. This claim too is likely to fail. The courts have denied their competence to determine the legality at international law of the use of force. In *Gentle*, Lord Hope identified the issue of legality as an issue of international law belonging to the area of relations between states and a matter of political judgement.[200] Baroness Hale thought it was a question which could only be authoritatively decided by the international institutions which police the international treaties governing the law of war.[201]

The approach in *Gentle* had been preceded by similar statements in earlier cases. In *CND*, counsel invited the court to issue an advisory declaration on the meaning of United Nations Resolution 1441 (which concerned the proposed invasion of Iraq), arguing that the courts are the surety that all public power be lawfully conferred and exercised. Simon Brown LJ rejected the argument, stating that the domestic courts are the surety for the lawful exercise of public power only with regard to domestic law. They are not charged with policing the United Kingdom's conduct on the international plane: 'That is for the International Court of Justice.'[202] Two other factors reinforced this finding. First, the court found that it would be detrimental to the UK's conduct of international relations for it to issue an advisory declaration on the meaning of Resolution 1441 because, as a matter of practical politics, other states do not make distinctions between legal assertions by governments and declarations of law by national courts. Secondly, even in respect of the issues over which the court might normally claim competence (such as issues as to legality or human rights), it is artificial and difficult, if not impossible, for the courts to isolate the legal issues from the other issues involved. In *CND* it was not possible to separate neatly the 'legal' issue from the intimately connected political, national security, and international relations considerations:[203]

the nature and subject matter of such a decision [the decision to deploy armed forces] require it to be treated as an indivisible whole rather than breaking it down into legal, political, military and other components and viewing those components in isolation for the purpose of determining whether they are suited to judicial determination.

---

[200] *Gentle* (n 41) [24]. For comment on the courts' approach to challenges to the legality of deployments at international law, see ND White, 'International Law, the UK, and Decisions to Deploy Troops Overseas' (2010) 59 International and Comparative Law Quarterly 814.

[201] *Gentle* (n 41) [58].

[202] *CND* (n 39) [36].

[203] *CND* (n 39) [59]. *CND* was considered in *R v Jones (Margaret)* [2004] EWCA Crim 1981, [2005] QB 259, a criminal case involving allegation of damaging property at an airbase. One of the defences pleaded was a defence of necessity: that they were damaging the airbase in an attempt to prevent the waging of an allegedly illegal war against Iraq. *CND* was considered, but the court held that it was not necessary to consider the issue of justiciability in relation to the claim of the illegality of the Iraq war. See also *Ayliffe v DPP* [2005] EWHC 684 (Admin), [2006] QB 227. Both cases were heard together on appeal in the House of Lords: *R v Jones (Margaret)* (n 135).

Irrationality

Under the head of irrationality, a claim could be made that the government's decision to go to war was an irrational response to a potential or actual threat. Assuming standing and justiciability are made out, the courts would probably apply a strict *Wednesbury* rationality test,[204] which catches only the most outrageous and perverse conduct.

It is extremely unlikely that the courts would find that the deployment of force was an irrational response to a claimed threat to national security. For the court to do so, it would have to assess the nature and extent of the claimed threat to national security and determine whether the decision to deploy was a rational response to that threat. The courts have in most cases held that the Crown is the sole judge of both the nature of the threat and the response necessary to avert it (subject to the provisos described shortly respecting evidential requirements and possible challenges in the extreme case). The classic statement is from *The Zamora*, where Lord Parker declared: 'Those responsible for the national security must be the sole judge of what the national security requires. It would obviously be undesirable that such matters be made the subject of evidence in a court of law or otherwise discussed in public.'[205] Similar was expressed nearly fifty years later by Lord Upjohn in *Burmah Oil*: 'It is clear that the Crown alone must be the judge of the precise emergency and exact point of time when it is necessary to exercise the prerogative in order to defend the country against apprehended invasion or, indeed, to take steps to prepare the country for war against a foreign power';[206] and another twenty years later in *GCHQ*: 'National security is the responsibility of the executive government; what action is needed to protect its interests is…as common sense itself dictates, a matter upon which those upon whom the responsibility rests, and not courts of justice, must have the last word.'[207]

The courts today continue to accord the executive a large degree of discretion, at least to the assessment of the nature of the threat posed to national security. In *Belmarsh* Lord Bingham said that 'great weight' should be attached to the government's evaluation of the nature and extent of the threat posed to national security because they were 'called on to exercise a pre-eminently political judgment'.[208]

The courts have required some evidence for the executive's claims about the threat posed and the response necessary.[209] In practice, though, the courts

---

[204] *Associated Provincial Picture Houses Ltd v Wednesbury Corp* [1948] 1 KB 223.
[205] *Zamora* (n 57) 107. [206] *Burmah Oil* (n 1) 102 (Lord Upjohn).
[207] *GCHQ* (n 89) 406. [208] *Belmarsh* (n 16) [29].
[209] See, eg, Lord Roskill in *GCHQ* (n 89), 420: 'The courts have long shown themselves sensitive to the assertion by the executive that considerations of national security must preclude judicial

have normally found the evidential point satisfied by an affidavit by a senior civil servant. In the *GCHQ* case, the Cabinet Secretary swore that the reason for not consulting the trade unions was that to do so might jeopardize national security by precipitating industrial action. The House of Lords would not go behind that assertion, although seeing as the argument was raised only before the House of Lords, and not the trial judge, it seems fair to be sceptical of the Cabinet Secretary's claim. Some judges have suggested that acceptance of the government's assertions is subject to challenges on the grounds of bad faith, unreasonableness, and abuse.[210] In *GCHQ*, Lord Scarman reserved the possibility that a ministerial decision could be set aside for irrationality,[211] but the other judges did not go so far and the majority decision has been applied. In *CND*, Simon Brown LJ considered it would be improper for the court to reject the government's views of the threat posed by judicial examination of the government's opinion of the legality of the Iraq military action, unless the court 'thought them plainly wrong'.[212]

There are a small number of cases where the courts have held that the executive did not make out its claim that its action was a necessary and proportionate response to a threat to national security. In the wartime case of *The Zamora*,[213] the Privy Council, sitting in Prize and applying international law, found that the government's requisitioning of a vessel carrying copper was unlawful: on the evidence presented, the Crown merely desired to requisition the copper without stipulating the reason or the urgency. In the *Belmarsh* case, Lord Hoffmann rejected the executive's assessment of the threat posed to national security and the rest of the majority rejected the executive's response to that threat when it found that indefinite detention of foreign suspects was discriminatory and disproportionate.[214] The House of Lords stressed that, although the courts should give great weight to the decisions of the executive and the legislature in the national security context, 'deference does not mean abasement'.[215] Recent litigation concerning the suppression of information revealing possible British complicity in torture is another striking example of the courts challenging head-on the executive's claims about

---

investigation of a particular individual grievance. But even in that field the courts will not act on a mere assertion that questions of national security were involved. Evidence is required that the decision under challenge was in fact founded on those facts.'

[210] *Re a Petition of Right* (n 56); *Chandler* (n 23) 809–11. For a recent authority on this point see, eg, *Corner House Research* (n 156).

[211] *GCHQ* (n 89) 406.   [212] *CND* (n 39) [42].
[213] *Zamora* (n 57).   [214] *Belmarsh* (n 16).
[215] *Belmarsh* (n 16) [176] (Lord Rodgers). For comment, see A Kavanagh, 'Judging the Judges under the Human Rights Act: Deference, Disillusionment and the "War on Terror"' [2009] Public Law 287; cf K Ewing, 'The Futility of the Human Rights Act' [2004] Public Law 829; K Ewing and J Tham, 'The Continuing Futility of the Human Rights Act' [2008] Public Law 668.

The War Prerogative and Individual Rights 149

national security.²¹⁶ The court ordered the publication of the information notwithstanding the Foreign Secretary's assertion, in several Public Interest Immunity certifications, that release of the information would lead to a real risk of serious harm to national security. The court considered the nature and content of the information in question and held that its publication would not create a real risk of serious harm to national security.²¹⁷

Although there are indications that in certain circumstances the courts will directly challenge the executive's assessment of a threat to national security and the response needed to avert that threat, it seems extremely unlikely that such challenges might extend to a situation where the executive determines that the required response to a threat is the deployment of armed forces. Where the courts have intervened in the executive's assessment of a threat or the response required, the case has concerned the infringement of an individual's right and both the threat and the response have been specific and targeted in nature. These types of situations are very different from the likely scenario in which the executive determines that the armed forces must be deployed to meet a threat. If the government claims there is a threat to national security which demands the deployment of force, it would be irresponsible of judges, with their lack of access to all of the relevant information, to presume that the threat is insignificant or false. The inherent uncertainty and potential drastic consequences of such a decision would also count against the court's intervention.²¹⁸ It is likely that the courts would not inquire into the evidence on which the executive bases its assessment of the threat, or consider whether the deployment of forces was a rational response to that threat. The courts may be more willing to intervene, however, in cases which are concerned with war, the armed forces, or national security, but not directly with the deployment of force.

Part V The War Prerogative and Individual Rights

Introduction

Even before the introduction of the HRA, the courts showed greater willingness to review the exercise of incidental war powers in cases involving the

---

²¹⁶ *Mohamed* (n 156).
²¹⁷ For examples of other cases indicating a lessening of the judicial subservience to the executive's assessment of a threat and the response required to meet that threat, see *A v Secretary of State for the Home Department* [2005] UKHL 71, [2006] 1 AC 221 (*Torture Evidence*); *JJ* [2007] UKHL 45, [2007] WLR 642; *Secretary of State for the Home Department v E* [2007] UKHL 47, [2007] 3 WLR 720; *MB* [2007] UKHL 46, [2007] 3 WLR 681. For comment, see Poole (n 179); A Tomkins, 'Legislating against Terror' [2002] Public Law 205.
²¹⁸ Kavanagh (n 139) 178–9.

infringement of individual rights. In the nineteenth century and for most of the twentieth century, the courts were most concerned with the protection of individual property rights, while in the late-twentieth century the courts became more involved with the protection of individual civil and political rights as against the exercise of the prerogative. In these cases, the courts identified the infringement of individual rights as a relevant factor both in deciding whether to embark on review of the exercise of the power in question and in determining the appropriate degree of deference to be accorded to the executive in relation to the particular issue in question.[219] In litigation under the HRA, the courts have identified the subject-matter of the war prerogative relevant to determining the scope and performance of the individual right.

The Case Law: Evaluation

In a series of cases during the two world wars, the courts, while upholding the king's prerogative to acquisition property, imposed certain conditions upon the lawful exercise of the power in protection of individual property rights. These cases have been discussed in the section on incidental war powers.[220]

Since the late-twentieth century the courts have focused on civil and political rights rather than property rights. The introduction of the HRA has obviously changed the courts' approach to cases involving individual rights in the national security context. In *Gentle*, Baroness Hale stated: 'As I understand it, it is now common ground that if a Convention right requires the court to examine and adjudicate upon matters which were previously regarded as non-justiciable, then adjudicate it must.'[221] However, the impact that the HRA has had in other cases in the national security sphere has been ameliorated in cases concerned with war. In these cases, the courts have applied different rules regarding the interpretation and protection of Convention rights. The courts' restraint in intervening in war and foreign relations has militated against the existence of the right, restricted its scope, or lowered the standard required for its performance.[222]

---

[219] Pre-HRA, members of the armed forces used rights-based arguments to challenge the policy banning homosexuals in the army: *ex parte Smith* (n 136). See also the ECtHR's decision on appeal in *Smith and Grady v United Kingdom* (1999) 29 EHRR 493.
[220] See the citations at nn 54–66.   [221] *Gentle* (n 41) [60].
[222] *Jones (Margaret)* (n 135) [30], [65]–[67]; *Gentle* (n 41) [8], [60]; *Smith* (n 162). For discussion of the position before these cases were decided, see P Rowe, *The Impact of Human Rights Law on Armed Forces* (CUP 2006) esp 137–41. The European Convention on Human Rights makes special provision for the recognition and protection of rights in times of war and public emergency: see arts 15(1) and 15(2). For comment see A Ashworth, 'Security, Terrorism and the Value of Human Rights' in Goold and Lazarus (n 165) 203, 212–13.

Three features of the HRA jurisprudence in cases concerned with war are noteworthy. First, the HRA's restrictive standing requirements mean that an individual making a claim under the HRA must show that the government's actions had a discrete and identifiable impact on him or her. Section 7 of the HRA provides that only the 'victim' of the impugned act may make a claim. Strasbourg law denies standing to representative bodies and pressure groups unless they themselves are victims of a breach of their Convention rights.[223] Members of the armed forces[224] and individuals directly affected by the conduct of war[225] will probably be able to establish standing. However, individuals falling outside of these two categories may have difficulty showing they were a 'victim' of the exercise of the war prerogative. This would probably rule out, for example, a claim by a UK resident that the decision to invade Iraq made terrorist attacks in the UK more likely, so violating UK residents' right to life.[226] It seems highly unlikely that the court would grant standing in such a claim.

Secondly, the subject-matter of the war prerogative is relevant to the scope and performance of rights, rather than to their existence. The House of Lords/Supreme Court recently considered these issues in *Gentle*[227] and *Smith*,[228] which each concerned soldiers' article 2 rights to life in the context of armed conflict. The court in each case treated the context of armed conflict to be relevant to the scope and performance of article 2 rights, rather than to their existence (or non-existence). The determination of the scope and performance of an individual right must take account of the exigencies of military life and what the exercise of the right would entail.[229] This is consistent with Strasbourg jurisprudence, which has held that 'when interpreting and applying the rules of the Convention' it is necessary to 'bear in mind the particular

---

[223] AW Bradley and KD Ewing, *Constitutional and Administrative Law*, 14th edn (Pearson Education 2007) 769–71.

[224] Members of the army used a claim under the HRA to challenge the discriminatory treatment of Gurka soldiers in relation to pay and pensions: *R (on the application of Purja) v Ministry of Defence* [2003] EWCH Civ 1345, [2004] 1 WLR 289. See also *Gentle* (n 41); *Smith* (n 162).

[225] eg *R (on the application of Al-Skeini) v Secretary of State for Defence* [2007] UKHL 26, [2008] AC 153 [79], [129]. See also judgment of the Grand Chamber: *Al-Skeini v United Kingdom* [2011] 53 EHRR 18.

[226] cf *Operation Dismantle v R* (1985) 18 DLR (4th) 494 (SCC), which dealt with a claim against the government's decision to test nuclear weapons, on the grounds that the testing increased the likelihood of war and the consequent violation of rights under the Charter of Rights and Freedoms. The claim was held to be arguable, but was dismissed on the grounds that there was no causal connection between the testing and any possible violation of rights and, in any case, the issues raised were unsuitable for judicial determination.

[227] *Gentle* (n 41).

[228] *Smith* (n 162).

[229] See *Smith* (n 162) [196] (Lord Mance); and *Gentle* (n 41) [60] (Baroness Hale).

characteristics of military life and its effects on the situation of individual members of the armed forces'.[230] Lord Hope in *Gentle* made clear that article 2 was not an absolute guarantee that nobody would be exposed by the state to situations where his or her life was in danger. The extent of article 2 protection owed to a member of the armed forces must take account of the characteristics of military life, the nature of the activities that they are required to perform, and the risks that they give rise to.[231] Similarly, Lord Rodger in *Smith* said it would be contrary to the very essence of active military service to expect the authorities to ensure that troops are not killed or injured by opposing forces. This fact, he thought, must be relevant in determining whether article 2 obligations have been performed.[232] Lord Mance also considered that the exigencies of military life go to the standard and performance, rather than the existence, of any Convention duty.[233] He recognized that the UK cannot be expected to provide in Iraq the full protective framework which it would be expected to provide domestically, 'but the UK could be expected to take steps to provide proper facilities and proper protection against risks falling within its responsibility or its ability to control or influence when despatching and deploying armed forces overseas.'[234]

Thirdly, the scope of Convention protection extends only to areas over which Britain (or the British armed forces) has actual or exclusive de facto control. Jurisdiction has been a key issue in the leading decisions concerning the application of Convention rights to the conduct of armed conflict. In *Smith* the majority of the Supreme Court thought that the protection of Convention rights extended only to areas over which the British armed forces had exclusive de facto control. These areas included a military base, military hospital, or detention centre, but excluded areas outside of those premises over which the armed forces did not have exclusive control. Paramount in the majority's reasoning was that issues relating to armed hostilities are essentially non-justiciable.[235] These findings were not, however, strictly necessary for the determination of the case before the Court.[236] In *R (on the application of Al-Skeini)*

---

[230] *Engel v The Netherlands* (1976) 1 EHRR 647 [54].
[231] *Gentle* (n 41) [18] (Lord Hope).
[232] *Smith* (n 162) [125].
[233] *Smith* (n 162) [192], [193], [196].
[234] *Smith* (n 162) [194].
[235] See *R Smith)* (n 162), Lord Rodger [125]–[127]; Lord Collins [308]. In addition, the majority gave the following reasons for this finding: the *travaux preparatoires* (Lord Collins [303]), consistency with public international law and state practice (Lord Collins [241]–[246]), the absence of special justification or other policy reasons to justify departure from the starting point of territorial jurisdiction (Lord Phillips [52]–[60]; Lord Hope [91], [104]).
[236] See the discussion of this in *Smith v Ministry of Defence* [2012] EWCA Civ 1365 (CA) esp at [9]–[16].

v Secretary of State for Defence[237] the House of Lords held that the HRA did not apply to the case of five men killed on the street or in their home by British troops in Basrah, because it could not be said that Basrah was under British control at the time, but it did apply in respect of a sixth man killed while in the custody of the British army. On appeal, the Grand Chamber of the European Court of Human Rights came to a different conclusion, but arguably on grounds that are consistent with the authorities of the House of Lords/Supreme Court.[238] The Grand Chamber held that the UK, through its armed forces, exercised such authority and control over the five men killed that those men were brought within the UK's Convention jurisdiction.[239] The Grand Chamber identified two features which, in combination, justified extra-territorial jurisdiction. The first is where state agents use force to bring an individual under the control of the state's authorities: 'What is decisive in such cases is the exercise of physical power over the person in question.'[240] The second is the effective control exercised over the area in question.[241]

Part VI Liability in Tort

Various common law and statutory rules have prohibited claims in tort against the Crown in relation to actions undertaken in war. Until 1947, actions against the Crown in tort were inhibited by two principles: the first that the king could not be impleaded in his own courts, and the second that the king could do no wrong. In 1947, a statutory prohibition on actions in tort by members of the armed forces was introduced by section 10 of the Crown Proceedings Act 1947. Section 10 prevented a claim in respect of the death or injury of a member of the armed forces caused by the negligence of another member of the armed forces provided that the Secretary of State certified that the death or injury was attributable to service. Section 10 acted as a bar to claims in tort even in peacetime conditions. The Crown Proceedings (Armed Forces) Act 1987 removed the blanket protection of section 10. The 1987 Act enables the Secretary of State to revive section 10 in respect of any 'warlike operation'. The Court of Appeal has held that the Ministry of Defence,

---

[237] *Al-Skeini* [2007] UKHL 26, [2008] AC 153 [79], [129]. See also *Al Jedda v Secretary of State for Defence* [2007] UKHL 58, [2008] 1 AC 322; *Al Saadoon v Secretary of State for Defence* [2009] EWCA Civ 7, [2010] QB 486.

[238] *Al-Skeini* [2011] 53 EHRR 18; in *Smith v Ministry of Defence* (n 236) [30] the Court of Appeal thought that the Grand Chamber's decision in *Al-Skeini* was not inconsistent with the Supreme Court's decision in *Smith* (n 162).

[239] *Al-Skeini* (n 238).   [240] *Al-Skeini* (n 238).

[241] *Al-Skeini* (n 238) [138]–[148].

as employer, holds a duty of care to the members of the armed forces, as employees. That duty includes a duty to provide safe systems of work and safe equipment. The fact such provision will involve operational policy issues does not preclude the existence of a duty of care, but will be relevant to the question of whether that duty has been breached.[242]

In addition to the statutory prohibitions on negligence claims against soldiers or the Crown, the courts have also developed a doctrine of combat immunity. The doctrine was established in English law by *Mulcahy v Ministry of Defence*,[243] where the court considered a claim by a soldier who, while serving in the Gulf war, suffered damage to his hearing when a fellow soldier fired a shell. M claimed that the Ministry of Defence was vicariously liable for the soldier's negligence. The court applied the decision of the High Court of Australia in *Shaw Savill*[244] to find that no duty of care was owed.

The case has since been interpreted as establishing a doctrine of combat immunity, which holds that no duty of care is owed in respect of the conduct of active operations in time of war.[245] The doctrine applies to claims made by a member of the armed forces against a fellow member of the armed forces and/or the Crown,[246] and to claims made by third parties against members of the armed forces.[247] Its precise scope is not clear, but Dixon J in the *Shaw Savill* case said: 'It covers attack and resistance, advance and retreat, pursuit and avoidance, reconnaissance and engagement.'[248] Its focus is 'actual engagement' or 'the heat of battle': 'Courts cannot adjudicate on decisions made in active operations.'[249] Issues concerning equipment and training of the armed force might fall outside of the combat immunity's scope.[250]

Part VII Conclusion

My conclusions are based on the premise that the decision to deploy the armed forces is a unique and extraordinary power. The war prerogative is distinguishable from other types of executive powers, including the executive's statutory powers in the sphere of national security, which are, and should be, subjected to judicial review. The courts play a vital role in scrutinizing the activities of the executive in the national security context and in helping to

---

[242] *Smith v Ministry of Defence* (n 236) [45]–[55].   [243] [1996] QB 732.
[244] *Shaw Savill and Albion Co Ltd v The Commonwealth* (1940) 66 CLR 344.
[245] *Bici v Ministry of Defence* [2004] EWHC 786; *Bell v Ministry of Defence* [2003] EWHC 1134.
[246] As in *Mulcahy* (n 243).   [247] *Bici v Ministry of Defence* (n 245).
[248] *Shaw Savill* (n 244) 361–2.   [249] *Smith v Ministry of Defence* (n 236) [59].
[250] *Smith v Ministry of Defence* (n 236) [62].

protect the rights of individuals. I commend recent cases, such as the *Binyam Mohamed* litigation, where the court carefully considered the evidence before it and the executive's claims as to what was necessary in the interests of national security. The Divisional Court held that the executive had failed to make its case for maintaining secrecy over the information which revealed possible British complicity in the torture of Mr Mohamed. Also to be commended are statements such as Lord Bingham's response in the *Belmarsh* case[251] to the Attorney General's argument that courts must submit to the government's assessments of the threat facing the nation and the necessary response. Lord Bingham recognized that, while Parliament, the executive, and judges have 'different functions', 'the function of independent judges charged to interpret and apply the law is universally recognised as a cardinal feature of the modern democratic state, a cornerstone of the rule of law itself'.[252]

The courts in those cases could be seen as living up to David Dyzenhaus' concept of the 'culture of justification', in which 'a political order accepts that all official acts, all exercises of state power, are legal only on condition that they are justified by law where law is understood in an expansive sense, that is, as including fundamental commitments such as those entailed by the principle of legality and respect for human rights'.[253] Professor Dyzenhaus explains that the onus of justification falls on the legislature, the executive, and the judiciary, and is conditioned by their different constitutional roles.

The emphasis on the different constitutional roles of the legislature, the executive, and the judiciary is key. The courts are aware, and should be aware, of their relative institutional strengths and weaknesses and of the limits of their legitimacy. The potential for judicial intervention in the exercise of the war prerogative magnifies issues as to relative institutional competence and legitimacy. The criteria to be considered in the justiciability evaluation, as identified in this chapter, all point to the courts exercising their discretion to abstain from reviewing issues concerned with the executive's exercise of its power to deploy the armed forces. The result of that justiciability evaluation may, however, be different in cases where the issue in question is not directly concerned with how the executive exercised its power to deploy, but with incidental matters (such as the organization of the armed forces) or with the infringement of individual rights. Judicial review is no substitute for political control of the merits, expediency, or efficiency of governmental decisions about war. Half-hearted judicial oversight might be worse than no judicial oversight at all.[254] The onus should be on the legislature, not the courts,

---

[251] *Belmarsh* (n 16).   [252] *Belmarsh* (n 16) [29].   [253] Dyzenhaus (n 165) 137.
[254] Dyzenhaus (n 146) 3.

to scrutinize the executive's exercise of its war prerogative. My proposals for reform to the war prerogative, as outlined in chapters 5 and 6, seek to strengthen Parliament's involvement in, and scrutiny of, the exercise of the war prerogative, and to enable it to play its role in giving expression to the culture of justification.

5
Institutional Mechanisms

Part I Introduction

The proposals detailed in chapter 6 recommend reform of the institutions and processes involved in the exercise of the war prerogative. I propose a substantive role for Parliament, in particular the House of Commons, in the exercise of the power to deploy the armed forces and a 'constitutional back-stop' role for the courts. This chapter sets the theoretical framework for my proposals. It adopts Adrian Vermeule's concept of 'institutional design writ small', which I call 'institutional mechanisms'. Institutional mechanisms are small-scale rules and institutional arrangements, within existing institutions, which aim to advance certain normative goals. The normative goals of my proposed institutional mechanisms are the promotion of democratic values and efficiency in decision-making. I explain how the implementation of institutional mechanisms, within the existing institution of Parliament, can promote these normative goals while ensuring the continued effectiveness of the conduct of war.

Part II Institutional Design

Introduction

Institutional design is concerned with the arrangement and structuring of governmental institutions and processes. My proposals, detailed in the following chapter, recommend reforms of the institutions and processes involved in the exercise of the power to deploy the armed forces. These proposals are an example of what Adrian Vermeule labels 'institutional design writ small' or 'mechanisms of democracy': small-scale rules and institutional arrangements that structure the process by which laws and policies are made, within the context of existing institutions.[1] Vermeule observes that much of the

---

[1] A Vermeule, *Mechanisms of Democracy: Institutional Design Writ Small* (OUP 2007) 4. In this chapter, I draw on Vermeule's conception of 'institutional design writ small' or 'mechanisms of

literature on institutional arrangements focuses on 'institutional design writ large'—such as mass elections, the separation of powers, federalism, and other large-scale institutional structures.[2] In *Mechanisms of Democracy: Institutional Design Writ Small* Vermeule assumes the existence of these basic, large-scale institutional structures and instead turns his attention to smaller-scale institutional devices and innovations that promote normative goals.

Vermeule's ideas are both pragmatic and aspirational. He accepts, for example, that the UK is unlikely to switch from a parliamentary system to one of separated powers: these are 'background institutions' which are 'not going anywhere'.[3] However, assumption of the status quo at the large-scale level does not preclude change at the smaller-scale level, which is where 'institutional design writ small' can be aspirational. Achievable small-scale reforms, within the existing large-scale institutional arrangements, can have large democratizing effects.

My proposals recommend changes to the processes by which decisions are made about war and the establishment of a special joint parliamentary committee to oversee the decision-making process. These are both small-scale changes to institutional arrangements within the large-scale institutional arrangements of the parliamentary system. I call these small-scale changes 'institutional mechanisms'. A mechanism is a process or system by which something comes into being. Institutional mechanisms are small-scale rules and institutional arrangements within the existing large-scale constitutional framework aimed at advancing certain normative goals.

There is an uneasiness in the English context with the concept of institutional design. English constitutional structures and arrangements are largely the result of incremental historical evolution, rather than deliberate design.[4] Goodin labels this the 'evolution' model of social change: by the action of some type of selection mechanisms, certain variants are winnowed out in

democracy', and in particular his idea that small-scale reforms can promote and enhance substantive goals. However, I make use of these conceptions in different ways from Vermeule. Vermeule's identification of potential mechanisms of democracy include the use of sub-majority voting in certain preliminary and procedural questions (such as setting of the agenda, or the publication of certain information) to enable minorities to force public accountability upon majorities; the use of a presumption in favour of the interpretation of an executive or administrative agency unless a supermajority of the judges on a multi-membered panel votes against the agency; optimizing transparency and trying to suppress 'bad' deliberation by limiting transparency at certain stages in the policy-making process; and the establishment of a constitutional committee in Congress, tasked with assessing the constitutional impact of policy and legislative proposals.

[2] Vermeule (n 1) 3.

[3] Vermeule (n 1) 3. See also HP Olsen and S Toddington, *Architectures of Justice: Legal Theory and the Idea of Institutional Design* (Ashgate 2007) 1.

[4] A Tomkins, *Public Law* (OUP 2003) 38; V Bognador, 'Conclusion' in Bognador (ed), *The British Constitution in the Twentieth Century* (OUP 2003) 689, 719.

favour of others, and those that survive over a protracted period might be said to be 'better-fitted' to their environment than those that did not.[5] There is a strong tendency within English constitutionalism to distrust attempts to consciously 'fiddle' with this evolutionary model by deliberately restructuring constitutional arrangements and practices.[6]

I have two objections to this distrust of institutional design. First, the fact that a particular arrangement is historic and has existed for a long time is not, of itself, a reason for its continued existence. Some of our constitutional arrangements simply do not reflect the values that now underlie our constitution. This is particularly true of the constitutional arrangements governing the war prerogative which have prioritized operational concerns and efficiency over other goals, such as democratic values. Secondly, it is incorrect to suggest that English constitutional arrangements have evolved in isolation, without the influence of normative goals or intentional action. As Goodin explained, the selection mechanisms by which certain variants are winnowed out in favour of others are evaluative and involve indirectly or directly the intentional actions of agents.[7] The influence of these evaluative 'selection mechanisms' was demonstrated in chapter 2. As the analysis in that chapter showed, normative justifications (drawing on political theories) have been advanced for the constitutional arrangements governing the war prerogative, shaping our discourse about those arrangements and their practical ordering.

The Goals of Institutional Design

1 Introduction

Theories about institutional design are concerned with the arrangement of governmental institutions and their structures and processes. Their content is not confined to matters of practical ordering: theories about institutional design also have normative or evaluative content. Normative theories of institutional design propose how constitutional institutions and processes should be arranged. Assessments of the substantive goals of collective action inform these

---

[5] RE Goodin, 'Institutions and Their Design' in RE Goodin (ed), *The Theory of Institutional Design* (CUP 1996) 1, 24–5.

[6] See, eg, Edmund Burke, in exalting the evolutionary nature of the English constitution, who declared: 'And this is a choice, not of one day, or one set of people, not a tumultuary and giddy choice; it is a deliberate election of ages and of generations; it is a constitution made by what is ten thousand times better than choice; it is made by the peculiar circumstances, occasions, tempers, dispositions, and moral, civil, and social habitudes of the people, which disclose themselves only in a long space of time' (E Burke, *The Works of the Right Honourable Edmund Burke* vol 10 (Rivington edn 1826) 97).

[7] Goodin (n 5) 39.

theories.[8] Likewise, evaluations of existing constitutional arrangements must be based on normative goals: 'Any normative claims made by a constitutional writer must draw on political theory; there are no value-neutral assessments that can be made of constitutions, or, indeed, any other social practice.'[9] Some analytical theories of institutional design (theories which attempt to describe or analyze constitutional arrangements) might present a 'neutral' description of constitutional arrangements,[10] but even descriptive or analytical theories are shaped (implicitly or explicitly) by an evaluation of what the constitutional arrangements should be, or by what goal(s) such arrangements should serve.[11]

Normative goals must also inform proposals to reform constitutional arrangements. Talking about proposals for institutional design without a clear normative orientation is 'facile constitutional engineering', because, as Bruce Ackerman says, 'institutional arrangements serve as concrete expressions of ultimate ideals'.[12] Two goals inform my institutional mechanisms: democratic values and efficiency in decision-making.

2 Democratic Values

My proposed institutional mechanisms advance four core values of democratic decision-making: impartiality, accountability, transparency, and deliberation.[13] Democratic decision-making, as used here, goes beyond a formal, aggregative version of democracy, which centres itself on the idea of 'majority rule'. Democratic governments should be based on reasons and justification, not just votes and power.

A brief explanation is required of the selection of these four values. First, the values are essential to democratic decision-making: they are base-line values which all democratic decision-making procedures must incorporate. These values are 'procedural' in the sense that they are directed towards the procedures of

---

[8] DJ Galligan, 'The Paradox of Constitutionalism or the Potential of Constitutional Theory?' (2008) 28 Oxford Journal of Legal Studies 343, 345; NW Barber, 'Prelude to the Separation of Powers' (2001) 60 Cambridge Law Journal 59, 62; Goodin (n 5) 36–7.

[9] Barber (n 8) 63.

[10] See, eg, T Daintith and A Page, *The Executive in the Constitution: Structure, Autonomy, and Internal Control* (OUP 1999) 11–12, who claim to present a 'positive theory of the constitution': 'a theory of what the constitution is, as opposed to what it ought to be'.

[11] For a critique of constitutional theories which claim to be based upon 'empirical fact', see S Lakin, 'How to Make Sense of the HRA: The Ises and Oughts of the British Constitution' (2010) 30 Oxford Journal of Legal Studies 399. See also Galligan (n 8) for an exploration of the different approaches to constitutional theory.

[12] B Ackerman, 'The New Separation of Powers' [2000] 113 Harvard Law Review 633, 639. See also Barber (n 8) 63: 'Separation of powers is a theory of the ordering of collective action; it must be prefaced by a political theory if it is to possess any normative force.'

[13] I adopt the four core values of democratic constitutionalism as identified by Vermuele (n 1) 4–8, but with amendments to the description and content of those values.

democratic decision-making. Their content, however, is substantive, reflecting normative choices about how public decisions should be made.

Secondly, the selection of these four values reflects the nature of the war prerogative. For the exercise of other public powers, other democratic values may carry greater weight; for example, the rule of law, equality, or human rights. But impartiality, accountability, transparency, and deliberation are the most relevant values for the exercise of the war prerogative.

Thirdly, although the four values identified are fundamental to democratic decision-making, identifying their precise content and scope poses conceptual challenges.[14] Different democratic theories agree that these values are core to democratic decision-making but will have different conceptions of their content, scope, and relative importance. In addition, there may be conflicts between and within democratic values.[15] Democratic values trade off against one another, and against other values and goods. For example, there can be trade-offs between transparency and deliberation: transparency can harm deliberation, because the glare of public attention can cause those taking part in deliberations to pander to media attention or to interest groups and outside audiences; public attention might also deter individuals from dissenting. There can also be desirable and undesirable forms of these values.[16] For example, there can be 'good' deliberation and 'bad' deliberation: deliberation can sometimes lead to 'group-think' and group polarization.

There may be high-level disagreement about the particular content of democratic values and about their relationship with one another. However, all of the above concerns are incidental to the objective of institutional design. Its realistic objective is to secure the minimal conditions of democratic governance rather than the unachievable utopian or perfect system. There is common ground between different conceptions of democracy, and in a practical setting most democrats could agree on the base-line conditions of democratic decision-making.[17] Other writers have proposed similar solutions. Goodin calls these the 'theories of the middle range',[18] while Sunstein prefers the description 'incompletely theorized agreements'.[19]

A brief account is required of the meaning of the democratic values I identified: impartiality, accountability, transparency, and deliberation.

Impartiality means that public officials should be 'other-regarding': they should act to promote the public good rather than their own self interest. This principle is common to all theories of democracy. Leading deliberative democrat theorists regard impartiality as part of the 'principle of reciprocity': officials

---

[14] Vermeule (n 1) 10–13.   [15] RA Dahl, *On Democracy* (Yale University 1998) 43.
[16] Vermeule (n 1) 10–13.   [17] Vermeule (n 1) 13–14.   [18] Goodin (n 5) 39.
[19] CR Sunstein, *Designing Democracy: What Constitutions Do* (OUP 2001) 50–66.

must justify public policy by giving reasons which are mutually acceptable and public-regarding, rather than self-interested.[20] Consequentialist theories of democracy, such as Bentham's, require governments to weigh the interests of each citizen equally: 'the Public Good ought to be the object of the legislator; General Utility ought to be the foundation of his reasonings.'[21] Non-consequentialists identify impartiality as an aspect of the principle that each individual is of inherent equal worth and should be treated with equal concern and respect. A contractualist argument contends that impartial government would be chosen by reasonable persons deciding on arrangements for their common life.[22] These theories have clear differences, but they all share a commitment to the principle that governmental officials must act to promote the public good, and not their own self-interest.

Accountability means that officials must answer for their actions to other members of the political community. What accountability means exactly is contested by democrat theorists. For elitist democracy theorists, elections (and the ability of electors to vote out incompetent officials) exhaust the accountability of government officials.[23] For Habermas, a necessary aspect of institutional accountability is that public decisions are the result of 'formally structured political will-formation':[24] accountability requires clarity and certainty of process. Some theorists argue that an essential component of accountability is that the reasons that found official decisions be contestable by citizens.[25] Elections are a key aspect of democratic accountability, but they can be a blunt instrument, and inadequate in ensuring accountability for specific governmental actions. Other features also essential to ensuring accountability include governmental institutions being willing and able to hold to account other governmental institutions, a free and independent media, and access to information about governmental decisions and actions.

Transparency means that governmental secrecy is presumptively undesirable. The reasons that officials give to justify political actions and the information

---

[20] A Gutmann and D Thompson, *Democracy and Disagreement* (Belknap Press 1996) 52–94.
[21] Jeremy Bentham, 'An Introduction to the Principles of Morals and Legislation' in SM Cahn (ed), *Classics of Modern Political Theory: Machiavelli to Mill* (OUP 1997) 685, 685.
[22] Contractualism is a family of views that understand justice or rightness as constituted by facts about what would be agreed to in certain imaginary choice situations, in which all participants promoted their own personal reasons but no one presses their interests at the unreasonable cost of others.
[23] A contention advanced by, for example, Max Weber and Joseph Schumpeter: see D Held *Models of Democracy*, 3rd edn (Polity 2006) ch 5.
[24] J Habermas, 'Popular Sovereignty as Procedure' in J Habermas, *Between Facts and Norms: Contributions to a Discourse Theory of Law and Democracy* (Polity 1996) 57.
[25] P Pettit, 'Democracy, Electoral and Contestatory' in I Shapiro and S Macedo (eds), *Designing Democratic Institutions* (NY University Press 2000) 105, 119–20.

necessary to assess those reasons should be made public. I identify the inherent and instrumental values of publicity in the following chapter.[26] Transparency is not always desirable: in the context of national security, there may be good reasons why particular information should be kept secret. My proposals recommend the establishment of institutional arrangements and processes which secure the democratic benefits of transparency while reducing its costs.

Deliberation means that officials should make decisions on the basis of public-regarding reasons. Deliberation, in the sense used by some deliberative democrats, is a controversial idea. Some deliberative democrats believe that through the process of deliberation it is possible for all public decision-making to arrive at decisions agreed to by all on the basis of impartial and universally shared viewpoints.[27] This 'thick' conception of deliberation is rejected by other democrats who argue that 'incompatible values' and 'incomplete understanding' are inherent in human politics, and moral disagreements are unavoidable.[28] A 'thinner' conception of deliberation, however, has widespread support and is of much greater practical utility. This conception identifies the value of deliberation among political actors as enabling the exchange of information and opinions and as facilitating the giving of reasons for decisions. During deliberation, participants must think about the positions they hold, listen to others respectfully, give reasons for the decisions they reach, and be open to preference transformation as part of political interaction.[29] Gutmann and Thompson (deliberative democrats) call this the 'principle of reciprocity'.[30] Bargaining and majority voting is compatible with this thinner conception of deliberation.[31]

3 *Efficiency*

My proposed institutional mechanisms will also seek to enhance efficiency in decision-making about war. I use 'efficiency' here primarily to mean

---

[26] See citations at nn 28–33 in ch 6.

[27] See, eg, S Benhabib, *Situating the Self* (Polity 1992) 9–10, 121–47; J Rawls, *A Theory of Justice* (Harvard University Press 1971); Habermas, *Between Facts and Norms* (n 24); B Manin, 'On Legitimacy and Deliberation' (1987) 15 Political Thought 351.

[28] See, in particular, Gutmann and Thompson, *Democracy and Disagreement* (n 20) 25–6 and *Why Deliberative Democracy* (Princeton University Press 2004). See also I Young, *Justice and Politics of Difference* (Princeton University Press 1990).

[29] JS Dryzek, *Discursive Democracy: Politics, Policy, and Political Science* (CUP 1990) 54. See also J Fishkin, *Democracy and Deliberation: New Directions for Democratic Reform* (Yale University Press 1991) 37; JS Dryzek, *Deliberative Democracy and Beyond: Liberals, Critics, Contestations* (OUP 2000).

[30] Gutmann and Thompson, *Democracy and Disagreement* (n 20) 26, 79.

[31] Indeed, some models of deliberative democracy, most notably that of Gutmann and Thompson, allow for majority voting in the event of disagreement that persists after full, public deliberation. See Gutmann and Thompson, *Democracy and Disagreement* (n 20) 36.

rational, impartial, and informed decision-making. I argue that democratic decision-making processes are more likely to reach a 'good' decision (a decision which is rational, impartial, and informed).[32] 'Efficiency' also has a secondary, more general, meaning in the context of proposed institutional mechanisms. Institutional mechanisms are small-scale changes to rules and arrangements within the existing large-scale institutional arrangements. Institutional mechanisms must be 'efficient' in the sense that they must realistically fit into the existing large-scale arrangements. There is no utility in proposing utopian small-scale reforms that will not gel with existing arrangements.

Operational Concerns

Opponents of increased parliamentary involvement in the war prerogative focus on the claimed detrimental impact it would have on the efficiency and effectiveness of military operations. I refer to these arguments as 'operational concerns'. The key operational concerns are that parliamentary involvement could compromise operational security through public discussion prior to action, complicate the timetable for preparation if deployment were contingent on a parliamentary vote, impair the government's ability to react to emergency situations, interfere with military decision-making, and impair flexibility of operational response.[33] These operational concerns are not new: parliamentary involvement in decisions about war has been debated for over 350 years, and similar concerns raised.[34] Two assumptions have commonly underlied these operational concerns. First, that decision-making processes about war must be secret, speedy, and flexible. Secondly, that the government must maintain full control and authority over the decisions and conduct of war because it has the necessary expertise and experience.

In matters of war and foreign affairs, English constitutional arrangements and practices have typically prioritized operational concerns over other values, such as liberty and democracy. As shown in chapter 2, institutional arguments have been the dominant justification for the executive's exclusive powers over war. Other normative goals (such as democratic values) have been treated as irrelevant, or even 'dangerous', in matters touching the war

---

[32] See citations at nn 48–100 for how Commons' involvement would improve decision-making about war.

[33] See, eg, the evidence given to the House of Lords Select Committee on the Constitution, *Waging War: Parliament's Role and Responsibility* (HL 2005–06, 236-II) 60–9, esp 61–3, 68–9. See also the government's response to proposed reform of the war prerogative: Tony Blair in a written answer in the House of Commons on 15 June 2005, said that a formal requirement to consult Parliament before deploying the armed forces 'could prejudice the Government's ability to take swift action to defend our national security where the circumstances so require': HC Deb 15 June 2005, vol 435, col 348W.

[34] See the discussion of the 'institutional arguments' in citations at nn 150–74 in ch 2.

prerogative. Constitutional arrangements have empowered governments to make decisions 'in the national interest' in ways that clash with democratic methods of decision-making. Decisions about war and foreign policy have frequently been made in secret, without broad consultation or participation. Margaret Thatcher and Tony Blair are prime examples of leaders who regarded themselves as having a 'trust to rule' and as having the ability and authority to decide unilaterally what was in the national interest, and to take what action s/he considered necessary.[35]

'Elitist' theories of public decision-making might throw light on the English tradition of prioritizing operational concerns and enabling unilateral decision-making in foreign affairs. Elitist theories contend that government should be conducted by an elite group of experts. Plato, for example, considered democracy an inferior form of government, arguing that democracy undermines the expertise necessary to govern societies properly. Democracy, he thought, promotes those who are expert at winning elections rather than those with the ability to think well about the difficult issues that politics involve. He advocated rule by 'Guardians', committed to rule for the general good and superior to others in their ability to achieve it.[36] Contemporary elitist theories of democracy build upon Plato's work. John Stuart Mill thought that the functions of government are highly skilled activities which require experienced and well-trained individuals;[37] Max Weber spoke of the 'emotionality' of the electorate, which made most people incapable of understanding or judging public affairs, and advocated rule by an expert bureaucracy and political elite;[38] and Joseph Schumpeter argued for a very formal type of democracy in which the democratic citizens' lot was the right to vote in an electoral process for the purpose of selecting competing elites, the few who are sufficiently experienced and qualified to govern.[39]

These operational concerns of efficiency and expertise might be persuasive at first glance. It appears plausible to assume that secrecy, flexibility, and speed are essential to operational efficiency and effectiveness, that war and national

---

[35] J Michael Lee, 'Parliament and Foreign Policy: Some Reflections on Westminster and Congressional Experience' (1988) 2 Irish Studies in International Affairs 1; A Doig and M Phythian, 'The National Interest and the Politics of Threat Exaggeration: The Blair Government's Case for War against Iraq' (2005) 76 Political Quarterly 368; SB Dyson, 'Personality and Foreign Policy: Tony Blair's Iraq Decisions' (2006) 2 Foreign Policy Analysis 289.

[36] Plato, *Republic*, bk 6. See the discussion in Dahl (n 15) 69–80.

[37] JS Mill, 'Considerations on Representative Government' in *Three Essays: On Liberty, Representative Government, the Subjection of Women* (first published 1861, introduction by R Wolheim, OUP 1975) 233–5. See further citation at n 146 in ch 2.

[38] See the discussion in Held (n 23) 135–7.

[39] J Schumpeter, *Capitalism, Socialism and Democracy* (Allen and Unwin 1976). See the discussion in Held (n 23) 141–4.

security are matters of high specialization and expertise, and that both of these features demand decision-making by a small and elite group of experts. Most analyses of reform of the war prerogative base their proposals on these general assumptions and conclude that parliamentary involvement would impair operational effectiveness and efficiency. I argue that this approach is overly general and sweeping, and does not withstand scrutiny. I have three particular objections.

First, it is possible, with careful institutional design, to enhance democratic values and ensure the effectiveness and efficiency of military operations. Analyses of constitutional arrangements for war and foreign policy powers typically—and uncritically—assume that there is a necessary trade-off between the promotion of democratic values and the protection of operational efficiency and effectiveness. Operational concerns are prioritized over all other interests, including the intrinsic and instrumental values of democracy. I do not think that these assumptions are valid. Democratic values and operational concerns need not be treated as competing normative goals or justifications for institutional design. There should not be unthinking or implicit prioritization of operational concerns, without consideration as to whether this is genuinely necessary.

Secondly, analyses of potential reform of the war prerogative often cite the opinions of military leaders about how increased parliamentary involvement would impair operational effectiveness and efficiency.[40] The dominant 'objective control' theory of civil–military relations invariably shapes the opinions of military leaders. That theory holds that military leaders must be isolated from politics and be given as free a hand as possible in military matters.[41] Their opinions may also reflect an element of mutual mistrust between civilian and political leaders. Military and political leaders have different mindsets, experiences, and priorities, and different ideas about appropriate decision-making procedures.[42] Both of these factors make it likely that military leaders will oppose increased parliamentary involvement in the exercise of the war prerogative.

Thirdly, arguments opposing increased parliamentary involvement reflect a misplaced deference for executive expertise, based on an assumption of a unique and highly specialized executive. We should be wary of accepting without question exaggerated claims of executive expertise. The well-known

---

[40] See, eg, House of Lords Select Committee on the Constitution, *Waging War: Parliament's Role and Responsibility. Volume I: Report* (HL 2005–06, 236-I) 60–9, esp 61–3, 68–9.

[41] The classic authority on the 'objective control' theory of civil–military relations is SP Huntington, *The Soldier and the State: Theory and Politics of Civil–Military Relations* (Harvard University Press 1959).

[42] Huntington (n 41); EA Cohen, *Supreme Command: Soldiers, Statesmen, and Leadership in Wartime* (The Free Press 2002) 10–12.

intelligence failures post 9/11 provide good evidence for such wariness and vigilance. Further, it is not necessary nor desirable that all those involved in making decisions about war do have specialized expertise in war and national security. Robert Dahl points out that nearly all important decisions about policies are not solely about matters that can be reduced to 'scientific' judgements, or judgements in respect of which experts could claim to have superior knowledge. Nearly all major decisions about policy involve several types of ethical judgements: about the end that the policy should achieve, about trade-offs and the balancing of different ends, and about the means to be used to achieve those ends. Claims that experts have superior ability to make judgements, not just about 'scientific' matters but ethical matters also, is dubious.[43] Even if we do accept that certain individuals are particularly qualified to make decisions about a certain subject, it does not follow that those individuals *do* have authority to make those decisions for us, or *ought* to have that authority.[44] Legitimate authority does not follow simply from expertise.

The Athenian leader Pericles anticipated these arguments in a famous oration in 431 BCE:[45]

Our ordinary citizens, though occupied with the pursuits of industry, are still fair judges of public matters; ... and instead of looking on discussion as a stumbling block in the way of action, we think it an indispensable preliminary to any wise action at all.

Part III Application

Introduction

The remainder of the chapter identifies how the enhanced involvement of the House of Commons would promote democratic values and efficiency in decision-making about war. The Commons' involvement would help to secure the intrinsic value of democratic decision-making, increase the likelihood of a 'good' decision, improve accountability and scrutiny, strengthen public trust in the decision, and perhaps make recourse to war less likely.

My focus on the House of Commons' involvement is not intended to negate the democratic legitimacy of the government. The government comprises mainly of elected representatives and has the confidence of the House of Commons. The modern exercise of the royal prerogative by the government is

---

[43] Dahl (n 15) 71.
[44] DM Estlund, *Democratic Authority: A Philosophical Framework* (Princeton University Press 2008) 3–4; ch 3.
[45] Quoted in Dahl (n 15) 39.

democratically accountable to some degree.[46] However, I argue that increasing the Commons' role in war-making would promote and enhance democratic accountability and legitimacy in decision-making about war. The Commons is the institution that is the most democratically representative of the people. All of its members are elected, its composition is diverse, and it has long claimed to be representative of the community. The Commons' involvement would also promote the inherent and instrumental values of democracy in ways that the current constitutional arrangements do not.

Intrinsic Value

There would be intrinsic value in the Commons having substantive involvement in the exercise of the war prerogative. This assertion is based on the premise that there is intrinsic value in the participation of democratic representatives in public decision-making, independent of the consequences or outcomes of that participation. The nature and consequences of the decision to go to war reinforce the intrinsic value of the Commons' involvement. The decision to go to war is a momentous decision: it involves the use of state-sanctioned force against another nation or target, it mandates the killing of citizens and foreign nationals, and it potentially affects the whole of the nation. The democratic representatives of the community ought to be involved in making such a decision.

'Double democratic deficit' strengthens the intrinsic value of the Commons' involvement. Matters normally dealt with at a national level are increasingly being dealt with at the regional and international levels, creating a 'democratic deficit'. The 'deficit' created by increasing internationalization and regionalization is heightened in the context of foreign policy, where often Parliament has had a limited material role, so leading to a 'double democratic deficit'.[47] This makes parliamentary involvement in foreign policy at the national level even more important, to secure the intrinsic value of democratic decision-making and to accord democratic legitimacy to decisions.

The House of Commons' involvement in the war prerogative would promote democratic legitimacy. The inherent value of the Commons' involvement is important, but it is not sufficient on its own to justify the proposed reforms. It is necessary to look to the consequences and outcomes of democratic decision-making and to the instrumental values of the Commons' involvement.

---

[46] D Jenkins, 'Judicial Review under a British War Powers Act' [2010] 43 Vanderbilt Journal of Transnational Law 611, 619

[47] H Born and H Haenggi (eds), *The 'Double Democratic Deficit': Parliamentary Accountability and the Use of Force under International Auspices* (Aldershot 2004) 3. See also Dahl (n 15) 115, 183. For an earlier consideration of these issues, see K Kaiser, 'Transnational Relations as a Threat to the Democratic Process' (1971) 25 International Organization 706.

Instrumental Value

1 'Good' Decision-Making

The House of Commons' involvement will make it more likely that a good decision will be made. By 'good' decision, I mean a decision which is rational, and based on sound information and reasoned deliberation. The argument for good decision-making is based on the assertion that democratic decision-making is likely to reach a good decision, and can be justified in different ways. Epistemic democrats would use the Condorcet Jury Theorem and other mathematical proofs to show that majoritarian decision-making is most likely to reach a decision which is correct by the relevant external standard. Procedural democrats contest the existence of a procedure-independent-truth, and would say that democratic decision-making produces a correct result to the extent that the decision-making procedure embodies certain procedural virtues, such as impartiality, accountability, transparency, and deliberation. Deliberative democrats, also denying the existence of an external 'truth', would say that a decision is correct if it is the result of informed and reasoned deliberation, based on public reasons.

I accept the argument that there is no normative standard for evaluating social decisions that is independent of individual values or preferences. However, I do not accept the argument that there are no standards by which to evaluate political outcomes.[48] On the purely procedural view, the value of democratic decisions is entirely a matter of their being democratic. I agree with David Estlund when he questions whether purely procedural values alone can ground a normative account of politics, without any appeal to standards of better or worse outcomes or decisions.[49] Estlund's concept of 'epistemic proceduralism' accepts that there is reasonable disagreement about what is a 'just' outcome and rejects a 'correctness theory' of legitimacy (that an outcome is legitimate if it is correct). It asserts, instead, a modest epistemic claim: that properly arranged democratic institutions will tend to produce substantive just outcomes, whatever that just outcome might be.[50] Democratic

---

[48] See, eg, Habermas, who rejects the standard of reason by which to evaluate public decisions: 'We need not confront reason as an alien authority residing somewhere beyond political communication' (Habermas, *Between Facts and Norms* (n 24) 285).

[49] Estlund (n 44) 27–8.

[50] This is an example of a formal epistemic approach: it makes no appeal to any specific conception of justice or common good and is untroubled by the fact that there is reasonable disagreement about which conception is best or correct. Such disagreement does not hamper the epistemic approach, if it could be established that whatever the best or correct conception of justice or common good is, certain democratic procedures have a tendency to produce outcomes conducive to justice or common good. See Estlund (n 44) 169–71. See also A Vermeule, *Law and Limits of Reason* (OUP 2009) 8.

decision-making, therefore, is normatively desirable because it (1) satisfies certain procedural democratic virtues, and (2) is epistemically the best among the procedures that are better than random.[51]

Many-minds argument

I now turn back to the claim, which is made by various democratic theories, that democratic collective decision-making produces, or is likely to produce, a good decision. These theories advance the 'many-minds' argument: that many heads are better than one. The many-minds argument has a long history: Aristotle wrote of the benefits of the 'wisdom of the multitude',[52] it was present in classical republicanism theory,[53] John Stuart Mill regarded the collaborative method of making legislation as better than non-collaborative methods,[54] and it is a key feature of deliberative democratic theory.[55]

I want to focus on three claims of the many-minds argument: the statistical claim that a group is more likely to reach a 'correct' decision than an individual or a small group, the claimed benefits which flow from an aggregation of information and individual perspectives, and the claim that deliberation and argument among many contributes to a better policy than one could devise.

In its simplest form, the Condorcet Jury Theorem states that where there are two alternatives, one of which is 'correct' (somehow defined), and where in a choice between those alternatives the members of the group are even slightly more likely to be right than wrong, then as the number of members in the group increases, the probability that a majority vote of the group is correct tends towards certainty.[56] A sufficiently large group of people, all of whom have a 51 per cent chance of providing the right answer to a question, is more likely to provide that answer than a single expert who has a 75 per cent chance of being correct.[57]

There are several conceptual problems with the Theorem and its application to real-life decision-making.[58] A key uncertainty concerns the premise behind the Theorem, which is the independence of the group members' views or

---

[51] Estlund (n 44) 98.
[52] Aristotle, *The Politics* (trans by C Lord, University of Chicago Press 1985) 100–3, 111–12. See discussion in J Waldron, 'The Wisdom of the Multitude: Some Reflections on Book 3, Chapter 11 of Aristotle's *Politics*' (1995) 23 Political Theory 563.
[53] See, eg, Marsilius of Padua, *Defensor Pacis (Defender of Peace)* (1324).
[54] JS Mill, 'On Liberty', ch 2 in Cahn (n 21) 939.
[55] See, eg, Gutmann and Thompson, *Democracy and Disagreement* (n 20) 128–64; Habermas (n 24); CR Sunstein, *The Partial Constitution* (Harvard University Press 1993) 133–45.
[56] A Vermeule, 'Many-Minds Arguments in Legal Theory' (2009) 1 Journal of Legal Analysis 1, 4–5.
[57] Vermeule (n 50) 28.
[58] Vermeule (n 56) 6–9; Estlund (n 44) 15–16 and ch 12; N Barber, 'Two Meditations on the Thoughts of Many Minds' (2010) 88 Texas Law Review 807.

Application 171

guesses. Independence means 'statistical independence': an absence of correlation of individuals' guesses. Even if particular voters make biased guesses, the group as a whole will be unbiased on average if guessers' biases are uncorrelated. As Vermeule points out, it is unclear whether statistical independence is compromised by factors such as deliberation, discussion, or common social background or training.[59] Social or other pressures to vote in a particular way would also seem to undermine the requirement of independence.[60] In the Commons, party discipline and vote-whipping clearly undermine the requirement of independence, and therefore the application of the Theorem. Even if the decision to go to war were made a conscience vote, strong social and party pressures would probably compromise statistical independence.

The claimed benefit of information aggregation may prove more useful. A common claim in many-minds arguments is that collaborative decision-making is superior because it enables individuals to enhance their understanding of complex problems through the process of sharing information and pooling knowledge.[61] Through information aggregation, individuals may understand aspects of the situation which they had not appreciated before, such as the consequences of taking a certain course of action or the interrelationship of other public issues.[62]

A connected claim is that deliberation and argument contributes to a better decision than could be made by one individual or a small group. Deliberation and argument require individuals to test publicly their views against those of others and to modify their views to accommodate those of others. Informed deliberation might expose the one-sidedness and partiality of certain viewpoints or the way that individual preferences are shaped by a belief that a certain situation is fixed and unchangeable.[63] Aristotle championed the superiority of collective deliberation when diverse groups come together:[64]

> they may surpass—collectively and as a body, although not individually—the quality of the few best... When there are many who contribute to the process of deliberation, each can bring his share of goodness and moral prudence;... some appreciate one part, some another, and all together appreciate all.

Critics have condemned many-minds arguments as starry-eyed and overly optimistic. They say that real-world deliberations often lead to errors and

---

[59] Vermeule (n 56) 6–7. However, see Estlund (n 44) 225–6, where he asserts that the fact that voters share common influences is not fatal to the Theorem's applicability.
[60] Estlund (n 44) 228–30.
[61] See, eg, J Waldron, *The Dignity of Legislation* (CUP 1999) ch 5.
[62] Held (n 23) 237–8.
[63] J Cohen, 'Deliberation and Democratic Legitimacy' in A Hamlin and P Pettit (eds), *The Good Polity: Normative Analysis of the State* (Blackwell 1989) 25.
[64] Aristotle (n 52) 100–3.

pathologies or to indeterminacy.[65] Theories identifying the claimed virtues of deliberation are often based on the concept of an 'ideal speech situation', a model of an ideal collective deliberation.[66] In the model deliberative situation, all affected people (or their proxies) are given an equal say; are untainted by prejudice or by differences of wealth, power, or dishonesty; have full information; and share the goal of 'reaching understanding'.[67] The claimed virtues of this type of collective decision-making are that it brings together diverse perspectives, places a wide variety of reasons and arguments before the public, and prevents inequalities of power or status from skewing the results. However, real-world deliberations may be far removed from this ideal: behaviour is often strategic, people lack full information, and equality is absent. The ideals of deliberation and its claimed benefits are not fulfilled, and instead deliberation can lead to extremism, error, or incoherence. Cass Sunstein has shown how group deliberations can become skewed. Through group polarization, 'members of a deliberating group predictably move toward a more extreme point in the direction indicated by the members' pre-deliberation tendencies'.[68] He identifies two principal catalysts for group polarization. First, the social influences on behaviour (particularly people's desire to maintain their reputations and self-conceptions); and secondly, the role of reasons in deliberation (the limited 'argument pools' within any group and the limited directions in which those limited pools lead the group). Apart from extremism, there is another way in which group deliberation can fail to live up to ideals: deliberation may produce incoherence—a mishmash of views or unending debate.[69]

Application
With these criticisms in mind, how do the claims of information aggregation and deliberation apply to decision-making about war? Would information aggregation and deliberation in the Commons make it more likely to reach a 'good' decision about whether or not to go to war? Information aggregation raises particular issues in the context of decision-making about war. As the proposals detailed in the following chapter show, the Commons cannot have access to all the information relevant to decision-making about war (although I propose that a special joint committee of Parliament should have full access). The government possesses a unique monopoly over some

---

[65] See the citations at n 58.
[66] The 'ideal speech situation' comes from the work of Juergen Habermas.
[67] J Habermas, *A Theory of Communicative Action* (MIT Press 1984) 99.
[68] Sunstein (n 19) 15; see also CR Sunstein, 'Deliberative Trouble? Why Groups go to Extremes' (2000) 110 Yale Law Journal 71.
[69] Vermeule (n 56) 20.

information. However, that does not negate the usefulness of information aggregation in the House of Commons. Members of the Commons should be able to contribute other relevant information and perspectives. MPs have a range of backgrounds and experiences. Some will have experience in diplomacy, international law, or the military, while others, with experience in other fields, will also be able to make useful contributions. MPs will also be in a position to communicate the opinions and concerns of their constituents. In addition, information-pooling in the House of Commons may highlight 'gaps' in the information on which a decision is made. Criticisms of the decision-making process leading to the military invasion of Iraq were that the key decision-makers conducted a poor information search; processed information in a biased way; and failed to survey adequately alternatives and objectives, or work out contingency plans.[70] The input of a greater number of individuals, with a broader range of perspectives and experiences, might improve the information pool, both in terms of contributing information to the pool and in terms of highlighting what information is missing from the pool.

For the same reasons, deliberation and debate within the Commons might improve decisions about war by bringing greater impartiality and objective critical analysis to decision-making. If governmental decision-makers must explain and justify their strategic choices to a well-informed group of outsiders in the Commons, they will need to think carefully about their proposals and anticipate a broader range of options. There is a long history of decisions about war being made by an 'inner circle': a select, often informal, group of individuals close to the Prime Minister. Typically, cabinet as a whole has played a limited role in the decision-making process.[71] Decisions made by a small and select group of individuals carry attendant risks. When people who share points of view and frames of reference deliberate together they are likely to strengthen, rather than

---

[70] See Doig and Phythian (n 35); P Hennessy, 'Informality and Circumscription: The Blair Style of Government in War and Peace' (2005) 76 Political Quarterly 3. In the US context, see D Mitchell and TG Massoud, 'Anatomy of Failure: Bush's Decision-Making Process and the Iraq War' (2000) 5 Foreign Policy Analysis 265.

[71] A commentator in 1895 argued that, in practice, the formulation and implementation of foreign policy was in the hands of the Prime Minister and the Foreign Secretary. He wrote that 'in this Constitutional, democratic country of ours, we are almost as much at the mercy of two men, so far as foreign policy is concerned, as if we were the inhabitants of a Continental monarchy where foreign affairs are personally directed by a quasi-autocratic Emperor and a Chancellor not responsible to Parliament': S Low, 'A Foreign Affairs Committee' (1895) 38 The Nineteenth Century: A Monthly Review 506. Other contemporary commentators made similar observations: see, eg, HN Brailsford, 'The Control of Foreign Affairs: A Proposal' (1909) 4/13 English Review 122, 126. For good discussions of these issues in more recent contexts, see C Foster, 'Cabinet Government in the Twentieth Century' (2004) 67 Modern Law Review 753; N White, *Democracy Goes to War: British Military Deployments under International Law* (OUP 2009) 26–30.

test, their existing convictions. This can lead to group polarization, which is a tendency to move towards a more extreme viewpoint.[72]

A related phenomenon is 'group-think', where decision-makers seek to achieve concurrence among group members, rather than make calculated and carefully considered decisions.[73] Group-think arises in small groups of like-minded individuals. It is exhibited by a hesitation to dissent or voice misgivings, uncritical deference to group consensus, and an absence of methodical decision-making procedures for considering evidence and alternative options.[74] The decision-making methods of former Prime Minister Tony Blair arguably displayed some of these features. The key decisions were made by a select group of individuals close to the Prime Minister in an informal 'sofa' setting, with an absence or disregarding of alternative options or contrary information, and without the broader input of the cabinet.[75] The 'war cabinets' during the Suez, Korean, and Falklands wars also demonstrated elements of group-think. These war cabinets comprised of a small selection of cabinet members and high-ranking military officials, and exhibited a consequential risk of 'tunnel vision' (making decisions without sensitivity to the wider context) and of specialist military professionals dominating the political factors.[76]

Decision-making by an inner circle is particularly dangerous because other governmental institutions lack the capacity to scrutinize effectively their decision-outcomes. Cabinet has proven a relatively ineffectual counter-weight for two reasons. First, because few of its members have been included in the decision-making process; and secondly, because the doctrine of collective responsibility commits all cabinet members to support government decisions. Even if individual ministers criticize or challenge proposed policies in private cabinet discussions, collective responsibility requires them to defer in public

---

[72] Sunstein (n 19) 4.

[73] There is extensive political science literature on the impact of group-think in the context of crisis decision-making. See, eg, IL Janis, *Groupthink: Psychological Studies of Policy Decision and Fiascoes*, 2nd edn (Houghton Mifflin 1983); SA Yetiv, 'Groupthink and the Gulf Crisis' (2003) 33 British Journal of Political Science 419.

[74] Yetiv (n 73) 420–1.

[75] Doig and Phythian (n 35); Hennessy (n 70). See also the statement to the House of Commons by Clare Short, who resigned from the cabinet in protest at the handling of the Iraq situation: HC Deb 12 May 2003, vol 405, cols 36–9. See also Report of a Committee of Privy Counsellors, *Review of Intelligence on Weapons of Mass Destruction* (HC 898, 2004) ('Butler Report') [606]–[611]; House of Common Foreign Affairs Committee, *The Decision to go to War in Iraq* (HC 2002–03, 813-I) [606]–[611]. Both the Butler Report and the report of the Foreign Affairs Committee raised concern about Blair's informal decision-making procedures. In particular, the reports observed that, although cabinet was briefed frequently on Iraq issues, these briefings were oral and unscripted. Written papers were not circulated in advance, which limited the ability of cabinet members outside of the inner circle to prepare properly for discussion or to contribute meaningfully to deliberation.

[76] C Seymour-Ure, 'British "War Cabinets" in Limited Wars: Korea, Suez and the Falklands' (1984) 62 Public Administration 181.

to the collective cabinet decision. Resignation from cabinet is the strongest expression of dissent from a cabinet decision. Resignation will draw attention to the decision, but is unlikely to solve its perceived flaws.[77] The Commons' ability to scrutinize effectively government decisions about war has become limited and marginalized.[78]

The dominance of the inner circle, collective responsibility, and the weakness of the Commons have created a lacuna that needs addressing. There is a very real need for impartial criticism and challenge of the government's proposals for deployment. The Commons, together with the proposed joint committee, could fulfil a valuable role by broadening the number and diversity of the decision-making group and encouraging the challenging of assumptions of the inner circle decision-makers.[79]

I give two examples of how more impartial deliberation could improve decision-making. First, greater transparency and public deliberation might help to reveal if decisions about war are motivated by factors not concerned with genuine threats to national security, but by more self-interested political concerns. The traditional realist school of international relations did not distinguish between different actors within the state. Other strands of political science, however, such as political economy models and empirical assessments, recognize that the 'state' is not a unitary entity and that the interests of leaders and the broader community are not always synonymous. Policies that leaders adopt to enhance their hold on power may make citizens worse off.[80] War is costly and inefficient in terms of citizen welfare, but it can be beneficial for leaders: Margaret Thatcher faced poor prospects of re-election before the Falklands war, and it is likely that the UK's victory was instrumental to her re-election in 1983.[81] Even without ascribing such bald political motive to

---

[77] Three ministerial level cabinet members resigned prior to the Iraq vote: Robin Cook, John Denham, and Lord Philip Hunt. Clare Short resigned two months after.

[78] See citations at nn 234–276 in ch 3 for how the Commons has exerted retrospective scrutiny of the government's exercise of its war prerogative.

[79] B Ackerman, *Before the Next Attack: Preserving Civil Liberties in an Age of Terrorism* (Yale University Press 2006) 85–6. See also the discussion of diversity in legislative assemblies in J Waldron, *Law and Disagreement* (Clarendon Press 1999) 73–5.

[80] BB De Mesquita, 'Game Theory, Political Economy, and the Evolving Study of War and Peace' (2006) 100 American Political Science Review 637, 638–9.

[81] The 'rally round the flag' effect (an increase in support for the government caused by involvement in international conflict) has been well documented. Brian Lai and Dan Reiter show that the Falklands war and the 1990–91 Gulf war boosted support for the Conservative party and Prime Ministers Margaret Thatcher and John Major respectively: see B Lai and D Reiter, 'Rally 'Round the Union Jack? Public Opinion and the Use of Force in the United Kingdom, 1948–2001' (2005) 49 International Studies Quarterly 255. Some studies have even suggested that as support for the Prime Minister's party declined, the likelihood that Britain displayed, threatened, or actually used force significantly increased: see TC Morgan and CJ Anderson, 'Domestic Support and Diversionary External Conflict in Great Britain, 1950–1992' (1999) 61 Journal of Politics 799.

governments' choices about war, it is well documented that governments, motivated by political imperatives, tend towards overreaction in the national security sphere.[82] The political costs of under-reaction will be higher than the costs of overreaction.[83] Questioning of the government's proposals by well-informed MPs would help to test whether the government's proposals are a rational and proportionate response to the threat posed.

Secondly, requiring the government to explain to the Commons what they propose to do and why, and to address the concerns and questions raised by MPs, would benefit the decision-making process. It would also assist operational effectiveness of deployment by helping to clarify the objectives of the use of force.[84] According to military leaders, clarity of objectives is essential for operational effectiveness and success.[85] Under the proposed reforms, the government will retain control over operational matters—the 'means' used to achieve the ends—but the tough strategic choices about those ends will be made against a more robust and transparent backdrop than a small-group setting of like-minded executive officials.[86]

I recognize the limitations to these claims of the value of information aggregation and deliberation in the Commons. First, debate and deliberation in the Commons are strongly influenced and, often, controlled by party politics. MPs are not impartial and rational participants, motivated solely by their conscience or conception of the national interest.[87] Strategic and political considerations motivate and shape what MPs say and how they behave in the House, as opposed to a genuine desire to reach understanding or a 'good'

---

[82] T Poole, 'Courts and Conditions of Uncertainty in "Times of Crisis"' [2008] Public Law 234, 244–9 (on the government's use of risk discourse). See also D Feldman, 'Human Rights, Terrorism and Risk: The Roles of Politicians and Judges' [2006] Public Law 364, 379 (on how governments use risk to help foster a climate of fear).

[83] M Ignatieff, *The Lesser Evil: Political Ethics in an Age of Terror* (Edinburgh University Press 2005) 58.

[84] See CP Gibson, *Securing the State: Reforming the National Security Decisionmaking Process at the Civil–Military Nexus* (Ashgate 2008) esp 103, 122. Gibson proposes a 'Madisonian' approach to civil–military relations, whereby countervailing forces can be employed to maximize effectiveness and accountability. He advocates building friction and lively debate into the decision-making process about war through open and informed deliberation and collaboration between political and military leaders.

[85] Lords Committee on the Constitution, *Waging War* (n 33) 66, 67 (evidence of Field Marshal Lord Bramall and General Sir Rupert Smith).

[86] Ackerman (n 79) 85–6.

[87] cf the Burkean approach to representation, which identified the proper role of MPs as being a trustee for constituents, and an advocate for the national interest, rather than a voice for his constituents. For more on the different roles of a modern parliamentarian, see V Bognador (ed), *Representatives of the People? Parliamentarians and Constituents in Western Democracies* (Gower 1985), particularly Bognador, 'Introduction' 1; H Berrington, 'MPs and Their Constituents in Britain: The History of the Relationship' 15; and SE Finer, 'The Contemporary Context of Representation' 286.

decision. This is particularly true of the front-benchers in both the government and the opposition, who are required to toe the party line. However, it is a weaker factor in relation to the back-benchers, who will often openly criticize party policy.[88] On an issue as important as the decision to go to war, MPs might feel a greater and more acceptable imperative to speak and act according to their conscience, even if it contravenes the party policy.[89] On the House of Commons' motion in March 2003 on the decision to go to war in Iraq, 38 per cent of Labour MPs either voted against the motion or abstained, a higher dissension/abstention rate than usual.[90] This indicates that party-political considerations are not the sole motivation in shaping debate and deliberation in the Commons.[91]

Secondly, the Commons is relatively homogenous in its composition. The composition of the Commons does not reflect the diversity present in the community.[92] The extent of the homogeneity of a group affects the nature of its deliberations. According to Sunstein, the best protection against error and pathologies of deliberation is to insist on the advantages of heterogeneity, which helps to ensure a wide argument pool is placed before the deliberators.[93] The Speaker's Conference on Parliamentary Representation makes a similar point in explaining its case for widening representation. A more diverse House of Commons would make better decisions and solve problems more effectively, because it would be able to draw upon a wider range of experiences and insights.[94]

Despite these limitations, deliberation and debate will serve important purposes. The composition of the Commons is relatively homogenous (certainly in comparison to the community), but it is more diverse than the

---

[88] Bognador, *The British Constitution in the Twentieth Century* (n 4) 707–9.

[89] In debates in the House of Commons on the issue of military deployment to Iraq, a number of MPs asserted that the deployment vote should transcend party and career interests. See, eg, HC Deb 18 March 2003, vol 401, col 817 (Malcolm Savidge); col 875 (John McDonnell); col 822 (Barry Gardiner); col 885 (Lindsay Hoyle); col 867(Bill Tynan).

[90] On the substantive motion in the Commons on 18 March 2003, the breakdown of the Labour party voting was 254 in favour (62%), 69 did not vote (17%), and 84 against (21%). See the analysis in House of Commons Library, 'Commons Divisions on Iraq: 26 February and 18 March 2003' (Standard Note, SN/SG/2109, 19 March 2003) <http://www.parliament.uk/documents/documents/upload/snsg-02109.pdf>.

[91] For further on dissent in the House of Commons, see C Pattie, E Fieldhouse, and RJ Johnston, 'The Price of Conscience: The Electoral Correlates and Consequences of Free Votes and Rebellions in the British House of Commons, 1987–1992' (1994) 24 British Journal of Political Science 359; P Cowley, '"Crossing the Floor": Representative Theory and Practice in Britain' [1996] Public Law 214.

[92] See the recent survey and report of the Speaker's Conference on Parliamentary Representation, *Final Report* (HC 2009–10, 239) [3].

[93] Sunstein (n 19) 44–5.

[94] Speaker's Conference on Parliamentary Representation, *Final Report* (n 92) [7]–[14].

decision-makers in the 'inner circle' who make the key decisions about war. That diversity, in addition to the sheer number making up the Commons, means that there will be MPs with different expertise, experiences, and opinions. The aggregation of information and deliberation within the Commons will improve the decision made. Requiring the government publicly to explain and justify its proposals will improve the quality of the decision and consequent actions by encouraging reflection and reason-giving. It will ensure that the government will not act unless and until a broad range of people have an opportunity to consult and deliberate, and helps to counter the risk of group polarization within the government.[95]

2 Enhanced Accountability and Scrutiny

Substantive and informed parliamentary involvement in the exercise of the war prerogative will bolster the capacity of Parliament and the community to scrutinize the government's proposals and ensure that government officials answer for their actions. A special joint committee of Parliament, charged with scrutinizing the information on which the government bases its decisions, will also enhance accountability.

Since the advent of parliamentary government ministers have been accountable to Parliament for their actions.[96] However, the effectiveness of these accountability measures has long been questioned. The Government dominates the House of Commons through parliamentary majorities, use of the whips, and control of the parliamentary timetable.[97] The government's increasing control over the Commons has undermined the mechanisms of the Commons for scrutinizing the government's exercise of the war prerogative (as identified in chapter 3).[98] Recent practice in regards to the Iraq war illustrates how the Commons is essentially powerless in the face of the government's control over key aspects of Commons' procedures and processes, including the parliamentary timetable, the type of motion (adjournment or substantive) on which debates take place, and the information made available to the Commons. My proposed institutional mechanisms will counter the government's dominance of the Commons and ensure that its members can scrutinize effectively the government's decisions about war.

---

[95] Sunstein (n 19) 240–1.
[96] R Blackburn and A Kennon, *Parliament: Functions, Practice and Procedures*, 2nd edn (Sweet and Maxwell 2003) [1-009].
[97] See the discussion in, generally, M Russell and A Paun, *The House Rules? International Lessons for Enhancing the Autonomy of the House of Commons* (Constitution Unit, University College London 2007).
[98] See further citations at nn 234–276 in ch 3.

3 Two Further Instrumental Values

There are two further instrumental values of the Commons' involvement. First, the Commons' substantive involvement in the decision to go to war will enhance public trust in the decision. Greater transparency (through public debates and reports), interaction between MPs and their constituents, and public deliberation by elected representatives will engage the community more directly in a decision of obvious national importance.

Secondly, it has been suggested that substantive democratic involvement in the decision to go to war makes war less likely than if democratic decision-making was not involved. Immanuel Kant advanced this thesis, and it has been since restated and tested by many other writers.[99] The 'democratic peace' argument has two claims: first, that democracies are unlikely to fight wars with one another because of shared democratic norms and culture and a shared commitment to the peaceful adjudication of disputes. Secondly, institutional constraints in the domestic political structures of democracies mean that democracies are less likely to resort to war. Those institutional constraints are said to include the influence of public opinion and the greater reluctance of legislatures, in comparison to executives, to go to war.[100] Doubts have been raised as to whether domestic institutional constraints do make nations less likely to engage in war, but Kant's core assertion holds true regardless. In democratic systems, where decisions about war are debated openly, both the public and policy-makers are sensitized to the costs of waging war, and it makes it more likely that war really is a rational response to a perceived threat.

Part IV Conclusion

This chapter has identified the normative goals for my proposed small-scale changes to the institutional arrangements and processes involved in the exercise of the war power. The proposed institutional mechanisms seek to advance

---

[99] There is extensive literature on the 'democratic peace' argument. See, eg, MW Doyle, 'Kant, Liberal Legacies, and Foreign Affairs' (1983) 12 Philosophy and Public Affairs 205; Dahl (n 15) 57–8; B Russett, *Controlling the Sword: The Democratic Governance of National Security* (Harvard University Press 1990) ch 5; S Weart, *Why Democracies Will Never Fight One Another* (Yale University Press 1998); D Peters and W Wagner, 'Between Military Efficiency and Democratic Legitimacy: Mapping Parliamentary War Powers in Contemporary Democracies, 1989–2004' (2011) 64 Parliamentary Affairs 175, 177–8.

[100] But see studies which have cast doubt on this claim: eg, C Layne, 'Kant or Cant: The Myth of the Democratic Peace' (1994) 19 International Security 5; S Chan and W Safran, 'Public Opinion as a Constraint against War: Democracies' Responses to Operation Iraqi Freedom' (2006) 2 Foreign Policy Analysis 137.

the goals of impartiality, transparency, accountability, and deliberation, as the core values of democratic decision-making. The proposed mechanisms must address, in addition, the important operational concerns in decision-making about war and its conduct. This chapter argued against the assumption that there is a necessary trade-off between democratic values and operational efficiencies. I contend that it is possible, when designing the institutions and processes involved in decision-making about war, to promote both democratic values and operational efficiency and effectiveness. Collective democratic decision-making improves the likelihood of making good decisions, and ensures proper scrutiny and accountability. It also accords democratic legitimacy to the decisions made, by ensuring the effective participation of the national legislature with its greater diversity and deliberative pedigree and enhancing public trust in the decision made. It may also make recourse to war less likely. The following chapter will show how these aspirational normative goals can be translated into proposals for concrete practical arrangements.

6
Reform

Part I Introduction

This chapter outlines my proposals for reform of the constitutional arrangements for the war prerogative. The previous chapter established why I think reform is necessary and desirable; this chapter details those reforms. In summary, I propose the enactment of a statute which would require the government to obtain in the House of Commons a majority vote in support of deployment of the armed forces, except in identified situations; impose duties on the government to provide Parliament (and the public) with certain information about the proposed deployment; and establish a special joint committee of Parliament to scrutinize the relevant information and exercise a general oversight role over the deployment of forces. I also propose a limited role for the courts in enforcing particular aspects of these procedural requirements. These proposals show that, through careful institutional design, democratic values and the interests of national security and operational efficiency can be reconciled and promoted.

Summary of Recent Proposals for Reform

Following the controversy surrounding Britain's military intervention in Iraq in 2003, the government and various parliamentary and other bodies reviewed the prerogative power to deploy the armed forces. The then-Labour government published a series of consultation papers and white papers considering whether changes should be made to how the war prerogative is exercised,[1] the House of Lords Select Committee on the Constitution conducted an in-depth investigation into the war powers,[2] the Public Administration Select

---

[1] Ministry of Justice, *The Governance of Britain* (Green Paper) (Cm 7170, 2007); Ministry of Justice, *War Powers and Treaties: Limiting Executive Powers* (Cm 7239, 2007); Ministry of Justice, *The Governance of Britain—Constitutional Renewal* (White Paper) (Cm 7342-I, 2008); Ministry of Justice, 'The Governance of Britain. Review of the Executive Royal Prerogative Powers: Final Report' (October 2009).

[2] House of Lords Select Committee on the Constitution, *Waging War: Parliament's Role and Responsibility. Volume I: Report* (HL 2005–06, 236-I).

Committee reported on the place of the prerogative in a modern democracy,[3] and the Joint Committee on the Draft Constitutional Renewal Bill considered some of the broader issues concerning the war prerogative.[4] More recently, the Political and Constitutional Reform Committee (a select committee of the House of Commons) conducted an inquiry into parliamentary involvement in conflict decisions.[5] In addition, individual MPs attempted to introduce private members' legislation that would place upon the government an obligation to seek the approval of Parliament before deploying the armed forces;[6] and various campaign groups and think-tanks campaigned for greater parliamentary involvement in the exercise of the war prerogative.[7] These reviews and proposals for reform generally agreed that it was desirable to formalize in some way an enhanced role by Parliament (in particular the House of Commons) in the making of the decision to deploy the armed forces. I will focus here on the two most thorough reviews of the war powers: the reviews by the House of Lords Select Committee on the Constitution and the then-Labour government.

In July 2006 the House of Lords Select Committee on the Constitution (hereafter the 'Lords Committee') published its inquiry findings into the desirability and practicality of establishing legal limitations on the Crown's prerogative to deploy the armed forces.[8] The Lords Committee concluded that, for reasons of democratic legitimacy and accountability, the House of Commons should have an enhanced role in the exercise of the power to deploy the forces. It rejected the suggestion of a statutory requirement for parliamentary involvement on the ground that it presented practical difficulties and uncertainties that outweighed any constitutional merit.[9] Instead

---

[3] Public Administration Select Committee, *Taming the Prerogative: Strengthening Ministerial Accountability to Parliament* (HC 2003–04, 422).

[4] Joint Committee on the Draft Constitutional Renewal Bill, *Draft Constitutional Renewal Bill* (2007–08, HL 116-I, HC 551-I).

[5] Political and Constitutional Reform Committee, *Parliament's Role in Conflict Decisions* (HC 2010–12, 923). See also, from the same committee, *Parliament's Role in Conflict Decisions: Government Response to the Committee's Eighth Report of Session 2010–12* (HC 2010–12, 1477); *Parliament's Role in Conflict Decisions—Further Government Response* (HC 2010–12, 1673).

[6] Armed Forces (Parliamentary Approval for Participation in Armed Conflict) HC Bill (2004–05) [31]; Armed Forces (Parliamentary Approval for Participation in Armed Conflict) HC Bill (2005–06) [16]; Waging War (Parliament's Role and Responsibility) HC Bill (2006–07) [34].

[7] See, eg, Charter 88; and the Democracy Task Force launched by the Conservative party in February 2006, which published 'An End to Sofa Government: Better Working of Prime Minister and Cabinet' (2006).

[8] Lords Committee on the Constitution, *Waging War* (n 2).

[9] The Committee identified the following difficulties with putting the deployment power on a statutory basis: the possibility of subjecting the armed forces to criminal prosecution, the possibility of judicial review of the government's exercise of the war prerogative, and the need to provide for 'emergency' exceptions which could be exploited by future governments. See Lords Committee on the Constitution, *Waging War* (n 2) [104].

it recommended the creation of a constitutional convention that would determine the role Parliament should play in making decisions to deploy forces. Some commentators questioned the Lords Committee's proposal that a convention could be created or purposively developed, suggesting this reasoning was 'faulty'.[10] It is true that constitutional conventions are normally established over time, based upon established practice and normative acceptance of their binding force on the part of political actors.[11] However, Sir Ivor Jennings, who proposed a three-pronged test for the existence of a convention, considered that a 'single precedent with a good reason may be enough to establish the rule'.[12] A 'good reason', according to Jennings, is to be determined by reference to the needs of constitutional government: does the rule play a necessary constitutional role? It seems clear that a rule requiring the government to seek parliamentary approval before going to war serves a necessary role in promoting constitutional government. There are also historical examples of single precedents establishing a convention.[13] Therefore, although established practice and usage may be the main source of convention, it is incorrect to say that a convention could not be established by a single precedent: in this case, for example, by an assurance of the government that it would, in the future, seek parliamentary approval before deploying the armed forces. Unequivocal acknowledgment of the need to take such action would establish a binding conventional obligation for all future situations.[14]

The then-Labour government similarly concluded that the Commons should have a formal role in the exercise of the war prerogative, and also rejected the use of statute. The government's recommendations were set out in the Ministry of Justice report *The Governance of Britain—Constitutional Renewal* (hereafter the 'White Paper').[15] Instead of advocating the use of a constitutional convention, as did the Lords Committee, the government preferred a resolution of the House of Commons for implementing the proposed reform.[16] The suggested resolution would require the government to obtain a majority vote of the Commons in support of its proposed deployment, except in emergency situations or in respect of secret or special forces operations. The

---

[10] D Jenkins, 'Constitutional Reform Goes to War: Some Lessons from the United States' [2007] Public Law 258, 259.

[11] AV Dicey, *Introduction to the Study of the Law of the Constitution*, 10th edn (Macmillan and Co 1959) 417, 422; AW Bradley and KD Ewing, *Constitutional and Administrative Law*, 14th edn Pearson 2007) 20; PA Joseph, *Constitutional and Administrative Law in New Zealand*, 3rd edn (Thomson Brookers 2007) ch 8.

[12] Sir Ivor Jennings, *The Law and the Constitution*, 5th edn (University of London Press 1959) 136.

[13] See the examples described by Joseph (n 11) 221.

[14] See text and citations at nn 331–334 in ch 3 for the statements made by the government in 2011 acknowledging the existence of a constitutional convention in favour of parliamentary debate before deployment.

[15] Ministry of Justice, White Paper (n 1).   [16] Ministry of Justice, White Paper (n 1) [210].

government's White Paper recognized that establishing a statutory basis for a requirement of parliamentary approval would provide certainty and protect the proposed mechanism from being ignored or circumvented.[17] Nevertheless the government preferred (presumably in the interests of maintaining flexibility and discretion) the use of a resolution of the House of Commons, in the form of an Address to Her Majesty, and leaving it up to the Commons whether it formalized the resolution by Standing Order. The White Paper emphasized the need for any proposed mechanism to maintain a high degree of flexibility and to allow for emergency exceptions to the requirement for parliamentary approval. This was, it declared, 'vital to ensure that our national security, our ability to conduct effective operations and the safety of the UK Forces are not compromised by the implementation of the new mechanism'.[18] The government included in the White Paper a draft of a possible resolution.[19] It provided that the Commons would receive a report from the Prime Minister which set out the terms of the proposed approval and the information about objectives, locations, and legal matters that the Prime Minister thought appropriate in the circumstances. The Commons would be asked to give its approval by 'resolving to approve the terms set out in the Prime Minister's report'.[20] Approval would not be required if the deployment was necessary to deal with an emergency and there was insufficient time to seek approval; or if public disclosure about the decision could prejudice the effectiveness of military operations or the security or safety of members of the armed forces. Operations involving members of the special forces would also be exempt from the approvals process.

All of the reviews and reports seem to have come to naught. A government report, published nineteen months after the White Paper, stated that '[a]s promised in the ... White Paper, the Government is also preparing a draft of a detailed House of Commons resolution setting out processes the House of Commons should follow in order to approve any deployment of the Armed Forces in armed conflict overseas'.[21] However, the Labour government did not initiate such a resolution before it left office. The coalition government said in debate about military intervention in Libya that 'we will enshrine in law for the future the necessity of consulting Parliament on military action',[22] but it has not yet taken steps to do so, and it responded with little enthusiasm

---

[17] Ministry of Justice, White Paper (n 1) [210].
[18] Ministry of Justice, White Paper (n 1) [216].
[19] Ministry of Justice, White Paper (n 1) Annex A, 53.
[20] Ministry of Justice, White Paper (n 1) Annex A, 53.
[21] Ministry of Justice, 'The Governance of Britain. Review of the Executive Royal Prerogative Powers: Final Report' (n 1) [37].
[22] HC Deb 21 March 2011, vol 525, col 799.

or commitment to the Committee on Political and Constitutional Reform's recommendations that a parliamentary resolution be drafted and introduced by the end of 2011.[23]

In any event, I would argue, the proposals made so far have been inadequate because they failed to ensure that the House of Commons would be able to play an informed and substantive role in making the decision to go to war. The government's White Paper acknowledged that the current position, whereby the government can exercise the war prerogative without requiring any 'formal parliamentary agreement', was an outdated state of affairs in a modern democracy.[24] Yet, it seems that the government wanted to protect its extensive discretion and power over the decision to go to war and to restrict Parliament's involvement to a purely formal approval of the executive's decisions: essentially, to accord an appearance of democratic legitimacy and accountability to the decision while preventing Parliament from playing a material or substantive role in the decision-making process.

The White Paper's proposals reflected an adherence to a formal conception of democracy focused on democracy as an aggregation of votes, rather than on a more substantive conception of democracy focused on the nature and quality of democratic decision-making. By leaving extensive discretion to the government, the Commons' role would essentially be restricted to rubber-stamping an executive fait accompli.[25] Three aspects of the proposals are particularly problematic: (1) the recommendation that the Prime Minister should determine the scope and nature of any information provided to Parliament, (2) the absence of any special arrangements for the recall of Parliament if deployment were deemed necessary when Parliament was adjourned or dissolved, and (3) the acceptance that the Prime Minister should have total discretion as to the timing of when the government would seek parliamentary approval. The coalition government seems to support an even more restricted role for the Commons, in the form of a convention in favour of parliamentary debate before deployment. These proposals have given blind primacy to concerns of operational efficiency and effectiveness over the intrinsic and instrumental values of democratic decision-making. They have wrongly ignored or rejected

---

[23] Political and Constitutional Reform Committee *Parliament's Role in Conflict Decisions: Government's Response* (n 5) 3. See also *Parliament's Role in Conflict Decisions—Further Government Response* (n 5).

[24] Ministry of Justice, White Paper (n 1) [197].

[25] cf Jeremy Waldron, who argues, in the context of legislative law-making, that the executive's securing formal parliamentary approval of its legislative measures is an 'indispensable aspect of a measure's legitimacy and authority as *law*' and rejects political scientists who identify this as 'mere honorific decoration': J Waldron, *Law and Disagreement* (Clarendon Press 1999) 29. I contend that parliamentary involvement should be more than mere rubber-stamping of an executive measure.

the possibility of developing decision-making processes and institutions which could ensure both the meaningful participation of Parliament *and* operational efficiency and effectiveness.

A Reforming Statute: An Overview

I recommend legislation that will require the government to obtain a vote of approval in the House of Commons in advance of a deployment of armed forces except in identified circumstances. I also propose the establishment of a joint committee of the two Houses, which will play the key role in scrutinizing the information on which the government bases its case for war, and could also have an oversight role over operations which are exempted from prior approval of the Commons. The statute would define the types of deployments for which the government must obtain the prior approval of the Commons; provide exceptions for particular types of deployment, for which prior approval would not be required; require the government to supply to Parliament information about the proposed deployment; require the government to schedule a debate to enable deliberation in the Commons about the proposed deployment and to obtain a majority vote in support of its plans before the commencement of deployment; and establish a special joint committee of Parliament tasked with scrutinizing the information on which the government bases its case for war.

I have recommended the use of legislation (rather than convention, resolution of the Commons, or Standing Orders) to ensure that the proposed requirements are not ignored or circumvented. Non-legislative mechanisms would enable more room for manoeuvre by the government than a legislative mechanism: compliance with conventions cannot be legally enforced, and a majority vote in the Commons can circumvent Standing Orders. The greater room for manoeuvre would enable the government to sidestep, when politically convenient, the proposed procedural and substantive conditions on the exercise of its war prerogative. I recognize that the government must possess a necessary degree of discretion and flexibility in the exercise of its war powers, but I think that such discretion and flexibility can be adequately provided for in a legislative mechanism.

The proposed legislation would not replace royal prerogative as the source of the Crown's powers to deploy the armed forces: the power would continue to be based in the royal prerogative, with the statute superimposing conditions upon the exercise of the prerogative. There are precedents of statutes which leave the prerogative in place but control the manner in which it is used. The Royal Assent Act 1967 and the Constitutional Reform and Governance Act 2010 are two examples. The statute would explicitly state that the Crown's prerogative to deploy the armed forces is preserved intact (albeit qualified as to its exercise). This would help to avoid the confusion and uncertainty which has arisen in situations where a statute covers the same ground as the prerogative but is silent as to it.[26]

My focus in the following proposals is on the role of the House of Commons, rather than the House of Lords. This is for three reasons. First, there is the primacy of the House of Commons. The government draws its support and legitimacy from the Commons; its existence depends upon a majority in the Commons. Secondly, democratic principles are a key motivator for reform of the war prerogative. Unless or until the Lords undergoes reform, the Commons holds the clear claim to democratic legitimacy and accountability. Thirdly, it would be a difficult and undesirable situation if the Commons and the Lords disagreed on a vote on a proposed action. The determinative vote should be with the Commons, for the first two reasons. This does not mean that the Lords will have no role in the making of the decision to go to war. The Lords will play a key role in scrutinizing, questioning, and deliberating. I suggest that the Lords should conduct a debate on a proposed deployment without having a determinative vote. That debate will be valuable in informing public opinion and the Commons' deliberations. I also suggest, as detailed later in the chapter, the establishment of a special joint committee of Parliament, comprised of members of both the Commons and the Lords.

Part II Parliamentary Access to Information

General Principles

1 Introduction

Parliament's access to information is an issue of fundamental importance. Parliamentary access to information about war and national security has long been an issue of contention between the government and MPs.[27] The government's control over information about war and national security, and over who has access to that information, poses a real obstacle to Parliament's ability to play a substantive role in decision-making about war. Without access to the relevant information, MPs are limited in their ability to hold

---

[26] In such situations, depending on the statute, the prerogative might be regarded as being superseded by the statute (see, eg, *AG v De Keyser's Royal Hotel Ltd* [1920] AC 508 (HL)), or the prerogative and statute might be interpreted as being coterminous (see, eg, *R v Secretary of State for the Home Department, ex parte Northumbria Police Authority* [1988] 1 All ER 556 (CA)).

[27] See the discussion in citations at nn 258–267 in ch 3.

governments to account and to participate in the policy and decision-making processes, resulting in an imbalance of power between the executive and other governmental institutions. Only for genuine reasons of national security or individual safety should information justifiably be kept secret. This section proposes potential solutions for reconciling these competing interests in the exercise of the war prerogative.

2 *The Value of Publicity*

Instrumental and moral justifications support a presumption in favour of publicity. The presumption should be rebutted only where the interests of national security truly justify the withholding of information. Publicity is valuable because it enhances democratic values in various ways: it encourages citizens to deliberate about public policy, it enables public officials to learn about and from public opinion and a range of political and moral perspectives, it ensures that the reasons given for a particular decision or action are 'reciprocal' (mutually acceptable),[28] and it promotes democratic accountability.[29] Bentham recognized that it is natural for officials in a position of power to take less interest in others' affairs, and greater interest in their own affairs. Bentham thought the only way to overcome these 'dangerous motives' was 'respect for public opinion—dread of its judgment—desire of glory?—in one word, everything which results from publicity'.[30] Publicity is also valuable for its inherent moral worth, independently of its instrumental value. Kant regarded the principle of publicity as a test that any policy must pass in order to be just: a policy is unjust if making it public would defeat its purpose. The obligation to justify policies to those whom it affects provides the moral basis of the publicity principle.[31]

All of these reasons hold true in the context of the decision to go to war and national security more generally. Questions of national security involve issues of such importance that they should be the subject of public knowledge and deliberation. It will not be possible for the Commons to participate meaningfully in the decision-making process without access, in some way, to the key information on which the government bases its case for war. Parliamentary access to information is also necessary to enable Parliament to scrutinize effectively the government's use of information and conduct of war. The controversies

---

[28] A Gutmann and D Thompson, *Democracy and Disagreement* (Belknap Press 1996) 8.
[29] Jeremy Bentham, 'Essay on Political Tactics' in *The Works of Jeremy Bentham* vol 2 (John Bowring ed, William Tait 1843) 310–12.
[30] Bentham (n 29) 314.
[31] Gutmann and Thompson (n 28) 98–100; Immanuel Kant, 'Perpetual Peace' in SM Cahn (ed), *Classics of Modern Political Theory: Machiavelli to Mill* (OUP 1997) 571, 591.

surrounding the 'Arms to Iraq' affair[32] and the UK's military invasion of Iraq in 2003[33] highlight real concerns about how information (particularly intelligence information) can be manipulated to support a pre-existing political agenda and about the limited accountability and scrutiny of the use of that information. Publicity of government information and records can guard against abuses, mismanagement, and corruption. In addition to ensuring that MPs are adequately informed, it is also necessary to disseminate adequate information to the broader public. Publicity of government information encourages citizen trust in government action and enables citizens to assess whether the decision about war and the reasons advanced for it are mutually acceptable.

3 The Culture of Secrecy

National security and secrecy are commonly regarded as synonymous. It is often assumed that information about national security must necessarily be kept secret, and the claim that information touches on national security typically acts as a trump, to override all other interests. These assumptions, however, do not withstand scrutiny. The interests of national security or the safety of individuals will sometimes justify secrecy, but not all information which touches on national security or foreign policy interests should be kept secret. It is also clear that the interests of national security have been employed to justify secrecy in circumstances not warranting it (such as a desire to avoid embarrassment or the revelation of incompetence).

A variety of factors have combined to create this culture of secrecy in the national security context and the resulting monopoly of the government over access to information. These factors include the following:

- The government is the main source of information about foreign policy and national security.
- There is a long tradition of deference on the part of the legislature and the courts to the executive's claimed expertise over matters of foreign policy and national security.

---

[32] Lord Justice Scott, *Report of the Inquiry into the Export of Defence Equipment and Dual-Use Goods to Iraq and Related Prosecutions* (HC 115, 1996); see also A Tomkins, *The Constitution after Scott* (OUP 1998).

[33] Report of a Committee of Privy Counsellors, *Review of Intelligence on Weapons of Mass Destruction* (HC 898, 2004) ('Butler Report') 10–11; see also M Phythian, 'Hutton and Scott: A Tale of Two Inquiries' (2005) 58 Parliamentary Affairs 124; A Glees and PHJ Davies, 'Intelligence, Iraq and the Limits of Legislative Accountability during Political Crisis' (2006) 21 Intelligence and National Security 848; P Davies, 'Iraq, Intelligence and the Constitution' (2008) 14 Intelligence Studies Review 4.

- There is a long tradition of secrecy in matters of foreign policy, motivated by a desire to maintain maximum room for manoeuvre and the exercise of discretion, on the assumption that it would be detrimental to foreign policy interests to bring clarity and openness to foreign relations.[34]
- Decisions about war and national security are, in part, based on intelligence information, which is usually secret. Intelligence agencies' work normally depends on secrecy for success, which reinforces the culture of secrecy in matters affecting war and national security.[35] The fact that intelligence information is normally secret and difficult to challenge means there are significant imbalances of power between those who have direct access to it and those who do not.[36] David Omand has commented: 'If all knowledge is power, secret knowledge is turbo-charged power.'[37]
- Experimental evidence suggests that individuals overestimate the likelihood of harm and risk and accordingly overact to it, or disregard probabilities entirely and focus solely on avoiding an adverse potential outcome.[38] The tendency to overestimate risk dominates the national security sphere.[39] This tendency may explain why information is kept secret even where the interests of national security do not, in fact, require it.[40]
- Selective disclosure of information is purposefully employed as a powerful means of shaping public opinion. The executive will 'leak' or disclose information which is supportive of their position and withhold information which is no more sensitive, but which does not support their position.[41] The Scott Report on Arms to Iraq revealed how different intelligence agencies focused on information that was of interest to them and supplied only

---

[34] L Freedman, 'Even-Handedness, Guidelines and Defence Sales to Iraq' (1996) Public Law 391, 391–2.

[35] The former head of the Security Service explains that the role of the security agencies in the conduct of international relations is necessarily competitive, if not aggressive, and depends on secrecy for its success: Sir Stephen Lander, 'International Intelligence Cooperation: An Inside Perspective' (2004) 17 Cambridge Review of International Affairs 481, 481.

[36] MJ Smith, 'Intelligence and the Core Executive' (2010) 25 Public Policy and Administration 11.

[37] D Omand, *Securing the State* (Hurst and Co 2010) 191.

[38] CR Sunstein, 'Terrorism and Probability Neglect' (2003) 26 Journal of Risk and Uncertainty 121.

[39] SJ Schulofer, 'Secrecy and Democracy: Who Controls Information in the National Security State?' (19 August 2010) NYU School of Law Public Research Paper, 10–53, 16 <http://ssrn.com/abstract=1661964>; Smith (n 36).

[40] The Joint Committee on Human Rights noted in a report that 'protective anxiety' pervades the culture of the intelligence agencies and prevents the disclosure of information that does not in reality pose any threat of harm to intelligence sources or working methods. See JCHR, *Eighteenth Report of 2003–04* (2003–04, HL 158, HC 713) [19]. See also AM Schlesinger Jr, *The Imperial Presidency* (Houghton Mifflin 1989) ch 10.

[41] M Fenster, 'The Opacity of Transparency' (2006) 91 Iowa Law Review 885; Schulofer (n 39) 15–16.

that information which reinforced their institutional position.[42] Similar allegations have been made about the government's publication of information concerning Iraq's alleged possession of Weapons of Mass Destruction.

- Bureaucratic power struggles often motivate officials to keep important information secret. Max Weber showed how secrecy is both a consequence of bureaucracy and also one of its key tools—officials keep information secret to shield themselves from oversight.[43] They also withhold information from fellow officials in order to enhance political and bureaucratic power: 'every bureaucracy seeks to increase the superiority of the professionally informed by keeping their knowledge and intentions secret'.[44] The tendency towards secrecy is strongest in fields where the competitor is external; such as a foreign polity.[45]

4 Possible Solutions

The interests promoting publicity confront the culture of secrecy in the national security sphere. In relation to a particular piece of information, there may be good reasons supporting its publicity and also good reasons supporting its secrecy. How might this tension be reconciled, or at least ameliorated? I propose two potential solutions in the current context. The first is a requirement to submit information relevant to the case for deployment to a public interest test. This test would be similar to the balancing approach taken under the Freedom of Information Act 2000 (the 'FOI Act'), but with a more explicit focus on the relevance of the particular information to democratic deliberation about proposed policies or actions. The second is the establishment of a joint committee of Parliament, which would have access to all of the information on which the government is basing its case for war, and which would produce a report to Parliament based on that information.

A Revised Public Interest Test

1 Introduction

I propose that information relevant to the case for deployment should be submitted to a revised public interest test. The revised test would be similar to the balancing approach taken under the FOI Act, with a more explicit and stronger

---

[42] Tomkins (n 32) 137.
[43] Max Weber, 'Bureaucracy' in HH Gerth and C Wright Mills (eds), *Essays in Sociology* (Routledge 1948) 233–4.
[44] Weber (n 43) 233–4. For exploration of these issues in the British context, see I Leigh, *The Frontiers of Secrecy: Closed Government in Britain* (Junction Books 1980).
[45] Weber (n 43) 233.

focus on the relevance of the information to democratic deliberation about proposed policies or actions. This emphasis would establish a rebuttable presumption in favour of the disclosure of information relevant to the government's case for war.

2 *The Current Public Interest Test*

The claimed objectives of the FOI Act are to make public authorities more open and accountable, to assist understanding of their work, and to promote a culture of transparency and accountability.[46] The FOI Act seeks to achieve these objectives by giving rights of public access to information held by public authorities. Its effectiveness in the spheres of national security and foreign affairs is severely limited, however, as the FOI Act creates broad exemptions for information held by intelligence agencies and for information relating to national security, defence, and international relations. Section 23 excludes absolutely intelligence agencies from coverage under the FOI Act, while sections 24, 26, and 27 provide for a 'qualified exemption' for disclosure of information relating to national security, defence, and international relations. A 'qualified exemption' means that the exemption from publication is subject to the 'public interest test', which provides that the information should be released if the public interest in disclosure outweighs the interests of national security.

The Information Commissioner, who is charged with the enforcement of the FOI Act, recognizes the strong public interest in information about national security, defence, and international relations. In a guidance note, the Commissioner suggests a factor weighing in favour of disclosure of information about national defence is whether the information furthers the 'understanding of and participation in the public debate of issues of the day'.[47] The Commissioner provides, as a specific example of such an issue, the decision whether to deploy the armed forces. He acknowledges there is a strong public interest in facilitating an informed debate about the merits of decisions on national security: it would 'increase public confidence, promote decision makers' accountability to the public, and facilitate public understanding and debate'.[48] In a decision dealing with a request for information

---

[46] Objectives as identified on the website of the Information Commissioner: see <http://www.ico.gov.uk>. For further on the potential reasons for the adoption of the FOI Act, see S Palmer, 'Freedom of Information: A New Constitutional Landscape?' in N Bamforth and P Leyland (eds), *Public Law in a Multi-Layered Constitution* (Hart Publishing 2003) 221; S James, 'The Potential Benefits of Freedom of Information' in RA Chapman and M Hunt (eds), *Open Government in a Theoretical and Practical Context* (Ashgate 2006) 17, 21–31.
[47] Information Commissioner, 'Freedom of Information Act—Awareness Guidance No 10' (version 1, April 2006) <http://www.ico.gov.uk> 4.
[48] Case Reference FS50134653, 1 September 2008 [48].

about the government's 'dossier' (which set out the intelligence information which the government said supported its case for military action in Iraq), the Commissioner recognized the strong public interest in how the dossier was produced and in its contents:[49]

Allegations have been made that the dossier was politically manipulated so that it no longer constituted a 'technical' assessment capable of underpinning a 'neutral' assessment of the issues. There is therefore a strong public interest in a degree of exposure of the circumstances of the dossier's production, because that would facilitate public understanding of and participation in the debate about alleged Iraqi weapons capability and intentions, and promote accountability and transparency of the bodies responsible for producing the dossier and for taking decisions on the basis of its contents.

The Information Commissioner explicitly recognizes the public interest in publicity of information about national security and related matters. However, the apparatus of the FOI Act enables and, in some cases mandates, considerable deference to the executive's claims that secrecy is required for reasons of national security. The evidential burden placed on a public authority is relatively light. A public authority can establish that an exemption is required to safeguard national security by obtaining a signed certificate from a minister of the Crown. The certificate is taken as evidence that the exemption is required (subject to the public interest test). The certificate does not need to refer to a specific request or to specific information; it can refer to a category of information and can apply to future requests. In certain situations, a public authority can give a 'neither confirm nor deny' response to a request for disclosure of information, meaning the public authority does not have to confirm whether or not it holds the particular information requested.[50] The government also possesses an 'executive veto' under section 53 of the FOI Act, which enables a government minister to override a decision of the Information Tribunal ordering the release of information. This executive veto was used to override the decisions of the Information Commissioner[51] and the Information Tribunal[52] ordering the release of Cabinet minutes (in redacted form) relating to the March 2003 decision to take military action in Iraq.[53]

---

[49] Case Reference FS50134653, 1 September 2008 [61].
[50] See, as an example of a 'neither confirm nor deny' response, which was upheld by the Information Commissioner, Case Reference FS50102023, 28 February 2008, where the Cabinet Office refused to confirm or deny if it possessed information relating to the bombing of the *Rainbow Warrior*.
[51] Case Reference FS50165372, 18 February 2008.
[52] Case Reference EA/2008/0024 and EA/2008/0029, 27 January 2009.
[53] Secretary of State for Justice, 'Exercise of the Executive Override under section 53 of the Freedom of Information Act 2000, in Respect of the Decision of the Information Commissioner Dated 18 February 2008, as Upheld by the Decision of the Information Tribunal of 27 January 2009, Statement of Reasons' (23 February 2009).

3 The Revised Public Interest Test

The FOI Act takes an overly deferential approach to the claimed interests of national security and international relations. I do not think that its qualified exemption test should be applied when determining whether information relevant to the decision to deploy should be kept secret or disclosed. Rather, a more nuanced approach, based upon evaluation and justification, should be adopted. In particular, a certificate from a minister should not be treated as conclusive; the arguments for and against disclosure of the specific information should be reasoned through in each case, and not merely assumed; and greater weight should be given to the relevance of the specific information to public deliberation about the decision to go to war.

The presumption should be in favour of publicity of all information which is relevant to the government's case for deployment. The presumption may be rebutted if the publicity of particular information would cause identifiable harm to national security interests or individual safety, and that harm outweighs the public interest in publication. The balancing exercise shall accord particular weight to the information's relevance to democratic deliberation about the proposed policy or actions. National security may sometimes require secrecy; but there is a difference between operational security and a political desire to obscure and truncate debate about issues of war and the use of force.

Certain information may justifiably be withheld from publication.[54] In particular, two types of information might be kept secret: first, information which is unlikely to be of relevance to a politically interested person seeking to reach an informed judgement about the decision to deploy; and secondly, information which would undermine operational success or individual safety.[55] For example, it will normally be justified to suppress detailed information about the identity of active officers, agents, or sources working in circumstances where exposure could endanger their safety;[56] technical details about the components and capabilities of weaponry, targeting, order of battle, and other specific military matters;[57] and information about activities or operations which depend upon secrecy for their success, because they are susceptible to counter-measures. Publication of such information would probably be valueless to a politically interested person seeking to reach an informed judgement about defence policy, but would be detrimental to national security interests.

---

[54] On the types of information that should normally be withheld, see generally L Lustgarten and I Leigh, *In from the Cold: National Security and Parliamentary Democracy* (Clarendon Press 1994) 30–2.
[55] Lustgarten and Leigh (n 54) 30.   [56] Lustgarten and Leigh (n 54) 32.
[57] Lustgarten and Leigh (n 54) 31.

Information which is likely to be of particular relevance to public deliberation about the merits of the decision to go to war includes information about the objectives of the proposed deployment, the reasons why deployment is regarded as a suitable and necessary means for achieving those objectives, the legal bases of deployment, the geographical region of deployment, its expected duration, the expected number of forces participating, and the predicted cost and financing of the deployment. All these types of information are relevant to an assessment of the merits of the proposed decision to deploy. They address the overarching issues relating to deployment, but not specific operational or strategic matters, disclosure of which could be detrimental to operational success.

I propose that this revised public interest test should be employed in two separate contexts. The first is in relation to information, relevant to the government's case for deployment, which the government considers should be kept secret. In this context, the revised public interest test will be applied by the special joint committee of Parliament (on which, see the following section). The second context in which the revised test should be employed is in relation to applications under the FOI Act for the publication of information about the government's case for deployment. The revised balancing test will enable the maximization of the benefits of publicity (focusing on its enhancement of deliberation about key issues), while minimizing its costs (in particular, identifiable damage to national security interests or individual safety).

Joint Committee of the Houses of Parliament

1 Introduction

I propose that the establishment of a joint committee of the Houses of Parliament would be the best mechanism to reconcile the need to keep secret particular information about the government's case for deployment and the need to ensure that the Commons is sufficiently informed. I will call this committee the Joint Committee of the Lords and Commons on National Security ('JCNS'). I propose that the committee include selected members of the House of Lords (even though the committee will report to the House of Commons) in order to maximize the detached impartiality of the membership. Members of the Lords might also possess special expertise in and knowledge of national security matters.

The benefits of such a committee would be:

- To provide a forum of review for government intelligence policy, and, where necessary, challenge the uses to which the government applies intelligence information and intelligence resources.

- To enable the Commons to exercise democratic control over the executive and intelligence and security services in the making of decisions about deployment.
- To better inform the Commons by scrutiny of and report on the government's provision of information to the Commons and on the government's case for deployment.
- To enable a specialized committee with particular experience and expertise to scrutinize the government's policies and actions in relation to deployment.
- To keep secret information that should justifiably be kept secret.

There are historical and contemporary precedents for the establishment of parliamentary committees to scrutinize government decisions about foreign policy and national security. From the seventeenth century, Parliament has established ad hoc committees to consider specific issues of foreign policy, and, more recently, it has established select committees of the Commons to scrutinize government policy and expenditure in relation to foreign policy and security.[58] Of particular relevance for present purposes is the Intelligence and Security Committee ('ISC'), established by section 1 of the Justice and Security Act 2013 to examine the expenditure, administration, and policy of the Security Service, the Secret Intelligence Services, and the Government Communication Headquarters.[59] The ISC has since been given expanded powers of scrutiny over the Defence Intelligence Staff, the Joint Intelligence Committee, and the law enforcement agencies (police and customs). The ISC is not a committee of Parliament. It is established under statute, not Standing Orders, and it reports to the Prime Minister rather than to Parliament. It comprises nine members drawn from both Houses of Parliament, appointed by the Prime Minister following consultation with the leader of the opposition. No member may be a minister of the Crown. Committee members are 'notified' under the Official Secrets Act 1989 and operate within the 'ring of secrecy', according members access to highly classified information and obligating them to observe confidentiality.

The ISC enables Parliament to hold the government and security services to account for their activities, with the object of promoting democratic scrutiny and accountability. In the *Binyam Mohamed* litigation, the court described

---

[58] See citations at nn 247–257 in ch 3 for more on the scrutiny of foreign policy and war by parliamentary committees.

[59] For a useful overview of the ISC, see House of Commons Library, 'Intelligence and Security Committee' (SN/HA/2178, 21 April 2009). For more comprehensive examinations of the ISC, see A Glees, PHJ Davies, and JNL Morrison, *The Open Side of Secrecy: Britain's Intelligence and Security Committee* (Social Affairs Unit 2006); Omand (n 37) 264–5.

the ISC as a 'powerful means of ensuring that the SIS and Security Service can be made democratically accountable for their conduct and of ensuring that they act in accordance with the rule of law and do not facilitate action by other States which is contrary to our laws and values'.[60] The ISC, the court said, is in a position to hold the government and those in charge of the intelligence services to account in Parliament, and this 'is a very significant means of democratic accountability'.[61]

2 Functions of the JCNS

The JCNS would have three key functions. The focus of the first two functions would be the scrutiny of the information on which the government bases its case for deployment. First, the JCNS would scrutinize information relevant to the government's case for war, and produce a report to the Commons containing its assessment of that information. Secondly, the JCNS would ensure that the government presents as much information as possible to the Commons; that is, all information relevant to the decision to deploy, excepting that information that justifiably needs to be kept secret. The third function would be an oversight role in respect of deployments exempted from the requirement for prior parliamentary approval.

First Function
The first function of the JCNS would be to scrutinize the information relevant to the government's case for war and to report to the Commons on its assessment of this information. This would ensure that the government's case for deployment is subjected to independent democratic scrutiny, while also ensuring the secrecy of information which justifiably should be kept secret. In an analogous context, the Joint Committee on Human Rights has encouraged the government to consider whether the ISC could play a role in scrutinizing material on which the government bases its assessments of the nature and scale of threats posed to national security. The Committee thought that the ISC's view would be an important element of independent democratic scrutiny in evaluating whether particular measures were proportionate responses to the threat in question.[62] I propose that the JCNS would play a similar

---

[60] *R (on the application of Mohamed) v Foreign Secretary (No 2)* [2010] EWCA Civ 65, [2010] EWCA Civ 158, [2010] 3 WLR 554 [90].
[61] *Mohamed* (n 60) [90]. Some have questioned the effectiveness of the ISC's scrutiny: see R Booth and I Cobain, 'Security watchdog inadequate, human rights groups say' *The Guardian* (London 27 February 2010) 4.
[62] Joint Committee on Human Rights, *Prevention of Terrorism Bill* (2004–05, HL 68, HC 334) esp Ev 1–2, Ev 4. For discussion, see D Dyzenhaus, 'Deference, Security and Human Rights' in BJ Goold and L Lazarus (eds), *Security and Human Rights* (Hart Publishing 2007) 125, 149–52.

scrutiny role in relation to the government's assessment of the claimed threat to national security and its determination that the deployment of force was necessary to meet that threat. It is not possible for all information relevant to those assessments to be made publicly available to MPs, but a committee of parliamentarians is the next best thing.

To exercise this first function effectively, the committee must have authority to view and scrutinize all the key information relating to the government's case for deployment. The committee should also be empowered to request further information from the government and to ask questions of government ministers and other key officials about the information and their assessments. The information considered by the committee might include information sourced from the Joint Intelligence Committee, the Defence Intelligence Staff, the Foreign Office, and the intelligence agencies. The committee would require adequate research, investigatory, and administrative support. Having viewed and assessed the relevant information, the JCNS would produce a report for the Commons setting out its findings on the government's case for deployment. The JCNS' findings might include, for example, an evaluation of the strength of evidence for the assertion that nation X was developing nuclear weapons which posed a threat to the UK, or an evaluation of the government's stated objectives for military action and the likelihood of success in achieving those objectives. The committee's findings, as set out in the report, will probably be based on information that was laid before the committee but withheld from publication. As with select committees generally, the committee's findings would not be binding on the Commons. It would not be the JCNS' role to make the decision of whether MPs should support the government's proposal for deployment. However, it would be expected that MPs would accord considerable weight to the committee's findings on whether the government's case for deployment was justified and supported by sound evidence.

Second Function
The second function of the JCNS would be to ensure that the government publishes as much information as possible about its case for deployment. The committee will evaluate the government's proposed disclosure of information with reference to the revised public interest test and may recommend that further information be disclosed to the Commons. If the government declines to publish particular information as recommended, there should be a duty on the government to consult with the JCNS over the government's reasons for withholding the information. If the JCNS and the government continue to disagree, the committee may publish a finding that the government is withholding information which the committee considers should be made public. Although the information itself would not be made public, the

objective would be to bring parliamentary and public attention to bear on the government.

The government would retain the final right to determine whether or not to publish particular information. There will be no right of appeal to the courts or any other body from a decision by the government concerning the release of information to Parliament.[63] The government's decision will be final. It would be undesirable for two reasons to allow for a right of appeal: first, decisions about war might need to be made quickly, and appeal proceedings would probably not be completed in time for any judgment to take effect. Secondly, the courts would probably (and should) consider this to be a non-justiciable issue or an issue over which they lack jurisdiction.[64] It would also be undesirable for an applicant to be able to seek an urgent hearing for interim relief (such as an interim injunction or other restraining order) pending the hearing of the appeal. The proposed reforms seek to strengthen the parliamentary scrutiny of the government's exercise of its war prerogative. For reasons of institutional competence and legitimacy, this is an issue ill-suited to judicial determination.

Third Function

A third function for the JCNS would be an oversight role in respect of military action exempted from the requirements for prior parliamentary approval. The statute should impose a duty on the government to inform the JCNS of proposed covert action by special operations forces and of other operations exempted from the requirement of the Commons' prior approval. The government should also keep the JCNS informed about the performance and outcome of such operations. The JCNS would be restricted to an oversight role only.

3 Composition and Powers of the JCNS

The JCNS will require a particular composition and certain powers to be capable of fulfilling these three functions. The membership and leadership of the committee will be key. The committee must be composed of a cross-section of parliamentarians who can command widespread trust and public credibility; for example, senior politicians and leaders of parliamentary factions.[65] The committee must be seen to be independent of the government. To promote

---

[63] Although there will be no right of appeal, there is a potential for applications for judicial review. All rights of appeal are statutory. Judicial review, however, is based on the courts' inherent jurisdiction, and needs no statutory basis. Judicial review is dealt with in a separate section, in citations at nn 112–120.

[64] See the discussion in citations at nn 116–119.

[65] H Born and I Leigh, 'Democratic Accountability of Intelligence Services' (Geneva Centre for the Democratic Control of Armed Forces, Policy Paper No 19, 2007) <http://www.dcaf.ch/publications> 12.

public confidence in the committee's independence, the chair of the committee should be a parliamentarian from the opposition parties.[66] Committee members should be nominated by the Prime Minister, after consultation with the party leaders, and appointed by vote of the respective Houses of Parliament. This procedure will ensure that the members nominated to the committee are of suitable standing and experience and are formally approved and appointed by Parliament.

The JCNS should be free to establish its own procedures and practice. It will not be possible for the committee to hold hearings in public as it would curtail the evidence that the committee would be able to consider. It may be useful for the committee to hold public briefings, to help to increase the transparency of the committee without compromising national security or individuals' safety.[67] The secretariat to the committee should be clearly separate from the executive (unlike the ISC's secretariat, which is based in the Cabinet Office for security reasons).

Finally, the JCNS' effectiveness will depend largely on factors that cannot be provided for in rules. Much will turn on a willingness to make the necessary changes in culture and practice. The committee's success will depend, in particular, on the willingness and cooperation of the actors involved. It will need to earn the trust of MPs, the public, the government, and the intelligence agencies.[68] The establishment of such a committee, possessing the powers and functions proposed, would be a major change in practice. In particular, the government would have to submit all relevant information to the committee and ensure that the committee is kept fully informed of relevant matters and developments. In the case of the ISC, non-disclosure of information by the government has been a problem. The ISC has reported on occasion that in practice, it has been afforded access to highly sensitive and operational information that has gone further than required by the Intelligence Services Act 1994.[69] But on other occasions it has expressed concern that requested information had not

---

[66] The first chair of the ISC, Lord (Tom) King of Bridgwater, believes that the ISC should be chaired by a parliamentarian from one of the opposition parties, in order that the public be confident that the committee was not susceptible to political influence and that the chairmanship was not regarded merely as a consolation prize for an ex-cabinet minister from the governing party. Cited in Glees and Davies (n 33) 853. See also the similar proposals of B Ackerman, *Before the Next Attack: Preserving Civil Liberties in an Age of Terrorism* (Yale University Press 2006) 85.

[67] Similar proposals were made in respect of the ISC: see Ministry of Justice, White Paper (n 1) [236].

[68] For useful discussion of these issues in relation to parliamentary intelligence oversight committees, see Born and Leigh (n 65) 10–11.

[69] Intelligence and Security Committee, *Annual Report 2007–08* (Cm 7542, 2009) [15].

been disclosed.[70] The most highly profiled instance of non-disclosure of information concerned the alleged extraordinary rendition and torture of Binyam Mohamed. The ISC conducted an investigation into the matter and issued a report in July 2007.[71] It became apparent during subsequent litigation that the ISC had not been provided with several key documents concerning Binyam Mohamed's case during its original investigation in 2007.[72]

The government and intelligence agencies periodically express concern about whether parliamentarians are capable of keeping secrets. However, there have been no reported problems with the ISC leaking classified information.[73] Research into the functioning of parliamentary intelligence oversight committees has indicated that parliamentarians rarely leak classified information.[74] MPs know that if they do leak information, they will lose the trust and confidence of the intelligence services and the government, and the public as a whole. Leaking officially classified information is illegal, and it may constitute a breach of privilege to leak or publish unreported evidence and documents presented to committees.[75]

Part III Detail of the Proposed Legislation

Definitions: Deployment Requiring Prior Approval

The legislation will need to identify what types of deployment will require parliamentary deliberation and approval and to define the relevant terms in an appropriate way. One problem is that the nature of armed conflict has changed considerably in the last sixty years. States no longer make a declaration of war or make a formal recognition of a relationship of war.[76] The term 'war'

---

[70] See, eg, Intelligence and Security Committee, *Annual Report 2006–07* (Cm 7299, 2008) [123]–[126].

[71] Intelligence and Security Committee, *Rendition* (Cm 7171, 2007).

[72] *Mohamed* (n 60).

[73] Glees, Davies, and Morrison (n 59) 21.

[74] H Born and LK Johnson, 'Balancing Operational Efficiency and Democratic Legitimacy' in Born, Johnson, and I Leigh (eds), *Who's Watching the Spies? Establishing Intelligence Service Accountability* (Potomac Publishers 2005) 225–339.

[75] eg, in 1999 a member of the Foreign Affairs committee showed to two Foreign Office ministers a copy of a report on Sierra Leone before it was due to be published. The matter was referred to the committee on Standards and Privileges, who concluded that it was a serious interference with the select committee system, as it tended to undermine the committee's authority and call into question its independence from government influence. The House agreed to the committee's recommendation that the member be suspended for ten days. See Committee on Standards and Privileges, *Eighth Report* (HC 1998–99, 607).

[76] Hague Convention III 1907 (HC III), art 1 provides that hostilities should not commence 'without previous and explicit warning, in the form either of a declaration of war, giving reasons,

is now largely devoid of significance at international law, which now speaks of situations of 'armed conflict'. The demise of the declaration of war has obscured the boundary between peace and war and raises conceptual and practical uncertainty about when a situation of armed conflict exists. Several definitions of 'armed conflict' are used, but they often leave considerable room for interpretation and doubt. It can be difficult, in a factual or practical sense, to determine with certainty whether or not a situation of armed conflict exists. The types of operations in which the armed forces might be involved have also changed. These now include peacekeeping, disaster relief, humanitarian intervention, and peace enforcement operations.

One suggested approach has been to define armed conflict by reference to the Geneva Conventions and Protocols. Clare Short's Bill would require approval to be obtained when UK armed forces participate in 'armed conflict'. Armed conflict is defined in the Bill as meaning 'any use of force which gives rise, or may give rise, to a situation of armed conflict to which the Geneva Conventions of 1949 or the Additional Protocols of 1977 apply'.[77] The government's draft resolution also defined armed conflict by reference to the Geneva Conventions.[78] The problem with this definition is that the Geneva Conventions and Protocols do not themselves provide a definition of armed conflict. Further, the Geneva Conventions rules were last updated in 1977; since then, new types of military operations have developed.

Various definitions of the meaning of 'armed conflict' have been advanced in the context of the Geneva Conventions. However, these have not allayed the uncertainty. The International Criminal Tribunal for the former Yugoslavia defined armed conflict as existing 'whenever there is a resort to armed force between States or protracted armed violence between governmental authorities and organised armed groups within a State'.[79] Alternatively, the commentary to the Geneva Conventions defines armed conflict as meaning 'any difference arising between States and leading to the intervention of members of the armed forces.'[80] All of these definitions leave considerable uncertainty. It can be very

---

or of an ultimatum with conditional declaration of war'. Since 1939, most armed conflicts have commenced without any ultimatum or declaration: see LC Green, *The Contemporary Law of Armed Conflict*, 3rd edn (Manchester University Press 1993) 94.

[77] Armed Forces (Parliamentary Approval for Participation in Armed Conflict) HC Bill (2005–06) [16].

[78] Ministry of Justice, White Paper (n 1) Annex A.

[79] *Prosecutor v Tadic* (1996) 105 ILR 419, 488.

[80] J Pictet (ed), *Commentary on the Geneva Conventions of 12 August 1949* vol III (International Committee of the Red Cross 1958) 23. See also D Fleck (ed), *The Handbook of International Humanitarian Law*, 2nd edn (OUP 2008) [201]–[211]; Sir Arnold McNair and Sir Arthur Watts, *The Legal Effects of War*, 4th edn (CUP 1966).

Detail of the Proposed Legislation

difficult, in practice, to decide when violence has reached such a threshold that there is a 'conflict' between parties, as distinct from disorganized violence of low-level intensity.[81] A good example of this ambiguity is the application of the Geneva Conventions to the situation in Iraq: the Conventions clearly applied during the military intervention in Iraq in March 2003, but the US and UK maintain that they have not applied since the transfer of sovereignty in June 2004 and the end of major combat operations.

German law is useful in looking for an alternative reference to the Geneva Conventions. The German Parliamentary Participation Act of 18 March 2005[82] requires parliamentary consent for each military deployment abroad where soldiers are involved in armed force or where such involvement is expected. The Act explicitly excludes from the definition of 'deployment' preparatory or planning measures and the involvement of the armed forces in humanitarian relief or support operations, in which arms are borne solely for the purposes of self-defence.[83]

The German approach offers a sensible solution to the definition of deployments for which prior parliamentary approval should be required. Under my proposed legislation, the definition will be based on a distinction between military deployments where the use of force is not involved and is not expected to be involved, and military deployments where the use of force is to be, or expected to be, involved. The former deployments would cover the deployment of the armed forces for humanitarian relief and peacekeeping operations in which arms are borne solely for self-defence. These kinds of operations are carried out with the general consent of the parties involved. They are based upon the minimum necessary use of force; for example, peacekeeping forces will normally have sufficient combat compatibility for use in self-defence only, and the use of force must be a measure of last resort and proportional to the threat posed.[84] Peace enforcement operations (also known as peace support operations) are distinct from peacekeeping operations,[85] and would most likely fall within the category of deployments requiring prior Commons' approval. Peace enforcement operations are generally carried out under the authority of the United Nations and their objective is to maintain

---

[81] UK Ministry of Defence, *Manual of the Law of Armed Conflict* (OUP 2004) 379.

[82] For a useful summary and translation of the relevant German statutory law, see the evidence of Katja Ziegler, House of Lords Select Committee on the Constitution, *Waging War: Parliament's Role and Responsibility* (HL 2005–06, 236-II) 31–46, 48–52, 56–9. I rely here on Dr Ziegler's translation of the Parliamentary Participation Act of 18 March 2005 (Germany), which is at 44–6.

[83] Parliamentary Participation Act of 18 March 2005 (Germany), s 2.

[84] See further 'United Nations Peacekeeping Operations: Principles and Guidelines' ('Capstone Doctrine') (2008) <http://www.un.org/en/peacekeeping/>.

[85] Peace enforcement operations are normally established under Chapter VII of the UN Charter.

or restore peace between belligerent parties, who may not consent to the intervention. They are coercive in nature and use force or its threat against any party to enforce norms, sanctions, or agreements reached by the parties themselves. A peace enforcement force will normally be equipped to enable it to achieve its operational objectives in the face of real or potential threats, and will have the capability to conduct full-scale military operations.[86]

The potential for 'mission creep' poses another definitional challenge. Mission creep is where the dynamics of the situation change, with the effect that the nature and intensity of operations change. Somalia in 1993–94 is often cited as a prime example of mission creep, as the peacekeeping operation shifted into peace enforcement with a need to employ a much higher degree of force.[87] In the context of proposed reform, the key issue is whether or not the government, in the event of mission creep, should be required to seek parliamentary approval for the continued involvement of the armed forces on the basis that the nature and intensity of operations has materially changed. I think the government should be required to do so, if the nature of the operation has shifted such that it has changed from an operation where prior approval was not required to one where prior approval is required. The government should keep Parliament and the JNSC informed of developments, and, if the nature and intensity of an operation changes, the government should seek the Commons' approval for the continued involvement of the UK armed forces.

In summary, the proposed statute should require the government to obtain the approval of the Commons before deployment of the armed forces abroad in circumstances where force will be, or is expected to be, involved, except in certain specified circumstances. The statute should exclude from the definition of 'deployment' preparatory or planning measures and the involvement of the armed forces in humanitarian relief or support operations in which arms are borne solely for the purposes of self-defence.

Exceptions to the Requirement for Prior Approval

The proposed statute must make exceptions to the requirement for prior approval of the Commons in respect of three types of deployment: (1) deployment which is a necessary response to an emergency situation and/or immediate threat ('emergency exception'), (2) special forces operations or other operations where publicity would probably undermine their success, and (3) minor and low-scale deployments.

---

[86] See further 'United Nations Peacekeeping Operations: Principles and Guidelines' (n 84).
[87] See Fleck (n 80).

I will take each exception in turn. The government must be able to deploy the armed forces, without obtaining parliamentary approval, in response to an emergency or immediate threat. Although the proposed statute must make such provision, experience from other European countries suggests that the need to take immediate action in response to emergency situations is in fact often overstated. In evidence to the Lords Committee, Professor Bell said that he was not aware of any situation where a European country, in which the legislature has a formal constitutional role in making decisions about deployment, has had to rely on an emergency provision. He observed that the nature of the international legal order and of regional and security treaties made it unlikely that emergencies would arise, because deployments of armed forces tend to be dependent upon debate within the UN, NATO, or other regional or security organizations.[88]

The two key issues in drafting an emergency exception are, first, formulating an appropriate definition of an 'emergency situation'; and secondly, determining whether or not retrospective parliamentary approval should be required. The emergency exception provision must be drafted in such a way to ensure that the executive retains sufficient flexibility to enable it to react to an emergency or immediate threat. For this reason, the provision should be drafted using relatively broad language rather than overly detailed and prescriptive language. I suggest that the statute should provide that prior consent of the Commons is not required for deployments in response to an emergency or imminent threat, where a requirement to obtain the approval of the Commons would or would be likely to undermine the effectiveness of the deployment. For the purposes of the proposed statute, it will be for the executive to determine whether or not an emergency situation or imminent threat exists. The government should be required to keep the JCNS informed of developments so that the JCNS is able to exercise oversight over the government's actions. The government should inform Parliament about the deployment as soon as is possible.

On the second issue, I recommend that retrospective approval should not be required for deployments made in reliance on the emergency exception. There are two reasons. First, if retrospective parliamentary approval is required, it seems very unlikely that the Commons would vote against the deployment, seeing as the deployment has already occurred and the armed forces are on the ground. If the parliamentary involvement is essentially a formal rubber-stamping of a fait accompli, it serves no substantive purpose. It might serve a symbolic function, by expressing support of the operation and the armed forces, but that symbolic function would be outweighed by the

---

[88] Professor J Bell, evidence to Lords Committee on Constitution, *Waging War* (n 82) 51.

repercussions in the potential (albeit unlikely) situation where the Commons did not vote in support of the deployment. Those repercussions form the basis of my second reason. In Germany, deployments made in response to imminent danger do not require prior approval of the *Bundestag*, but the government must seek *ex post* consent, without 'undue delay'. If the *Bundestag* does not give consent, the government must terminate the ongoing operation.[89] I think this would be an undesirable situation. It could be dangerous for the armed forces in the field to be required to terminate the operation and withdraw. It would also have severe political repercussions, internationally and domestically.

On balance, I think it is better to exempt deployments made in reliance of the emergency provisions from either prior or retrospective parliamentary approval. However, this does not exclude parliamentary involvement in potential ongoing operations. If the nature of the operation changes materially from one focused on responding to an imminent threat to an operation focused on, for example, regime change, then the government should be required to seek the approval of the House of Commons for the change in the nature of the deployment.

The second type of deployment for which exception should be made is special forces operations or other operations, where publicity would probably undermine their success. Such operations could not be subjected to prior parliamentary involvement for obvious reasons. As already noted, the JCNS should play an oversight role in respect of such operations.

Aside from emergency and special forces deployment, the statute could also provide for an exception for deployments of low scale and intensity.[90] A deployment could be defined as of 'minor scope and intensity' if the number of service personnel deployed is small, it is apparent from the circumstances that the deployment is of minor significance, and it does not entail any participation in warfare. The benefit of such a provision is that only politically significant deployments need to be discussed by the Commons.

Timing of the Commons' Involvement

To ensure that parliamentary involvement is substantive and meaningful, the issue of deployment must not be presented to the House of Commons as a

---

[89] Parliamentary Participation Act of 18 March 2005 (Germany), s 5.
[90] Section 4 of the Parliamentary Participation Act of 18 March 2005 (Germany) makes provision for a simplified procedure in respect of minor deployment. The simplified procedure requires the government to apply to the chairmen of the political groupings in the *Bundestag* and the chairmen of the Foreign Affairs and Defence committees, as well as one member of each political grouping represented on those committees. Consent is deemed to have been granted unless a parliamentary group or five per cent of the members of the *Bundestag* demand that the *Bundestag* hold a debate.

fait accompli. This means, for example, that the deliberation and vote in the Commons should take place before the major mobilization of forces into the conflict region. If major mobilization of the armed forces has already taken place, it is unlikely that the Commons would be willing to put at risk the armed forces, or the UK's credibility and reputation, by voting against the proposed military action.

The 2003 invasion of Iraq illustrated the critical nature of the timing of parliamentary involvement. Subsequent inquiries and leaks have revealed that military invasion was a long-developing strategy of the US and the UK. At a visit by Tony Blair to President Bush's ranch in April 2002, a commitment was made to participate in enforced regime change in Iraq. By July 2002, military action was seen as 'inevitable'. However, this planning was kept secret from the wider cabinet, Parliament, and the public. Claire Short MP's diary entry of 9 September 2002 records Blair assuring her that no final decisions had been taken and there was no need to discuss Iraq in cabinet. It later emerged that on that same day Tony Blair had asked for 20,000 British troops to be made available for the Gulf.[91] In March 2003 the House of Commons debated and voted on the military invasion of Iraq. However, by this point British troops had already mobilized into the region. MPs questioned whether Britain could withdraw from the region without a massive loss of credibility and authority. One MP believed it would destroy the credibility of British military and foreign policy to withdraw on the verge of battle.[92]

These considerations must be balanced, however, against strategic and security considerations. In a crisis situation, military and diplomatic moves do not follow a simple pattern: both are made strategically and in combination in order to achieve a particular objective—it is hoped the avoidance of war.[93] International crisis could be escalated if the government sought parliamentary authorization for the use of force too early. Another consideration is that mass deployment takes substantial planning, which might take place months in advance of actual deployment. Military planners need to be reasonably certain of what kind of conflict is envisaged and how intensive and extensive it will be. To reveal those plans for deployment at an early stage could undermine the strategic efficacy of the deployment.

Strategic deployment concerns, while potentially pressing, are ameliorated in the contemporary international context. Most proposed military operations will be (or should be) conducted under the authority of the United Nations,

---

[91] A Doig and M Phythian, 'The National Interest and the Politics of Threat Exaggeration: The Blair Government's Case for War against Iraq' (2005) 76 The Political Quarterly 368, 372.
[92] See the discussion on this point in citation at n 329 in ch 3.
[93] See GA Craig and AL George, *Force and Statecraft: Diplomatic Problems of Our Time*, 3rd edn (OUP 1995) 215–16 for an analysis of the diplomatic and military requirements in order that crises do not deteriorate to war.

and, where applicable, regional organizations such as the European Union, or treaty organizations such as NATO. Most deployments will also be coalition operations, where two or more nations join forces. Both these factors mean that, apart from deployments made in response to an immediate threat, armed forces deployments will require substantial forward planning and will be the subject of international publicity and attention. Plans for proposed military action are normally well publicized in advance of mobilization or deployment.[94] There are two further factors that allay concerns that operational effectiveness will be undermined by advance parliamentary approval. First, concerns as to the need to maintain maximum secrecy and surprise are undermined by the reality of instantaneous global media coverage and satellite and other technologies. Plans for deployment and the preparations for mobilization and deployment become known very quickly. Secondly, it is not proposed that the Commons should get involved, at least at the approval stage, in detailed military operational or strategic matters. Information about particular strategies or specific targets will not be publicly debated in the Commons at the approval stage.

The proposed legislation should accord a degree of discretion to the government as to the precise timing of parliamentary involvement. The discretion should be subject to three limitations. First, the government should seek the approval of the Commons prior to the start of major deployment, which will normally mean prior to the start of major mobilization of the armed forces to the specific region. Secondly, the JCNS should be kept informed of the government's plans and proposed actions and should consult with the government as to when the government should seek parliamentary approval. Thirdly, if Parliament is adjourned or in recess, the government should be required to recall Parliament.

Legal Advice

As the 2003 invasion of Iraq demonstrated, issues as to the legality of a proposed military action are key. I recommend that the House of Commons should be entitled to obtain its own legal advice on the legality of the proposed action. The events leading up to the Iraq war support this proposal. Before the war, only a summary was published of the Attorney General's legal advice to the government on the legality of the proposed action. It was subsequently revealed that the published summary was misleading and did not accurately represent the Attorney General's advice.

---

[94] Lords Committee on the Constitution, *Waging War* (n 2) [101] noted that recent history has shown that the processes leading up to deployments are generally protracted and conducted under full media coverage, 'rendering arguments about security and secrecy more theoretical than real'.

It is unlikely that the Attorney General or the government could be required to publish the whole of the Attorney General's advice, because the Attorney General is a member of the government and is not an independent legal officer. The Attorney General must normally answer questions put to him or her in Parliament, but he or she is not obliged to disclose his or her opinion where the government will not allow it, or where there would be a conflict of interest. The Attorney General's advice is probably subject to client–lawyer privilege.[95] The former Attorney General, Lord Goldsmith, has said that legal advice given to the government should not be disclosed for strong public interest reasons. He warned that if advice did have to be published, then the government might not ask for advice when it should or might not reveal all the facts when it does. The Attorney General might also be wary of disclosing to the government all the risks and doubts that the government ought to know before taking its decision.[96] In the *CND* case, the Divisional Court also recognized that disclosure of the government's opinion on the legality of a proposed deployment could have detrimental repercussions for its conduct of international relations.[97]

As the Attorney General's legal opinion cannot be disclosed in full, the House of Commons should be entitled to access an independent source of legal advice as to the legal issues raised by a proposed deployment.[98] The best option would be to appoint a legal adviser to the JCNS who would have access to the same information as the committee. This position would be similar to the legal adviser to the Joint Committee on Human Rights. Concern has been raised by the prospect of having conflicting sets of advice as to the legality of a proposed action, and the potential impact that it could have on the morale of the armed forces.[99] I do not regard this as a legitimate concern. Issues as to the legality of a proposed action will be a material consideration in deciding whether or not to support the proposed action. If there are serious disagreements or conflicts between legal advisers about the legality of a proposed action, then I think those disagreements ought to be deliberated and debated. This will improve the decision-making process and increase the likelihood of making a good decision.

---

[95] See the evidence given by two former Attorneys General to the Lords Committee on the Constitution, *Waging War* (n 82) 107. See also the discussion in T Daintith and A Page, *The Executive in the Constitution: Structure, Autonomy, and Internal Control* (OUP 1999) 8.
[96] Lords Committee on the Constitution, *Waging War* (n 82) 116.
[97] *R (on the application of Campaign for Nuclear Disarmament (CND)) v Prime Minister* [2002] EWHC 2777 (Admin). See the discussion of this case in citation at n 182 in ch 4.
[98] There is a Legal Services Office headed by Speaker's Counsel in the House of Commons, but this does not appear to be regarded as an authoritative source of advice on such matters: D Feldman (ed), *Oxford Principles of English Law: English Public Law*, 2nd edn (OUP 2009) 119.
[99] See Lord Goldsmith's evidence to the Lords Committee on the Constitution, *Waging War* (n 82) 118.

Treaty Obligations and Coalition Effectiveness

Most of the military operations in which the UK will be involved will be coalition operations, some of which will be constituted under treaties to which the UK is a signatory. None of the treaties to which the UK is party impose a legal requirement on the UK to provide military support to other countries. Although the UK's treaty obligations and relationships might give rise to a strong political expectation of military support, every deployment of UK armed forces requires a separate and independent decision by the UK government. The Foreign and Commonwealth Office has identified four multilateral treaties which create the strongest political expectation:[100] the North Atlantic Treaty (NATO),[101] the Treaty of the European Union,[102] the United Nations Charter,[103] and the Brussels Treaty.[104] All four preserve the principle that the UK armed forces cannot be deployed without a sovereign decision by the UK government.

Some have expressed concern that parliamentary involvement might have an adverse effect on the operational efficiency and effectiveness of coalition operations. The key concern is that parliamentary involvement would undermine efficiency and effectiveness by making the decision-making process lengthier and more complicated, and by the prospect that Parliament might impose conditions and constraints on the scope of the armed forces' operations. Dr Kim Howell, former Secretary of State for Foreign and Commonwealth Affairs, said in evidence to the Lords Committee that these constraints make operations 'very, very difficult'.[105] He noted that NATO developed an 'OPlan', an annex to its original plan of operations in Afghanistan, to try to urge other countries to take a more active role in operations by removing as many nationally-imposed constraints as possible. Evidence was also heard that new entrants to NATO are encouraged to have quick parliamentary decision-making processes in order to facilitate the bringing together of coalitions as rapidly as possible.[106]

I think these concerns are overstated and possibly also misguided. NATO itself recognizes that obtaining parliamentary and public support for military

---

[100] Lords Committee on the Constitution, *Waging War* (n 2) [25]; *Waging War* (n 82) 131. For detailed consideration of how treaties affect decision-making about the deployment of force, see N White, *Democracy Goes to War: British Military Deployments under International Law* (OUP 2009) esp ch 3, 4, and 5.
[101] North Atlantic Treaty (4/4/1949, TS 056 1949, Cmd 7789).
[102] Consolidated Treaty on European Union (7/2/1992, TS 012 1994, Cm 2485), amended by the Treaty of Nice (26/2/2001, TS 022 2003, Cm 5879).
[103] Charter of the United Nations (26/6/1945, Treaty Series No TS 067 1946, Cmd 7015).
[104] (17/3/1948, TS 001 1949, Cm 7599).
[105] Lords Committee on the Constitution, *Waging War* (n 82) 130.
[106] Lords Committee on the Constitution, *Waging War* (n 82) 131.

operations is vital to their success. A recent strategic review recommended that, through transparency and effective public communications, the Alliance must strive to attract and maintain public and legislative backing for its operations:[107]

The more open NATO leaders are in their deliberations, and the more clearly they explain the specific goals and rationale for NATO participation in any operation, the more likely it is that the Alliance will be able to attract the level of popular and parliamentary support it must have to fulfil its missions.

NATO's decision-making process accommodates the need for governments to seek parliamentary approval for military operations.[108] NATO's decision-making relies on negotiation, deliberation, and consensus. Decisions are rarely taken in one go, but instead usually after several rounds of deliberation, which allow for communications between national representatives and their national governments and legislatures, and subsequent negotiations and discussions. If national representatives remain in doubt, they often agree to a compromise, subject to a reservation which can be lifted after further consultation with their national government or legislature. Another option is to register a dissent to a decision (for example, by a dissenting footnote to communiques), without preventing its adoption.[109] Finally, it is not a necessary element of parliamentary involvement that the Commons should have the power to restrict or place conditions on the use of the armed forces. I do not suggest that the Commons should hold such power.

Part IV Role of the Courts

Introduction

Statutory codification of reform of the war prerogative raises the potential for judicial intervention to enforce the statutory provisions. For some of the reviews and inquiries into reform of the war prerogative, the potential for judicial intervention was a strong disincentive counting against a statutory

---

[107] NATO, 'NATO 2020: Assured Security; Dynamic Engagement. Analysis and Recommendations of the Group of Experts on a New Strategic Concept for NATO' (17 May 2010) 33 <http://www.nato.int/ebookshop>.

[108] NATO, 'The Comprehensive Political Guidance Endorsed by NATO Heads of State and Government on 29 November 2006' [8], reproduced in 'Towards the New Strategic Concept: A Selection of Background Documents' (NATO Public Diplomacy Division 2006) <http://www.nato.int/ebookshop>.

[109] W van Eekelen, 'Sending Troops Abroad' (Democratic Control of Armed Forces 2006) 5–6 <http://www.dcaf.ch/Publications/Sending-Troops-Abroad>.

requirement for parliamentary involvement. I believe these concerns were overstated, as they failed to take account of how the courts approach issues relating to the exercise of the war prerogative (and national security more broadly), or how parliamentary privilege would limit the courts' jurisdiction to consider claims that were based on parliamentary proceedings. The introduction of the proposed statute is unlikely to change materially the courts' approach to attempted challenges to the exercise of the war prerogative on the established grounds of judicial review. It is likely that the courts will continue to find the issues raised to be non-justiciable, or, if justiciable, to be subject to the lightest of scrutiny.[110] The only possible change might concern the courts' approach to challenges on the grounds of illegality.

As Lord Diplock said in the *GCHQ* case, the decision-maker must understand correctly the law that regulates his decision-making power and give effect to it.[111] A claim that the government failed to comply with a statutory condition regulating its war prerogative might potentially found a challenge on the ground of illegality. I will identify here four possible challenges and hypothesize as to the likely judicial response. I contend that the courts would continue to tread lightly in cases involving challenges to the exercise of the war prerogative. The courts are aware, and ought to be aware, of their institutional competence and expertise and the limits of their legitimacy. In addition, issues as to parliamentary privilege are likely to rule out judicial consideration of matters arising in proceedings of Parliament and the JCNS. However, cases involving flagrant disregard by the government of the statutory requirements might entice the courts into playing a vital role in holding the government to account for their non-compliance. The courts' intervention in such cases, as a constitutional 'backstop', would reinforce public accountability and the rule of law, and would supplement the political controls which the statute imposes on the government's war prerogative.

Potential Judicial Intervention

The first possible claim might arise where the government failed to obtain a majority vote in the Commons in support of deployment but went ahead and deployed regardless. In this situation, it would be a simple exercise for the court to determine whether or not a majority in the Commons voted in support of the government's proposed deployment. Parliamentary privilege would not preclude the court from making such a finding. The courts have the right to prove the occurrence of an event (but not to question its propriety),

---

[110] See ch 4 for how the courts have dealt with challenges to the exercise of the war prerogative on the established grounds of judicial review.
[111] *CCSU v Minister for the Civil Service* [1985] AC 374, 408.

by reference to the House records and *Hansard*.[112] The courts' approach in the context of legislative law-making reinforces this conclusion. They have held they have the power of determination of a question concerning compliance with 'manner and form' provisions which are directed at law-making procedures, rather than the substance or powers of law-making.[113] The European Parliamentary Elections Act 2002 provides a good precedent for judicial intervention of this type: section 12 of that Act makes statutory approval a condition precedent to the ratification of any treaty which provides for an increase in the powers of the European Parliament. In *R (on the application of Wheeler) v Prime Minister*[114] the Divisional Court commented, obiter, that a decision to ratify without such approval would be amenable to review.

A second potential claim might be that the government improperly relied on the 'emergency exception', exempting the government from seeking parliamentary support for a deployment. I expect that the courts would approach the issue with a high level of deference. As long as the executive offered credible evidence, it is likely that the courts would accept the executive's claims that there existed an emergency situation and that it would be detrimental to national security to comply with the standard statutory requirements. If there patently was no emergency, the courts would (and should) intervene and hold that the government failed to comply with its statutory obligations. However, in the absence of such flagrant disregard, the courts should defer to the government's assessment of the threat posed to national security and the response necessary to meet that threat. The proviso is that the government must justify its assessment and offer evidence in support. More in-depth judicial consideration of whether there was in fact an emergency situation which required immediate action would involve the courts in matters over which they have deferred to the government on the grounds of institutional incompetence and democratic legitimacy.[115]

A third claim might be that the government improperly identified a particular deployment as one which did not require prior parliamentary approval. Such a claim could arise in a situation where the government deployed to what it said was a peacekeeping mission, which would not entail the use of force, when the evidence suggested otherwise. The court might look to the authority under which a proclaimed peacekeeping mission was established,

---

[112] *Church of Scientology of California v Johnson-Smith* [1972] 1 QB 522; *Prebble v TVNZ Ltd* [1994] 3 NZLR 1, 11 (PC).
[113] *R (on the application of Jackson) v A-G* [2005] UKHL 56, [2006] 1 AC 262.
[114] [2008] EWHC 1409 (Admin) [55].
[115] For discussion of the unsuitability of judicial intervention in such issues in the American context, see LG Ratner, 'The Coordinated Warmaking Power: Legislative, Executive, and Judicial Roles' (1970–71) 44 Southern California Law Review 461, 481.

such as the specific articles of the UN Treaty. But the courts are unlikely to delve too deeply into the factual basis on which the government based its assessments that force was not expected. The courts would recognize that such situations are fluid and might change materially in a short time. In most cases, it would not be appropriate for the courts to seek and consider evidence about the context in which the deployment took place, the government's assessment about the nature of the situation, or other related matters.

A fourth potential claim is that the government improperly withheld information from either the JCNS or the Commons. But again, the courts are unlikely to find the issues justiciable. There are three reasons. First, the statute establishes the JCNS to administer and supervise the information disclosure obligations. This political control should be a sufficient safeguard, and the courts should be very slow to intervene in its operation. In a related context, the courts have held they should give 'great weight' to the decisions of Parliament about the 'devices of democratic process'. Elected politicians are best placed to judge the measures necessary to safeguard the integrity of democracy.[116]

Secondly, the courts are likely to defer to the executive's determinations as to what information should be withheld from Parliament on national security grounds. The only requirement the courts might insist upon is that the executive must adduce evidence to support its assertions.

Thirdly, parliamentary privilege, properly interpreted and applied, would preclude the courts from entering upon consideration of proceedings of Parliament or the JCNS. Article 9 of the Bill of Rights 1688 holds: 'That the freedom of speech, and debates or proceedings in Parliament, ought not to be impeached or questioned in any court or place out of Parliament.' Article 9 protects from challenge in the courts what is said or done within the walls of Parliament in performance of its legislative functions or in protection of its established privileges.[117] The courts cannot consider as evidence proceedings in Parliament if the purpose of admitting the evidence is to question or impeach what is said or done in those proceedings.[118] A plaintiff or defendant cannot use House records to establish that a party has misled the House or has acted with malice or an improper motive.[119]

Parliamentary privilege represents a powerful disincentive to judicial intervention. The courts should regard challenges to the adequacy or correctness of

---

[116] *R (on the application of Animal Defenders International) v Secretary of State for Culture, Media and Sport* [2008] UKHL 15, [2008] 2 WLR 781, [33] (Lord Bingham). These comments were made in the context of a case concerning a ban on political advertising.

[117] *Burdett v Abbott* (1811) 14 East 1; *Stockdale v Hansard* (1839) 9 Ad & E1; *Bradlaugh v Gossett* (1884) 12 QBD 271; *British Railways Board v Pickin* [1974] AC 765; *Pepper (Inspector of Taxes) v Hart* [1993] AC 593; *Prebble* (n 112).

[118] Joseph (n 11) 424–5.

[119] *Edinburgh and Dalkeith Rly v Wauchope* (1842) 8 Cl & F 710; *Pickin* (n 117); *Prebble* (n 112).

information provided to the Commons as raising issues that fall outside their jurisdiction by virtue of article 9. To show that the information provided to the Commons was inadequate or incorrect, the courts would need to examine Parliament's records to determine what information was provided, and then determine whether it was adequate or correct. It is likely that article 9 would bar the courts from doing so because it would involve the courts in questioning or impeaching what was said or done in the House. The ambit of parliamentary privilege has narrowed over recent years, but not so much as to allow judicial intervention in this context. On current case law, the use of *Hansard* is precluded where the speaker is potentially exposed to legal liability, or where there is an attempt to impugn the truth of the parliamentary statement or the speaker's motive for making it.[120]

Remedy

I propose that the statute would exclude all but one judicial remedy for contravention of the statutory provisions. I recommend that the only remedy available be a 'declaration of non-compliance', modelled on the comparable remedy of a declaration of incompatibility under the HRA. A declaration of non-compliance would have no legal effect on a government decision to deploy the armed forces, and no criminal or other liability would flow from the government action. Nor would a declaration of non-compliance require the government to recall the armed forces or halt the military operation. A declaration would engage the same sort of dialogue as occurs under the HRA when the courts issue declarations of incompatibility. By making such a declaration, the court would communicate its finding that the government acted in contravention of the statute, but the political branches (the government and Parliament) would determine the appropriate response.

Part V Conclusion

This chapter proposed that the participation of the House of Commons in the exercise of the war prerogative should be substantive. By substantive, I mean that the involvement of the Commons should be informed and based on a process of reasoned deliberation, and that the executive should be responsive to those deliberations. I am concerned to avoid confining parliamentary

---

[120] *Wilson v First Country Trust Ltd (No 2)* [2003] UKHL 40, [2004] 1 AC 816 [65]. For evaluation and comment of the courts' recent treatment of art 9 parliamentary privilege, see Philip A Joseph, 'Parliament's Attenuated Privilege of Freedom of Speech' (2010) 126 Law Quarterly Review 568.

involvement to a formal rubber-stamping of the executive's decision to commit to war. I have recommended that the courts play a limited, constitutional 'backstop' role in situations where the government has flagrantly disregarded the statutory requirements and the political controls have failed.

Recent proposals for the Commons' involvement have focused on whether the decision to go to war should be the subject of a vote in the Commons. However, these proposals fail to consider adequately the processes leading up to the vote; for example, MPs' access to relevant information, the timing of parliamentary involvement, and the nature of the debate in the Commons leading to the vote. Confining the House of Commons' involvement to a vote on whether or not to support the government's decision to deploy, without ensuring that the vote is part of a process of informed and reasoned deliberation, represents a formalistic approach to democratic decision-making. It reduces the legitimacy of political decision-making to an aggregation of votes and simply adds a veneer of democratic legitimacy to an executive fait accompli. The issues posed by reform of the war prerogative are challenging, but this chapter has shown that they can be met by careful institutional design.

7
Conclusions

I introduced this book by posing three questions. The first focused on why the war prerogative is identified as axiomatically an 'executive' power. I was interested to identify the theoretical justifications that have been and are advanced for the constitutional arrangements for the war power. My historical research, presented in chapter 2, showed that there has been an ongoing assertion in political and theoretical discourses of exclusive executive power over war and the related spheres of foreign policy and defence. However, the justifications advanced for this arrangement have evolved over the past four centuries. Two points are of significance: first, although the design of English constitutional arrangements is commonly identified as an 'evolutionary' model, my analysis of historical orthodox discourses shows how political theories and values have shaped thinking about those arrangements. Our constitutional arrangements are not solely the end-result of political pragmatism and organic evolution. Secondly, 'institutional' arguments have been to the fore since the eighteenth century. These arguments are founded on the special demands of the war and foreign policy powers and the institutional competence and expertise of the executive. The same arguments continue to be raised today to justify executive control over the war prerogative and to reject calls for increased parliamentary involvement in its exercise.

The second question asked how the war prerogative has been exercised in practice. Has the making of war and deployment of force been exclusively for the executive, to the exclusion of Parliament and the courts? The historical analysis in chapter 3 showed that Parliament (particularly the House of Commons) has played an active and substantive role in the exercise and scrutiny of the war prerogative. Its role has evolved as political power shifted from the monarch to ministers responsible to Parliament, and ideas changed concerning the relationship between the governing and the governed. These findings revealed a deep dichotomy between orthodox political and theoretical discourses and how the war prerogative has been exercised in practice. Furthermore, they revealed that Parliament's role in decisions about war has been contested for over four hundred years. The concerns raised in the fall-out from Iraq are not new.

Chapter 4 showed that the courts have consistently refused to intervene in the exercise of the war prerogative. They have, however, been more willing to intervene in the exercise of incidental war powers and powers not intimately connected with the deployment of force or conduct of war. I argued that the courts possess jurisdiction to review the exercise of the war prerogative, but that, in all but the most extreme case, they should find non-justiciable issues intimately connected with war. The courts, relative to Parliament, are ill-equipped to scrutinize issues concerning the deployment of force or conduct of war. These are paradigm 'polycentric' issues over which the courts lack institutional competence, expertise, and legitimacy.

The third question asked whether there were better ways to organize our constitutional arrangements concerning the war prerogative. In chapter 5, I showed that reforms to institutional design need not be directed at large-scale constitutional arrangements. The more realistic and achievable option is to focus on small-scale reforms which work within existing large-scale arrangements. Institutional mechanisms can promote democratic values while avoiding the need for extensive institutional change. I argued that there need not be a trade-off between democratic values and 'efficiency' (which in this context means operational concerns) in institutional design. Institutional mechanisms can promote both.

In chapter 6, I explained my proposals to reform the constitutional arrangements for the war prerogative. These proposals accept that the executive should retain primary responsibility for decisions about war, national security, and foreign policy. But this does not discount the capacity and legitimacy of other governmental institutions to ensure that the executive exercises its war powers responsibly and justifiably. Parliament should play the key role in scrutinizing the government's conduct of war. Its institutional competence to do so stems from its processes of decision-making and its relationship and interactions with the executive, while its legitimacy is founded on its democratic and representative character. I propose that the courts play a secondary scrutinizing role in the form of a 'constitutional backstop' in cases where the government flagrantly disregards the statutory provisions. In more peripheral issues concerning the war prerogative, the courts have, and should, intervene, particularly when individual rights are in play. In relation to issues closer to the heart of the exercise of the war prerogative, however, the courts lack the institutional competence and legitimacy to adjudicate on the issues raised.

I finish by making two comments of broader consequence. The first is the need to revisit the prioritization of national security over all other interests and goals; a prioritization which is seen across a range of our constitutional arrangements, practices, and rules. It is axiomatic that the state must protect itself, its citizens, and their ways of life. It also seems that the threats posed to our national security are materially different from the types of threats previously posed. However, that should not lead to an unthinking prioritization of claimed national security interests over all others. We should look to ways that we can ensure the protection of national security while also protecting and promoting other fundamental goals and values of our ways of life. Two particular examples considered in this thesis are subjecting information relevant to national security to a revised balancing test; and strengthening the capacity of Parliament to make and scrutinize decisions about national security. My concern has been to propose workable and pragmatic reforms to particular arrangements, practices, and rules, which reconcile and promote different (and sometimes conflicting) interests and values.

The second broader implication is the value of historical analysis in constitutional law. The English constitution is undeniably the product of historical evolution. Its arrangements, institutions, and practices have evolved over centuries. An understanding of that evolution is essential to an understanding of our present arrangements. The historical nature of the English constitution should be valued and appreciated, but it should not be misused: we should not equate the fact of long practice with its continued relevance or authority. Some of our constitutional arrangements, institutions, and practices are no longer appropriate for our needs: some simply do not reflect the values that now shape our constitutional thinking and practice. I have argued that we should look to institutional mechanisms (small-scale reform to arrangements, institutions, and practices), that can promote normative goals, within the existing large-scale arrangements.

The decision to deploy the armed forces is too important and solemn a decision to leave to the Prime Minister and an inner cabal of government ministers. In a constitution such as ours, which enshrines democratic values, we must revise our constitutional arrangements. The executive, Parliament, and the courts must all contribute, in accordance with their respective institutional competence and legitimacy, to the making and scrutiny of decisions about war.

Bibliography

BOOKS, JOURNAL ARTICLES, AND CONTRIBUTIONS TO EDITED COLLECTIONS

Ackerman B, 'The New Separation of Powers' [2000] 113 *Harvard Law Review* 633
——, *Before the Next Attack: Preserving Civil Liberties in an Age of Terrorism* (Yale University Press 2006)
Adams G, *Constitutional History of England* (Jonathan Cape 1921)
Adams S, 'Spain or the Netherlands? The Dilemmas of Early Stuart Foreign Policy' in H Tomlinson (ed), *Before the English Civil War: Essays on Early Stuart Politics and Government* (MacMillan Press 1983)
Adamson J, 'The Triumph of Oligarchy: The Management of War and the Committee of Both Kingdoms, 1644–45' in C Kyle and J Peacey (eds), *Parliament at Work: Parliamentary Committees, Political Power and Public Access in Early Modern Britain* (Boydell Press 2002) 101
Allan T, 'Human Rights and Judicial Review: A Critique of Due Deference' [2006] *Cambridge Law Journal* 671
Allison J, 'History in the *Law of the Constitution*' (2007) 28 *The Journal of Legal History* 263
——, *The English Historical Constitution: Continuity, Change and European Effects* (Cambridge University Press 2007)
Amery L, *Thoughts on the Constitution* (Oxford University Press 1947)
Anderson C and Morgan T, 'Domestic Support and Diversionary External Conflict in Great Britain, 1950–1992' (1999) 61 *Journal of Politics* 799
Anderson M and Hatton R (eds), *Studies in Diplomatic History: Essays in Memory of David Bayne Horn* (Longman 1970)
Anon, 'Our Foreign Policy' (1882) 5 *Scottish Review* 332
Anson W, *The Law and Custom of the Constitution*, 4th edn (Clarendon Press 1935)
Aristotle, *The Politics* (translated by C Lord, University of Chicago Press 1985)
Ashworth A, 'Security, Terrorism and the Value of Human Rights' in BJ Goold and L Lazarus (eds), *Security and Human Rights* (Hart Publishing 2007) 203
Bagehot W, *The English Constitution* (The World's Classics edn, Oxford University Press 1974)
——, 'The House of Commons' (1867) in P Norton (ed), *Legislatures* (Oxford University Press 1990)
Bamforth N and Leyland P (eds), *Public Law in a Multi-Layered Constitution* (Hart Publishing 2003)
Banks W and Raven-Hansen P, 'Pulling the Purse Strings of the Commander in Chief' (1994) 80 *Virginia Law Review* 833

Barber N, 'Prelude to the Separation of Powers' (2001) 60 *Cambridge Law Journal* 59
—, 'Two Meditations on the Thoughts of Many Minds' (2010) 88 *Texas Law Review* 807
Barendt E, 'Separation of Powers and Constitutional Government' [1995] *Public Law* 599
Barry B, *Theories of Justice* (Harvester Wheatsheaf 1989)
—, *Justice as Impartiality* (Oxford University Press 1995)
Baxter S, 'Recent Writings on William III' (1966) 38 *Journal of Modern History* 256
Beer S, 'The British Legislature and the Problem of Mobilising Consent' in E Frank (ed), *Lawmakers in a Changing World* (Englewood Cliffs 1966)
Benhabib S, *Situating the Self* (Polity 1992)
Bentham J, *The Works of Jeremy Bentham* (J Bowring ed, William Tait 1843)
—, 'An Introduction to the Principles of Morals and Legislation' in SM Cahn (ed), *Classics of Modern Political Theory: Machiavelli to Mill* (Oxford University Press 1997) 685
Berrington H, 'MPs and Their Constituents in Britain: The History of the Relationship' in *Representatives of the People? Parliamentarians and Constituents in Western Democracies* (Gower 1985) 15
Birch T (ed), *Works of Sir Walter Raleigh* (Oxford University Press 1829)
Black J, *British Foreign Policy in the Age of Walpole* (John Donald Publishers 1985)
—, *A System of Ambition? British Foreign Policy 1660–1793* (Longman 1991)
—, *Parliament and Foreign Policy in the Eighteenth Century* (Cambridge University Press 2004)
—, 'Hanover and British Foreign Policy 1714–60' (2005) 120 *English Historical Review* 303
Blackburn R and Kennon A, *Griffith and Ryle on Parliament: Functions, Practice and Procedures*, 2nd edn (Sweet and Maxwell 2003)
Blackstone W, *Commentaries on the Laws of England, in Four Books* vol 1, 13th edn (E Christian ed, Strahan 1800)
Blanning T, '"That Horrid Electorate" or "Ma Patrie Germanique"? George III, Hanover, and the Fuerstenbund of 1785' (1977) 20 *Historical Journal* 20
Bognador V (ed), *Representatives of the People? Parliamentarians and Constituents in Western Democracies* (Gower 1985)
— (ed), *The British Constitution in the Twentieth Century* (Oxford University Press 2003)
—, 'Conclusion' in *The British Constitution in the Twentieth Century* (Oxford University Press 2003)
Born H and Haenggi H (eds), *'The Double Democratic Deficit': Parliamentary Accountability and the Use of Force under International Auspices* (Ashgate 2004)
Born H, Johnson L, and Leigh I (eds), *Who's Watching the Spies? Establishing Intelligence Service Accountability* (Potomac Publishers 2005)
Boynton G and Kim CL (eds), *Legislative Systems in Developing Countries* (Duke University Press 1975)
Bradley A and Ewing K, *Constitutional and Administrative Law*, 14th edn (Pearson Education 2007)

Brailsford H, 'The Control of Foreign Affairs: A Proposal' (1909) 4/13 *English Review* 122
Brazier R, *Ministers of the Crown* (Clarendon Press 1997)
Brazier R and de Smith S, *Constitutional and Administrative Law*, 8th edn (Penguin Books 1998)
Brown S, 'Public Interest Immunity' [1994] *Public Law* 579
Bueno De Mesquita B, 'Game Theory, Political Economy, and the Evolving Study of War and Peace' (2006) 100 *American Political Science Review* 637
Burall S, Donnelly B, and Weir S *Not In Our Name: Democracy and Foreign Policy in the UK* (Politico's 2006)
Burgess G, *Absolute Monarch and the Stuart Constitution* (Yale University Press 1996)
Burke E, *The Works of the Right Honourable Edmund Burke* vol 10 (Rivington edn 1826)
Cahn S (ed), *Classics of Modern Political Theory: Machiavelli to Mill* (Oxford University Press 1997)
Canavan F, 'Edmund Burke' in L Strauss and J Cropsey (eds), *History of Political Philosophy*, 2nd edn (Rand McNally and Company 1972)
Cane P, 'Prerogative Acts, Acts of State and Justiciability' (1980) 29 *International and Comparative Law Quarterly* 680
—— and Tushnet M (eds), *The Oxford Handbook of Legal Studies* (Oxford University Press 2003)
Carlyle E, 'Clarendon and the Privy Council, 1660–67' (1912) 27 *English Historical Review* 251
Carnall G and Nicholson C (eds), *The Impeachment of Warren Hastings* (Edinburgh University Press 1989)
Carter J, 'The Revolution and the Constitution' in G Holmes (ed), *Britain after the Glorious Revolution 1689–1714* (Macmillan 1969)
Chan S and Safran W, 'Public Opinion as a Constraint against War: Democracies' Responses to Operation Iraqi Freedom' (2006) 2 *Foreign Policy Analysis* 137
Chapman R and Hunt M (eds), *Open Government in a Theoretical and Practical Context* (Ashgate 2006)
Chitty J, *A Treatise on the Law of the Prerogative of the Crown: And the Relative Duties and Rights of the Subject* (Butterworth 1820)
Chubb B, *The Control of Public Expenditure: Financial Committees of the House of Commons* (Clarendon Press 1952)
Clarke J, *British Diplomacy and Foreign Policy 1782–1865: The National Interest* (Unwin Hyman 1989)
Cohen EA, *Supreme Command: Soldiers, Statesmen, and Leadership in Wartime* (The Free Press 2002)
Cohen J, 'Deliberation and Democratic Legitimacy' in A Hamlin and P Pettit (eds), *The Good Polity: Normative Analysis of the State* (Blackwell 1989)
Collingwood R, *The Idea of History* (Oxford University Press 1946)
Collins L, 'Foreign Relations and the Judiciary' (2002) 51 *International and Comparative Law Quarterly* 485
Cope E, *Politics without Parliaments: 1629–40* (Allen and Unwin 1987)

Lord Courtney, *The Working Constitution of the United Kingdom and Its Outgrowth* (London 1910)

Cowley P, '"Crossing the Floor": Representative Theory and Practice in Britain' [1996] *Public Law* 214

Craig G and George A, *Force and Statecraft: Diplomatic Problems of Our Time*, 3rd edn (Oxford University Press 1995)

Craig P, 'Prerogative, Precedent and Power' in C Forsyth and I Hare (eds), *The Golden Metwand and the Crooked Cord: Essays on Public Law in Honour of Sir William Wade QC* (Clarendon Press 1998) 65

Crick B, *The Reform of Parliament*, 2nd edn (Weidenfeld and Nicholson 1968)

Cromwell V, 'The Losing of Initiative by the House of Commons, 1780–1914' (1968) 18 *Transactions of the Royal History Society* 1

Cropsey J and Strauss L, *History of Political Philosophy*, 2nd edn (Rand McNally and Company 1972)

Dahl R, *On Democracy* (Yale University 1998)

Daintith T and Page A, *The Executive in the Constitution: Structure, Autonomy, and Internal Control* (Oxford University Press 1999)

Daly P, 'Justiciability and the "Political Question Doctrine"' [2010] *Public Law* 16

Davies G, *Essays on the Later Stuarts* (The Huntington Library 1958)

Davies P, 'Iraq, Intelligence and the Constitution' (2008) 14 *Intelligence Studies Review* 4

de Lolme J, *The Constitution of England, or an Account of the English Government* (Robinson 1796)

Dicey A and Wade ECS, *Introduction to the Study of the Law of the Constitution* (first published 1895, 10th edn, MacMillan and Company 1959)

Doig A and Phythian M, 'The National Interest and the Politics of Threat Exaggeration: The Blair Government's Case for War against Iraq' (2005) 76 *The Political Quarterly* 368

Doyle M, 'Kant, Liberal Legacies, and Foreign Affairs' (1983) 12 *Philosophy and Public Affairs* 205

Dryzek J, *Discursive Democracy: Politics, Policy, and Political Science* (Cambridge University Press 1990)

——, *Deliberative Democracy and Beyond: Liberals, Critics, Contestations* (Oxford University Press 2000)

Dunleavy P and Jones G, 'Leaders, Politics and Institutional Change: The Decline of Prime Ministerial Accountability to the House of Commons, 1868–1990' (1993) 23 *British Journal of Political Science* 267

Dworkin R, *Taking Rights Seriously* (Harvard University Press 1978)

Dyson S, 'Personality and Foreign Policy: Tony Blair's Iraq Decisions' (2006) 2 *Foreign Policy Analysis* 289

Dyzenhaus D, *The Constitution of Law: Legality in a Time of Emergency* (Cambridge University Press 2006)

——, 'Deference, Security and Human Rights' in BJ Goold and L Lazarus (eds), *Security and Human Rights* (Hart Publishing 2007) 125

Elliot M, 'Judicial Review's Scope, Foundations and Purposes: Joining the Dots' [2012] *New Zealand Law Review* 75

Ely J, 'Suppose Congress Wanted a War Powers Act That Worked' [1988] 88 *Columbia Law Review* 1379

Emden C (ed), *Selected Speeches on the Constitution* vol 1 (Oxford University Press, Humphrey Milford 1939)

Endicott T, 'The Reason of Law' (2003) 48 *American Journal of Jurisprudence* 83

Erskine J, *The Fatal Consequences of Ministerial Influence* (London 1736)

Estlund D, *Democratic Authority: A Philosophical Framework* (Princeton University Press 2008)

Ewing K, 'The Futility of the Human Rights Act' [2004] *Public Law* 829

—— and Tham J, 'The Continuing Futility of the Human Rights Act' [2008] Public Law 668.

Feldman D, Human Rights, Terrorism and Risk: The Roles of Politicians and Judges' [2006] *Public Law* 364

—— (ed), *Oxford Principles of English Law: English Public Law*, 2nd edn (OUP 2009)

Fenster M, 'The Opacity of Transparency' (2006) 91 *Iowa Law Review* 885

Fieldhouse E, Pattie C, and Johnston R, 'The Price of Conscience: The Electoral Correlates and Consequences of Free Votes and Rebellions in the British House of Commons, 1987–1992' (1994) 24 *British Journal of Political Science* 359

Finer H, 'The British Cabinet, The House of Commons and the War' (1941) 56 *Political Science Quarterly* 321

Finer S, 'The Contemporary Context of Representation' in *Representatives of the People? Parliamentarians and Constituents in Western Democracies* (Gower 1985) 286

Firth C, *The Last Years of the Protectorate 1656–1658* vol 1 (Longmans, Green and Company 1909)

Fisher H (ed), *Collected Papers of Frederic William Maitland* (first published 1888, Cambridge University Press 1911)

Fishkin J, *Democracy and Deliberation: New Directions for Democratic Reform* (Yale University Press 1991)

Fleck D (ed), *The Handbook of International Humanitarian Law*, 2nd edn (OUP 2008)

Flournoy F, *Parliament and War* (PS King and Son 1927)

Forsyth C, 'Judicial Review, the Royal Prerogative and National Security' (1985) 36 *Northern Ireland Legal Quarterly* 25

—— and Hare I (eds), *The Golden Metwand and the Crooked Cord: Essays on Public Law in Honour of Sir William Wade QC* (Clarendon Press 1998)

Foster C, 'Cabinet Government in the Twentieth Century' (2004) 67 *Modern Law Review* 753

Foster ER (ed), *The Proceedings in Parliament: 1610* (Yale University Press 1966)

Frank E (ed), *Lawmakers in a Changing World* (Englewood Cliffs 1966)

Fraser P, 'The Growth of Ministerial Control in the Nineteenth Century House of Commons' (1960) 75 *The English Historical Review* 444

Fredman S, 'From Deference to Democracy: The Role of Equality under the Human Rights Act 1998' (2006) 122 *Law Quarterly Review* 53

Freedman L, 'Even-Handedness, Guidelines and Defence Sales to Iraq' [1996] *Public Law* 391

Friedman D, 'Torture and the Common Law' (2006) 2 *European Human Rights Review* 180

Fuller L, 'The Forms and Limits of Adjudication' (1978–79) 92 *Harvard Law Review* 353

Fussner F, 'William Camden's "Discourse Concerning the Prerogative of the Crown"' (1957) 101 *Proceedings of the American Philosophy Society* 204

Galligan D, 'The Paradox of Constitutionalism or the Potential of Constitutional Theory?' (2008) 28 *Oxford Journal of Legal Studies* 343

Gardiner S (ed), *History of England under Buckingham and Charles I* (Longmans, Green and Company 1875)

——, *The Constitutional Documents of the Puritan Revolution, 1625–1660*, 3rd edn (Oxford University Press 1906)

Gee G and Webber GCN, 'What is a Political Constitution?' (2010) 30 *Oxford Journal of Legal Studies* 273

Gerth H and Wright Mills C (eds), *Essays in Sociology* (Routledge 1948)

Gibbs G, 'Parliament and Foreign Policy in the Age of Stanhope and Walpole' (1962) 77 The English Historical Review 18

——, 'The Revolution in Foreign Policy' in G Holmes (ed), *Britain after the Glorious Revolution* (Macmillan 1969) 59

——, 'Laying Treaties before Parliament in the Eighteenth Century' in R Hatton and M Anderson (eds), *Studies in Diplomatic History: Essays in Memory of David Bayne Horn* (Longman 1970) 116

Gibson C, *Securing the State: Reforming the National Security Decisionmaking Process at the Civil–Military Nexus* (Ashgate 2008)

Glees A and Davies P, 'Intelligence, Iraq and the Limits of Legislative Accountability during Political Crisis' (2006) 21 *Intelligence and National Security* 848

Glees A, Davies PHJ, and Morrison JNL, *The Open Side of Secrecy: Britain's Intelligence and Security Committee* (The Social Affairs Unit 2006)

Goldsworthy J, *The Sovereignty of Parliament: History and Philosophy* (Clarendon Press 1999)

Goodin R (ed), *The Theory of Institutional Design* (Cambridge University Press 1996)

——, 'Institutions and Their Design' in *The Theory of Institutional Design* (Cambridge University Press 1996) 1

Goold B and Lazarus L (eds), *Security and Human Rights* (Hart Publishing 2007)

Gordley J, 'Why Look Backward' (2002) 50 *American Journal of Comparative Law* 657

——, 'Comparative Law and Legal History' in M Reimann and R Zimmerman (eds), *The Oxford Handbook of Comparative Law* (Oxford University Press 2006) 753

Green L, *The Contemporary Law of Armed Conflict*, 3rd edn (Manchester University Press 1993)

Grey H, 'Parliamentary Government' (1858) in H Hanham (ed), *The Nineteenth-Century Constitution 1815–1914: Documents and Commentary* (Cambridge University Press 1969) 13

Griffith J, 'The Political Constitution' (1979) 42 *Modern Law Review* 1
Grotius H, *Law of War and Peace* (1625)
Gutmann A and Thompson D, *Democracy and Disagreement* (Belknap Press 1996)
Habermas J, *A Theory of Communicative Action* (MIT Press 1984)
——, *Between Facts and Norms: Contributions to a Discourse Theory of Law and Democracy* (Polity 1996)
Halsbury's Laws of England, 'Armed Forces', vol 3, 5th edn (2011)
——, 'International Relations Law', vol 61, 5th edn (2011)
——, 'Constitutional Law and Human Rights', vol 8(2), 4th edn (1996 reissue)
——, 'Armed Conflict and Emergency', vol 3, 5th edn (2011)
Hamlin A and Pettit P (eds), *The Good Polity: Normative Analysis of the State* (Blackwell 1989)
Haenggi H, 'The Use of Force under International Auspices: Parliamentary Accountability and "Democratic Deficits"' in H Born and H Haenggi (eds), *The 'Double Democratic Deficit': Parliamentary Accountability and the Use of Force under International Auspices* (Aldershot 2004) 3
Hand G, 'AV Dicey's Unpublished Materials on the Comparative Study of the Constitution' in G Hand and J McBride (eds), *Droits Sans Frontieres: Essays in Honour of L. Neville Brown* (Holdsworth Club 1991)
Hanham H (ed), *The Nineteenth-Century Constitution 1815–1914: Documents and Commentary* (Cambridge University Press 1969)
Hardie F, *The Political Influence of the British Monarchy: 1868–1952* (BT Batsford 1970)
Harling P and Mandler P, 'From "Fiscal-Military" State to Lassez-Faire State, 1760–1850' (1993) 32 *Journal of British Studies* 44
Harrington J, 'The Commonwealth of Oceana', *The Political Works of James Harrington* (J Pocock ed, Cambridge University Press 1977).
Harris B, 'Judicial Review, Justiciability and the Prerogative of Mercy' (2003) 62 *Cambridge Law Journal* 631
Harris S, *Out of Control: British Foreign Policy and the Union of Democratic Control, 1914–1918* (University of Hull Press 1996)
Hart H, *The Concept of Law* (Clarendon Press 1961)
Hart Jnr J, *The Rule of Law 1603–1660* (Pearson Education 2003)
Hawkins A, '"Parliamentary Government" and Victorian Political Parties, c. 1830–c. 1880' (1989) 104 *The English Historical Review* 638
Held D, *Models of Democracy*, 3rd edn (Polity Press 2006)
Henkin L, 'Is There a "Political Question" Doctrine?' (1976) 85 *Yale Law Journal* 597
Hennessy P, 'Informality and Circumscription: The Blair Style of Government in War and Peace' (2005) 76 *Political Quarterly* 3
Hicks G, 'Don Pacifico, Democracy, and Danger: The Protectionist Party Critique of British Foreign Policy 1850–1852' (2004) 26 *The International History Review* 515.
Hill C, *The English Revolution 1640* (Lawrence and Wishart 1940)
Lord Hoffmann, 'The COMBAR Lecture 2001: Separation of Powers' [2002] *Judicial Review* 137

Holdsworth W, *Some Lessons from Our Legal History* (Macmillan 1928)
Holdsworth W, *A History of English Law*, 7th rev edn (Sweet and Maxwell 1956)
Holmes G (ed), *Britain after the Glorious Revolution 1689–1714* (Macmillan 1969)
Hood Phillips O, *The Principles of English Law and the Constitution* (Sweet and Maxwell 1939)
Horwitz M, *The Transformation of American Law 1870–1960: The Crisis of Legal Orthodoxy* (Oxford University Press 1992)
Hudson AH, 'Effect on Commercial Law of Non-Declaration of War' in P Rowe (ed), *The Gulf War 1990–91 in International and English Law* (Routledge 1993) 333
Hugh M, *The Making of Modern British Politics 1867–1939* (Basil Blackwell 1982)
Hunt M, 'Sovereignty's Blight: Why Contemporary Public Law Needs the Concept of "Due Deference"' in N Bamforth and P Leyland (eds), *Public Law in a Multi-Layered Constitution* (Hart 2003) 349
Huntington S, *The Soldier and the State: Theory and Politics of Civil–Military Relations* (Harvard University Press 1959)
Hyde E (Earl of Clarendon), *Selections from the History of the Rebellion and the Life by Himself* (G Huens ed, Oxford University Press 1978)
Ibbetson D, 'Historical Research in Law' in P Cane and M Tushnet (eds), *The Oxford Handbook of Legal Studies* (Oxford University Press 2003) 863
Ignatieff M, *The Lesser Evil: Political Ethics in an Age of Terror* (Edinburgh University Press 2005)
James S, 'The Potential Benefits of Freedom of Information' in R Chapman and M Hunt (eds), *Open Government in a Theoretical and Practical Context* (Ashgate 2006)
Janis I, *Groupthink: Psychological Studies of Policy Decision and Fiascoes*, 2nd edn (Houghton Mifflin 1983)
Jenkins D, 'Constitutional Reform Goes to War: Some Lessons from the United States' [2007] *Public Law* 258
——, 'Judicial Review under a British War Powers Act' (2010) 43 *Vanderbilt Journal of Transnational Law* 611
——, 'The Lockean Constitution: Separation of Powers and the Limits of Prerogative' (2011) 56 *McGill Law Journal* 543
Jennings I, *The Law and the Constitution*, 5th edn (University of London Press 1959)
Jones J (ed), *The Restored Monarchy 1660–1688* (MacMillan Press 1979)
Joseph P, 'Parliament's Attenuated Privilege of Freedom of Speech' (2010) 126 *Law Quarterly Review* 568
——, *Constitutional and Administrative Law in New Zealand*, 3rd edn (Thomson Brookers 2007)
Jowell J, 'Judicial Deference: Civility, Servility or Institutional Capacity?' [2003] *Public Law* 601
Jowell J, Le Sueur A, and Woolf H, *De Smith's Judicial Review*, 6th edn (Sweet and Maxwell 2007)
Judge D, *Representation: Theory and Practice in Britain* (Routledge 1999)
Judson M, *The Crisis of the Constitution: An Essay in Constitutional and Political Thought in England 1603–1645* (Rutgers University Press 1949)

Kaiser K, 'Transnational Relations as a Threat to the Democratic Process' (1971) 25 *International Organization* 706

Kant I, 'On the Old Saw: That May be Right in Theory but It Won't Work in Practice' (translated by EB Ashton) in S Cahn, *Classics of Modern Political Theory: Machiavelli to Mill* (Oxford University Press 1997) 555

——, 'Perpetual Peace' (translated by M Campbell Smith) in S Cahn, *Classics of Modern Political Theory: Machiavelli to Mill* (Oxford University Press 1997) 571

Kavanagh A, 'Judging the Judges under the Human Rights Act: Deference, Disillusionment and the "War on Terror"' [2009] *Public Law* 287

——, 'Defending Deference in Public Law and Constitutional Theory' (2010) 126 *Law Quarterly Review* 222

——, 'Constitutionalism, Counterterrorism, and the Courts: Changes in the British Constitutional Landscape' (2011) 9 *International Journal of Constitutional Law* 172.

Keir D, *The Constitutional History of Modern Britain 1485–1937* (Adam and Charles Black 1938)

——, 'The Case of Ship-Money' (1936) 52 *Law Quarterly Review* 546

Kelsey S, 'The Foundation of the Council of State' in C Kyle and J Peacey (eds), *Parliament at Work: Parliamentary Committees, Political Power and Public Access in Early Modern Britain* (Boydell Press 2002) 129

Kennedy M, 'Legislation, Foreign Policy, and the "Proper Business" of the Parliament of 1624' (1991) 23 *Albion: A Quarterly Journal Concerned with British Studies* 41

Kenyon J (ed), *The Stuart Constitution: Documents and Commentary*, 2nd edn (Cambridge University Press 1986)

King J, 'The Justiciability of Resource Allocation' (2007) 70 *Modern Law Review* 197

——, 'Institutional Approaches to Judicial Restraint' (2008) 28 *Oxford Journal of Legal Studies* 409

Kleinnijenhuis J, Oegena D, and van Noije L, 'Loss of Parliamentary Control Due to Mediatization and Europeanization: A Longitudinal and Cross-Sectional Analysis of Agenda Building in the UK and the Netherlands' (2008) 38 *British Journal of Political Science* 455

Komesar N, *Imperfect Alternatives: Choosing Institutions in Law, Economics and Public Policy* (University of Chicago Press 1997)

Kornberg A and Musolf L (eds), *Legislatures in Developmental Perspective* (Duke University Press 1970)

Korr C, *Cromwell and the New Model Foreign Policy* (University of California Press 1975)

Ku C and Jacobson HK, *Democratic Accountability and the Use of Force in International Law* (Cambridge University Press 2003)

Kyle C and Peacy J (eds), *Parliament at Work: Parliamentary Committees, Political Power and Public Access in Early Modern England* (Boydell Press 2002)

Lachs P, 'Advise and Consent: Parliament and Foreign Policy under the Later Stuarts' (1975) 7 *Albion: A Quarterly Journal Concerned with British Studies* 45

Lai B and Reiter D, 'Rally 'Round the Union Jack? Public Opinion and the Use of Force in the United Kingdom, 1948–2001' (2005) 49 *International Studies Quarterly* 255

Lakin S, 'How to Make Sense of the HRA: The Ises and Oughts of the British Constitution' (2010) 30 *Oxford Journal of Legal Studies* 399

Lander S, 'International Intelligence Cooperation: An Inside Perspective' (2004) 17 *Cambridge Review of International Affairs* 481

Landis J, *The Administrative Process* (Yale University Press 1938)

Langford P, 'Prime Ministers and Parliaments: The Long View; Walpole to Blair' (2006) 25 *Parliamentary History* 382

Layne C, 'Kant or Cant: The Myth of the Democratic Peace' (1994) 19 *International Security* 5

Le Sueur A, 'The Nature, Powers, and Accountability of Central Government' in D Feldman (ed), *Oxford Principles of English Law: English Public Law*, 2nd edn (OUP 2009)

Lee J, 'Parliament and Foreign Policy: Some Reflections on Westminster and Congressional Experience' (1988) 2 *Irish Studies in International Affairs* 1

Leigh D, *The Frontiers of Secrecy: Closed Government in Britain* (Junction Books 1980)

Leigh I, 'The Security Service: The Press and the Courts' [1987] *Public Law* 12

Leigh I and Lustgarten L, *In from the Cold: National Security and Parliamentary Democracy* (Clarendon Press 1994)

Locke J, 'Second Treatise of Civil Government' in S Cahn (ed), *Classics of Modern Political Theory: Machiavelli to Mill* (Oxford University Press 1997) 261

Loewenstein K, *Political Power and the Governmental Process*, 2nd edn (University of Chicago Press 1965)

Loughlin M, 'Theory and Values in Public Law: An Interpretation' [2005] *Public Law* 48

——, 'Constituent Power Subverted: From English Constitutional Argument to Constitutional Practice' in M Loughlin and N Walker (eds), *The Paradox of Constitutionalism: Constituent Power and Constitutional Reform* (Oxford University Press 2006)

Low S, 'A Foreign Affairs Committee' (1895) 38 *The Nineteenth Century: A Monthly Review* 506

——, 'The Foreign Office Autocracy' (1912) 91 *Fortnightly Review* 1

Madison J, 'The Federalist Papers' in S Cahn *Classics of Modern Political Theory: Machiavelli to Mill* (Oxford University Press 1997)

Magid H, 'Jeremy Bentham and James Mill' in L Strauss and J Cropsey (eds), *History of Political Philosophy*, 2nd edn (Rand McNally and Company 1972) 679

Maitland F, 'Why the History of English Law is Not Written' in H Fisher (ed), *Collected Papers of Frederic William Maitland* (Cambridge University Press 1911)

——, *The Constitutional History of England: A Course of Lectures Delivered by F. W. Maitland* (Cambridge University Press 1913)

Manin B, 'On Legitimacy and Deliberation' (1987) 15 *Political Thought* 351

Marshall G, 'Justiciability' in A Guest (ed), *Oxford Essays in Jurisprudence* (Oxford University Press 1961) 265

——, *Constitutional Theory* (Oxford University Press 1971)

Massoud T and Mitchell D, 'Anatomy of Failure: Bush's Decision-Making Process and the Iraq War' (2000) 5 *Foreign Policy Analysis* 265

May E, *Parliamentary Practice*, 20th edn (Butterworths 1983)

McBain G, 'Abolishing Crown Prerogatives Relating to the Military' (2011) 20 *Nottingham Law Journal* 14

McCrudden C, 'Legal Research and the Social Sciences' (2006) 122 *Law Quarterly Review* 632

McGoldrick D, 'The Boundaries of Justiciability' (2010) 59 *International and Comparative Law Quarterly* 981

McGovern E, 'The Report of the House of Commons Select Committee on Procedure: Scrutiny of Public Expenditure and Administration' (1970) 33 *Modern Law Review* 190.

McNair A and Watts A, *Legal Effects of War*, 4th edn (Cambridge University Press 1966)

Melanson G, 'Honour in Opium? The British Declaration of War on China, 1839–40' (1999) 21 *The International History Review* 855

Mendle M, 'The Great Council of Parliament and the First Ordinances: The Constitutional Theory of the Civil War' (1992) 31 *The Journal of British Studies* 133

Mill J, *An Essay on Government* (first published 1820, Cambridge University Press 1937)

Mill JS 'Considerations on Representative Government' in *Three Essays: On Liberty, Representative Government, the Subjection of Women* (first published 1861, introduction by R Wolheim, Oxford University Press 1975)

——, 'On Liberty' in S Cahn (ed), *Classics of Modern Political Theory: Machiavelli to Mill* (Oxford University Press 1997) 939

Miller J, 'The Later Stuart Monarchy' in JR Jones (ed), *The Restored Monarchy 1660–1688* (MacMillan Press 1979) 30

Milsom S, *Historical Foundations of the Common Law*, 2nd edn (Butterworths 1981)

Milward J, *The Diary of John Milward, Esq, Member of Parliament for Derbyshire September, 1666 to May, 1668* (Caroline Robbins ed, Cambridge University Press 1938)

Montesquieu, 'L'Espirit des Lois' in S Cahn (ed), *Classics of Modern Political Theory: Machiavelli to Mill* (Oxford University Press 1997) 347

Mosse G, *The Struggle for Sovereignty in England* (Michigan State College Press 1950)

Nenner H, 'The Later Stuart Age' in J Pocock (ed) (with G Schochet and L Schwoerer), *The Varieties of British Political Thought 1500–1800* (Cambridge University Press 1993) 39

Norton P, 'Parliament and Policy in Britain: The House of Commons as a Policy Influencer' (1984) 13 *Teaching Politics* 198

—— (ed), *Parliament in the 1980s* (Basil Blackwell 1985)

——, *Legislatures* (Oxford University Press 1990)

Olsen HP and Toddington S, *Architectures of Justice: Legal Theory and the Idea of Institutional Design* (Ashgate 2007)

Omand D, *Securing the State* (Hurst and Company 2010)

Ottee T, 'Avenge England's Dishonour: By-Elections, Parliament and the Politics of Foreign Policy in 1898' (2006) 121 *English Historical Review* 385

Packenham R, 'Legislatures and Political Development' in A Kornberg and L Musolf (eds), L*egislatures in Developmental Perspective* (Duke University Press 1970) 521

Palmer S, 'Freedom of Information: A New Constitutional Landscape?' in N Bamforth and P Leyland (eds), *Public Law in a Multi-Layered Constitution* (Hart Publishing 2003)

Parrish J, 'A Guide to the American Legal History Methodology' (1994) 86 *Law Library Journal* 105

Paun A and Russell M, *The House Rules? International Lessons for Enhancing the Autonomy of the House of Commons* (Constitution Unit, UCL 2007)

Perreau-Saussine A, 'British Acts of State in English Courts' [2007] *British Yearbook of International Law* 176

Peters D and Wagner W, 'Between Military Efficiency and Democratic Legitimacy: Mapping Parliamentary War Powers in Contemporary Democracies, 1989–2004' (2011) 64 *Parliamentary Affairs* 175

Pettit P, 'Democracy, Electoral and Contestatory' in I Shapiro and S Macedo (eds), *Designing Democratic Institutions* (NY University Press 2000)

Phillipson N, 'Politeness and Politics in the Reigns of Anne and the Early Hanoverians' in J Pocock (ed) (with G Schochet and L Schwoerer), *The Varieties of British Political Thought 1500–1800* (Cambridge University Press 1993) 214

Phythian M, 'Hutton and Scott: A Tale of Two Inquiries' (2005) 58 *Parliamentary Affairs* 124

Pictet J (ed), *Commentary on the Geneva Conventions of 12 August 1949* vol III (International Committee of the Red Cross 1958)

Pitt W, *Orations on the French War* (JM Dent 1906)

Pocock J, *The Ancient Constitution and the Feudal Law* (Cambridge University Press 1957)

——, 'Machiavelli, Harrington and English Political Ideologies in the Eighteenth Century' (1965) 22 *The William and Mary Quarterly* 549

——, *The Political Works of James Harrington* (Cambridge University Press 1977)

—— (ed), *Harrington: 'The Commonwealth of Oceana' and 'A System of Politics'* (Cambridge University Press 1992)

——, 'Introduction' in Pocock (ed) (with G Schochet and L Schwoerer), *The Varieties of British Political Thought 1500–1800* (Cambridge University Press 1993) 1

——, Schochet G, and Schwoerer L (eds), *The Varieties of British Political Thought 1500–1800* (Cambridge University Press 1993)

Pollard A, *The Evolution of Parliament* (Longmans, Green and Company 1920)

Ponsonby A, *Democracy and Diplomacy* (Metheun 1915)

Poole T, 'Courts and Conditions of Uncertainty in "Times of Crisis"' [2008] *Public Law* 234

Pugh M, *The Making of Modern British Politics 1867–1939* (Basil Blackwell 1982)

Raleigh W, 'The Cabinet-Council' in *Works of Sir Walter Raleigh* vol I (T Birch ed, 1751)

Ratner L, 'The Coordinated Warmaking Power: Legislative, Executive, and Judicial Roles' (1970–71) 44 *Southern California Law Review* 461

Rawls J, *A Theory of Justice* (Harvard University Press 1971)

Reimann M and Zimmerman R (eds), *The Oxford Handbook of Comparative Law* (Oxford University Press 2006)

Reiss H (ed), *Kant's Political Writings* (Cambridge University Press 1970)

Rhys Lovell C, *English Constitutional and Legal History: A Survey* (Oxford University Press 1962)

Risius G, 'Prisoners of War in the United Kingdom' in P Rowe (ed), *The Gulf War 1990–91 in International and English Law* (Routledge 1993)

Robinson A, *Parliament and Public Spending: The Expenditure Committee of the House of Commons, 1970–76* (Heinemann 1978)

Rousseau J, 'Of the Social Contract' (translated by G Cole) in S Cahn, *Classics of Modern Political Theory: Machiavelli to Mill* (Oxford University Press 1997) 370

Rowe P, *The Gulf War 1990–91 in International and English Law* (Routledge 1993)

——, *The Impact of Human Rights Law on Armed Forces* (Cambrige University Press 2006)

Russell C, 'The Foreign Policy Debate in the House of Commons in 1621' (1977) 20 *The Historical Journal* 289

——, *Parliaments and English Politics 1621–1629* (Clarendon Press 1979)

——, 'The Nature of a Parliament in Early Stuart England' in H Tomlinson (ed), *Before the English Civil War: Essays on Early Stuart Politics and Government* (MacMillan Press 1983) 123

Russett B, *Controlling the Sword: The Democratic Governance of National Security* (Harvard University Press 1990)

Schlesinger Jr A, *The Imperial Presidency* (Houghton Mifflin 1989)

Schulofer S, 'Secrecy and Democracy: Who Controls Information in the National Security State?' (19 August 2010) NYU School of Law Public Research Paper 10-53 <http://ssrn.com/abstract=1661964>

Schumpeter J, *Capitalism, Socialism and Democracy* (Allen and Unwin 1976)

Schwartzberg M, *Democracy and Legal Change* (Cambridge University Press 2007)

Schweizer K, 'An Unpublished Parliamentary Speech by the Elder Pitt, 9 December 1761' (1991) 64 *Historical Research* 98

Seaward P, 'The Cavalier Parliament, the 1667 Accounts Commission and the Idea of Accountability' in C Kyle and J Peacy (eds), *Parliament at Work: Parliamentary Committees, Political Power and Public Access in Early Modern England* (Boydell Press 2002) 149

Sedley S, 'The Sound of Silence: Constitutional Law without a Constitution' (1994) 110 *Law Quarterly Review* 270

Seymour-Ure C, 'British "War Cabinets" in Limited Wars: Korea, Suez and the Falklands' (1984) 62 *Public Administration* 181

Shapiro I and Macedo S (eds), *Designing Democratic Institutions* (NY University Press 2000)

Simpson A, *In the Highest Degree Odious: Detention without Trial in Britain* (Oxford University Press 1992)

Smith K and McLaren J, 'History's Living Legacy: An Outline of 'Modern' Historiography of the Common Law' (2001) 21 *Legal Studies* 251

Smith M, 'Intelligence and the Core Executive' (2010) 25 *Public Policy and Administration* 11

Smith T, *De Republica Anglorum* (Mary Dewar ed, Cambridge University Press 2009)

Somerville J, *Politics and Ideology in England 1603–40* (Longman 1986)

Steiner Z, *The Foreign Office and Foreign Policy 1898–1914* (Cambridge University Press 1969)

——, 'The Foreign Office before 1914: A Study in Resistance' in G Sutherland (ed), *Studies in the Growth of Nineteenth Century Government* (Routledge and Kegan Paul 1972) 161

Lord Steyn, 'Deference: A Tangled Story' [2005] *Public Law* 346

Straka G, 'The Final Phase of Divine Right Theory in England, 1688–1702' (1962) 77 *English Historical Review* 638

Sunstein C, *The Partial Constitution* (Harvard University Press 1993)

——, *Legal Reasoning and Political Conflict* (Oxford University Press 1996)

——, 'Deliberative Trouble? Why Groups go to Extremes' (2000) 110 *Yale Law Journal* 71

——, *Designing Democracy: What Constitutions Do* (Oxford University Press 2001)

——, 'Terrorism and Probability Neglect' (2003) 26 *Journal of Risk and Uncertainty* 121

Supperstone M, *Brownlie's Law of Public Order and National Security*, 2nd edn (Butterworths 1981)

Sustein R, *Legal Reasoning and Political Conflict* (Oxford University Press 1996)

Sutherland G (ed), *Studies in the Growth of Nineteenth Century Government* (Routledge and Kegan Paul 1972)

Tanner J (ed), *Tudor Constitutional Documents A.D. 1485–1603 with an Historical Commentary* (Cambride University Press 1922)

——, *Constitutional Documents of the Reign of James I 1603–1635* (Cambridge University Press 1960)

——, 'The Succession Question and Divine Right—Commentary' in *Constitutional Documents of the Reign of James I 1603–1625* (Cambridge University Press 1960)

Thomas D, 'Financial and Administrative Developments' in H Tomlinson (ed), *Before the English Civil War: Essays on Early Stuart Politics and Government* (MacMillan Press 1983) 103

Thomas P, *The House of Commons in the Eighteenth Century* (Oxford University Press 1971)

Todd A, *On Parliamentary Government in England: Its Origin, Development and Practical Operation*, vol II, 2nd edn (1887–89)

Tomkins A, *The Constitution after Scott* (Oxford University Press 1998)

——, 'Legislating against Terror' [2002] *Public Law* 205

——, *Public Law* (Oxford University Press 2003)

——, 'What is Parliament For?' in N Bamforth and P Leyland (eds), *Public Law in a Multi-Layered Constitution* (Hart Publishing 2003) 53

Tomlinson H (ed), *Before the English Civil War: Essays on Early Stuart Politics and Government* (MacMillan Press 1983)

——, 'The Causes of War: A Historiographical Survey' in H Tomlinson (ed), *Before the English Civil War: Essays on Early Stuart Politics and Government* (MacMillan Press 1983) 7

Towle P, *Going to War: British Debates from Wilberforce to Blair* (Palgrave MacMillan 2009)

Turner E, 'Parliament and Foreign Affairs, 1603–1760' (1919) 34 *The English Historical Review* 172

Twysden R, *Certaine Considerations upon the Government of England* vol xlv (John Mitchell Kemble ed, 1849)

UK Ministry of Defence, *Manual of the Law of Armed Conflict* (Oxford University Press 2004).

Van Harten G, 'Weaknesses of Adjudication in the Face of Secret Evidence' (2009) 13 *International Journal of Evidence and Proof* 1

Vermeule A, *Mechanisms of Democracy: Institutional Design Writ Small* (Oxford University Press 2007)

——, 'Many-Minds Arguments in Legal Theory' (2009) 1 *The Journal of Legal Analysis* 1

——, *Law and Limits of Reason* (Oxford University Press 2009)

Vile M, *Constitutionalism and the Separation of Powers*, 2nd edn (Liberty Fund 1998)

Vital D, *The Making of British Foreign Policy* (George Allen and Unwin 1968)

Wade E, 'Act of State in English law' (1934) 15 *British Yearbook of International Law* 98

Waldron J, 'The Wisdom of the Multitude: Some Reflections on Book 3, Chapter 11 of Aristotle's Politics' (1995) 23 *Political Theory* 563

——, *Law and Disagreement* (Clarendon Press 1999)

——, *The Dignity of Legislation* (Cambridge University Press 1999)

Walker C, 'Review of the Prerogative: The Remaining Issues' [1987] *Public Law* 62

Ward I, *The English Constitution: Myths and Realities* (Hart Publishing 2004)

Watt D, 'Foreign Affairs, the Public Interest and the Right to Know' (1963) 34 *The Political Quarterly* 124

Weart S, *Why Democracies Will Never Fight One Another* (Yale University Press 1998)

Weber M, 'Bureaucracy' in H Gerth and C Wright Mills (eds), *Essays in Sociology* (Routledge 1948) 233

Weinbaum M, 'Classification and Change in Legislative Systems' in C Kim and G Boynton (eds), *Legislative Systems in Developing Countries* (Durham 1975) 43

Western J, *The English Militia in the Eighteenth Century: The Story of a Political Issue 1660–1802* (Routledge and Kegan Paul 1965)

Weston C, 'English Constitutional Doctrines from the Fifteenth Century to the Seventeenth: II. The Theory of Mixed Monarchy under Charles I and after' (1960) 75 *The English Historical Review* 426

——, *English Constitutional Theory and the House of Lords 1556–1832* (Routledge and Kegan Paul 1965)

White G, 'Truth and Interpretation in Legal History' in *Intervention and Detachment: Essays in Legal History and Jurisprudence* (Oxford University Press 1994)

White N, *Democracy Goes to War: British Military Deployments under International Law* (Oxford University Press 2009)

——, 'International Law, the UK, and Decisions to Deploy Troops Overseas' (2010) 59 *International and Comparative Law Quarterly* 814

Yetiv S, 'Groupthink and the Gulf Crisis' (2003) 33 *British Journal of Political Science* 419

Younder K, 'Public Opinion and British Foreign Policy' (1964) 40 *International Affairs* 22

Young I, *Justice and Politics of Difference* (Princeton University Press 1990)

Zagor M, 'Judicial Rhetoric and Constitutional Identity: Comparative Approaches to Aliens' Rights in the United Kingdom and Australia' (2008) 19 *Public Law Review* 271

Zaller R, *The Parliament of 1621: A Study in Constitutional Conflict* (University of California Press 1971)

Zimmerman R, 'Savigny's Legacy: Legal History, Comparative Law, and the Emergence of a European Legal Science' (1996) 112 *Law Quarterly Review* 576

RECORDS OF PARLIAMENTARY DEBATES

All references to parliamentary debates before 1803 are to *Cobbett's Parliamentary History* (referred to in the footnotes as 'Parliamentary History'), which is available online: <http://www2.odl.ox.ac.uk/gsdl/cgi-bin/library?site=localhost&a=p&p=about&c=modhis06&ct=0&l=en&w=iso-8859-1>.

All references to parliamentary debates from 1803 onwards are to Hansard's Parliamentary Debates (referred to in the footnotes as 'HC Deb').

SELECT COMMITTEE REPORTS

Committee on Standards and Privileges, *Eighth Report* (HC 1998–99, 607)

House of Commons Foreign Affairs Committee, *The Decision to go to War in Iraq* (HC 2002–03, 813)

House of Commons Public Accounts Committee, *Ministry of Defence: Chinook Mk 3* (HC 2008–09, 247)

——, *Ministry of Defence: Support to High Intensity Operations* (HC 2008–09, 895)

——, *Ministry of Defence: Type 45 Destroyer* (HC 2008–09, 372)

——, *The UK's Future Nuclear Deterrent Capability* (HC 2008–09, 250)

House of Lords Select Committee on the Constitution, *Waging War: Parliament's Role and Responsibility. Volume I: Report* (HL 2005–06, 236-I)

House of Commons Select Committee on Procedure, *Scrutiny of Public Expenditure and Administration* (HC 1968–69, 410)

Joint Committee on Human Rights, *Eighteenth Report of 2003–04* (2003–04, HL 158, HC 713)

——, *Tenth Report of Session 2004–05, Prevention of Terrorism Bill* (2004–05, HL 68, HC 334)
——, *The Justice and Security Green Paper* (2010–12, HL 286, HC 1777)
Joint Committee on the Draft Constitutional Renewal Bill, *Draft Constitutional Renewal Bill* (2007–08, HL 116-I, HC 551-I)
Political and Constitutional Reform Committee, *8th Report—Parliament's Role in Conflict Decisions* (HC 2010–12, 923)
——, *9th Report—Parliament's Role in Conflict Decisions: Government Response to the Committee's Eight Report of Session 2010–12* (HC 2010–12, 1477)
——, *12th Report—Parliament's Role in Conflict Decisions—Further Government Response* (HC 2010–12, 1673)
Public Administration Select Committee, *Ministerial Accountability and Parliamentary Questions* (HC 2003–04, 355)
——, *Taming the Prerogative: Strengthening Ministerial Accountability to Parliament* (HC 2003–04, 422)
Reform of the House of Commons Select Committee, *First Report: Rebuilding the House* (HC 2008–09, 1117)
Speaker's Conference on Parliamentary Representation, *Final Report* (HC 2009–10, 239)

COMMAND PAPERS

Hutton Lord, *Report of the Inquiry into the Circumstances Surrounding the Death of Dr David Kelly CMG* (HC 247, 2004)
Intelligence and Security Committee, *Rendition* (Cm 7171, 2007)
——, *Annual Report 2006–07* (Cm 7299, 2008)
——, *Annual Report 2007–08* (Cm 7542, 2009)
Ministry of Justice, *Governance of Britain* (Green Paper) (Cm 7170, 2007)
——, *War Powers and Treaties: Limiting Executive Powers* (Cm 7239, 2007)
——, *The Governance of Britain—Constitutional Renewal* (White Paper) (Cm 7342-I, 2008)
——, 'The Governance of Britain. Review of the Executive Royal Prerogative Powers: Final Report' (October 2009)
Report of a Committee of Privy Counsellors, *Falklands Island Review* (Cmnd 8787, 1983)
——, *Review of Intelligence on Weapons of Mass Destruction* (HC 898, 2004)
Scott LJ, *Report of the Inquiry into the Export of Defence Equipment and Dual-Use Goods to Iraq and Related Prosecutions* (HC 115, 1996)
Secretary of State for Constitutional Affairs and the Lord Chancellor, *Government Response to the House of Lords Constitution Committee's Report, Fifteenth Report of the Session 2006–06* (Cm 6923, 2006)
Secretary of State for Justice, 'Exercise of the Executive Override under Section 53 of the Freedom of Information Act 2000, in Respect of the Decision of the Information Commissioner Dated 18 February 2008, as Upheld by the Decision of the Information Tribunal of 27 January 2009, Statement of Reasons' (23 February 2009)

OTHER

'Iraq's Weapons of Mass Destruction: The Assessment of the British Government' (24 September 2002) <http://webarchive.nationalarchives.gov.uk/+/http://www.number10.gov.uk/>

'Iraq: Its Infrastructure of Concealment, Deception and Intimidation' (3 February 2003) <http://webarchive.nationalarchives.gov.uk/+/http://www.number10.gov.uk/>

Written Evidence to the Committee's Inquiry into the Role and Powers of the Prime Minister, 17 May 2011 (2010–12) <http://www.publications.parliament.uk/pa/cm201011/cmselect/cmpolcon/writev/842/m11.htm>

Booth R and Cobain I, 'Security watchdog inadequate, human rights groups say' *The Guardian* (London 27 February 2010) 4

Born H and Leigh I, 'Democratic Accountability of Intelligence Services' (Geneva Centre for the Democratic Control of Armed Forces, Policy Paper No 19, 2007) <www.dcaf.ch/publications>

Butt D, 'The Capacity of Courts to Handle Complexity: Report and Analysis of a Workshop Held at St Hugh's College, Oxford' (Foundation for Law, Justice and Society, 5 December 2008) <www.fljs.org>

Cabinet Office, *The Cabinet Manual*, 1st edn (October 2011)

Democracy Task Force, 'An End to Sofa Government: Better Working of Prime Minister and Cabinet' (2006) <http://image.guardian.co.uk/sys-files/Politics/documents/2007/03/27/DemocracyTaskForce.pdf>

Evans R and Leigh D, 'WikiLeaks cables: secret deal let Americans sidestep cluster bomb ban' *The Guardian* (London 1 December 2010) <http://www.guardian.co.uk/world/2010/dec/01/wikileaks-cables-cluster-bombs-britain>

House of Commons Library, 'Commons Divisions on Iraq: 26 February and 18 March 2003' (Standard Note, SN/SG/2109, 19 March 2003) <http://www.parliament.uk/documents/documents/upload/snsg-02109.pdf>

——, 'Impeachment' (Research Briefing, SN/PC/2666, 30 November 2004) <http://www.parliament.uk/documents/commons/lib/research/briefings/snpc-02666.pdf>

—— 'Intelligence and Security Committee' (SN/HA/2178, 21 April 2009) <http://www.parliament.uk/briefing-papers/SN02178>

Information Commissioner, 'Freedom of Information Act—Awareness Guidance No 10' (Version 1, April 2006) <www.ico.gov.uk>

Intelligence and Security Committee, 'Press Release, 27 March 2012' <http://isc.independent.gov.uk/news-archive/27march2012>

Norton-Taylor R, 'Revealed: the government's secret legal advice on Iraq war' *The Guardian* (London 28 April 2005) <http://www.guardian.co.uk/politics/2005/apr/28/uk.world3>

NATO, 'The Comprehensive Political Guidance endorsed by NATO Heads of State and Government on 29 November 2006' reproduced in 'Towards the

New Strategic Concept: A Selection of Background Documents' (NATO Public Diplomacy Division, 2006) <www.nato.int/ebookshop>
——, 'NATO 2020: Assured Security; Dynamic Engagement. Analysis and Recommendations of the Group of Experts on a New Strategic Concept for NATO' (17 May 2010) <www.nato.int/ebookshop>
'United Nations Peacekeeping Operations: Principles and Guidelines' ('Capstone Doctrine') (2008) <www.un.org/en/peacekeeping/>
van Eekelen W, 'Sending Troops Abroad' (Democratic Control of Armed Forces 2006) <http://www.dcaf.ch/Publications/Sending-Troops-Abroad>

Index

ancient constitution 29–30
Afghanistan conflict (2001–) 72, 103–4

Civil War (1642–1651) 45–7
consultation with Parliament about war 96–106
Crown's responsibility for general welfare 27–9, 112–3

democratic decision making
  intrinsic value 167–8
  instrumental values 169–79
democratic justifications for executive's powers 35–6, 137–9
democratic values 160–3
Divine Right 23–5

Falklands conflict (1982) 73, 93, 103–4, 175

impeachment 89–91
incidental war powers 117–24
institutional arguments for executive's powers 36–41, 139–41
institutional design 157–67
  goals 159–64
interactions between Parliament and executive in exercise of war and foreign policy powers 51–107
Iraq conflict (1990–1) 73
Iraq conflict (2003–) 76, 78, 91, 93, 96, 105–6, 117, 141, 146, 148, 152, 173, 174, 175, 177, 193, 203, 207, 208

Joint Committee on National Security (JCNS) 195, 197, 198, 199, 200, 205, 206, 208, 209, 212, 214
judicial review of war prerogative see, generally, ch 4
  hypothetical challenges to war prerogative on established grounds 144–9
  and individual rights 149–53
  jurisdiction 124–6
  proposed legislative reform 211–5
  see also justiciability
justiciability 126–143
  continued relevance and utility 132–4

development of 127–32
evaluation of 134–49

Korean War (1950–3) 66–7, 103
Kosovo conflict (1998–9) 67, 71, 103–4

legal advice to Parliament 208–9
legal history
  see, generally, ch 2, ch 5
  criticisms of 10–13
  internal legal history 8–9
  methodology 8–13
  objectives of 6–8

many-minds arguments 170–8
mixed government 30–2

operational concerns 164–7, 210–1
see also institutional arguments 36–41

paradigm 'kingly' power 25
parliamentary access to information 67–74, 93–4, 187–201
parliamentary appropriation and audit 85–8
parliamentary committees 91–3, 195–201
  Intelligence and Security Committee 196–7, 200–1
  Joint Committee on National Security 195–201
  and retrospective scrutiny 91–3
parliamentary freedom of speech 51–79
  limitations on 67–79
  'mouthpiece function' 63–7
  and parliamentary government 58–67
  scrutiny function 60–3
  secrecy in parliamentary debates 69–74, 189–91
  in seventeenth century 52–8
parliamentary power of supply 79–88
  in 1620s 802
  and parliamentary government 82–5
  see also parliamentary appropriation and audit 85–8
  see also prerogative taxation 81–2, 119

prerogative imprisonment and
    deportation 122
prerogative taxation 81–2, 119
publication of information about war and
    national security
  Freedom of Information Act public interest
    test 192–3
  revised public interest test 194–5
  value of publicity 188–9

reform of war prerogative
  recent proposals 181–6
  proposed legislative reform 201–11
requisition and acquisition of
    property 120–1
restrictions on trade and other relations
    with enemy 121–2
retrospective scrutiny of exercise of war
    prerogative 88–96
Revolutionary period
    (1649–60) 47–51

secrecy of information about war and
    national security 69–74, 141, 189–91
social contract 32–3
Suez conflict (1956) 67, 71, 77, 103–4

theoretical and political discourses
  assertion of executive's powers over war
    and foreign policy 15–22
  justifications for executive's powers over
    war and foreign policy 22–41
tort liability of Crown 153–4
treaty obligations 210–1

Whig parliamentary government
  assertion of executive power 19–20
  as justification for executive's powers over war
    and foreign policy 33–5
World War One (1914–18) 66, 70, 84,
    101–2, 120
World War Two (1939–45) 63, 73, 77,
    102–3, 122